BLACK FIRE
THIS TIME

VOLUME 2

Derrick Harriell, Ph.D., Editor
Kofi Antwi, Asst. Editor

Introduction by Mona Lisa Saloy, Ph.D.

WILLOW BOOKS
a Division of AQUARIUS PRESS
Detroit, Michigan

BLACK FIRE THIS TIME

Volume 2

© 2024 AQUARIUS PRESS

All rights reserved. No part of this publication may be reproduced, stored in a retrieval system, or transmitted in any form, or by any means, electronic, mechanical, recording, photocopying or otherwise without the prior written permission of the publisher.

Editor: Derrick Harriell, PhD

Assistant Editor: Kofi Antwi

Disclaimer: This is a collection of original works and reprints. The views and opinions within this collection are solely the creators' and do not necessarily reflect the opinions and beliefs of the editors and publisher, nor its affiliates.

Cover source image: Nelson Stevens

Cover design by Aquarius Press LLC

ISBN 9798988165583

Acknowledgments:
Thank you to Dr. Kim McMillon, Kofi Antwi, Dr. Liselli Fitzpatrick and Lakiba Pittman for their additional help.

WILLOW BOOKS, a Division of AQUARIUS PRESS
www.WillowLit.net

AQUARIUS PRESS LLC
PO Box 23096
Detroit, MI 48223

Printed in the United States of America

Contents

Introduction	Mona Lisa Saloy, Ph.D.	9
Judy Juanita	we	13
	Reparations Approved	15
	Dave Chappelle	16
Aneb Kgostisile	Come Justice	18
	Sacraments	19
	For Breonna	21
Everett Hoagland	An Elder BAM Poet...	22
	Amiri's Last Set	25
Kalamu ya Salaam	Homecoming	27
Val Gray Ward	Talking Drum	51
Raymond Nat Turner	Just Ms. Brooks and Me	53
Gideon Young	kwansaba crown	54
	the river	58
	what is it i hide from myself	59
Gerardo Del Guercio	Interview with Karina Griffith	59
Audre Lorde	Poetry Is Not a Luxury	62
	Power	65
Michael S. Harper	Dear John, Dear Coltrane	67
bell hooks	Appalachian Elegy	70
Carolyn Rodgers	Translation	77
	U Name This One	78
Ed Bullins	Clara's Ole Man	79
Jayne Cortez	The Oppressionists	97

June Jordan	1977: Poem for Mrs. Fannie Lou Hamer	98
Larry Neal	The Black Arts Movement	100
devorah major	valued colors	103
	salt water crossings	104
Liseli A. Fitzpatrick	Tell Me at 90!	106
	Tell Me II/African brothers like you...	109
Raymond Patterson	To a Weathercock	111
Etheridge Knight	The Bones of My Father	112
	For Malcolm, A Year After	113
Mari Evans	I Am A Black Woman	114
	Who Can Be Born Black?	116
Maya Angelou	The Mothering Blackness	117
	Caged Bird	118
Sarah Webster Fabio	The Hand That Rocks	119
Angela Jackson	Miz Rosa Rides the Bus	120
Alvin Aubert	The Revolutionary	122
	Nat Turner in the Clearing	123
Heather Buchanan and Kim McMillon	"We're Bringing You Black Theatre": Remembering Ed Bullins	123
Thulani Davis	backstage drama	124
Aldon L. Nielsen	All The Places We've Been	136
Jimmy Garrett	And We Own the Night	138
James E Cherry	A SURVEY OF AMERICAN HISTORY	151
	A BLACK BOY WAS HERE	151
Mwatabu S. Okantah	i, too, am a witness	153
	A blue-black on black crime	153

Herina Ayot	Baby Butterflies	154
C. Liegh McInnis	"Mississipppi Like…"	161
El-Ra Radney	The Dawn-Song: The Rising of the Astro-Afro Time Traveler	166
Megha Sood	Topography of a Wound	173
Jacquese Armstrong	sister sonia	174
Connie Owens Patton	TROUBLE	175
	Historical Rewind	177
Regina YC Garcia	Afro-futures Unnamed Nonce…	178
	Speculation	179
Tamara Madison	Afrotica	182
	Wake	183
Bill Marable	I have seen dreams come true…	184
Joan Cartwright	Blues Women…	187
Cynthia Manick	Eintou for the Matriarchs	196
	Dear "Is the Rainbow Enuf?"	197
i.c.y.	daughters of the lost tribe	198
Curtis L. Crisler	LAST STOP TO DINE	200
	Looking for Hurston in a Triptych	218
Conrad Pegues	waiting	222
Naomi Wilson	As Mardou	223
Lakiba Pittman	The Dreamers	224
Karla Brundage	Katrina	225
	She Roars	226
Doug Curry	Mickey	228
Amoja Sumler	Afro Futurist	231

Charlois Lumpkin	Going Cotton	232
Tureeda Mikell	LIFE LIGHT REMEMBERED	236
Thurman Watts	30 African Triplets	238
Mark Allan Davis	Why is Monumental Reckoning, "Monumental?"	241
Keisha-Gaye Anderson	Cuckoo	246
	Mama Lovie	247
Malik Abduh	Two Strikes	248
Paulette P. Jones	detail of flying african survival song…	256
	cynthia sequence	260
	a toast to the people	267
Syvilla Woods	All Praises to African Women Everywhere	270
Cole Eubanks	Driving South	271
	What Kind of Blue?	272
Ewuare Osayande	The Underground Railroad	273
Erik Andrade	Black Magic	277
	Where Do We Go?	280
Vanessa Silva	Untitled	282
Elijah Pringle	Washing Stockings: Around Midnight	283
Sheila Smith McKoy	Far Enough	284
Lamont Lilly	letter to Pan America	292
	bloodline	293
Mali Collins	Young Margaret	293
Raheem Curry	This is for my brothers…	301
Chantal James	Upon Alleyways	303

C. Prudence Arceneaux	Austin Police Department and Nazi Cowboys…	309
Regina Harris Baiocchi	Scuppernong	310
Wendy Mercer	Young, Beaten, and Black	320
Angela Clear	Lost Girls	320
Theodore A. Harris	1999 COLLAGE EULOGY FOR AMADOU DIALLO	322
Kalamu Chaché	Onetta May Harris	324
	Justice, Freedom, Equality!	325
	Before They Go Away	326
Ashley Rose	America's Dried Up Well	327
	Black Joy	328
Michael Warr	Her Words (for Gwendolyn Brooks)	331
	Searcching for Bob Kaufman	332
Dasan Ahanu	To My People of Ash and Soot	333
	Family Affair	337
	Protection	338
Kim McMillon	Somebody Stole My History	343
Kofi Antwi	Akwaaba	345
	All Hail the City of Doom	346
avotcja	I SING A SONG OF MAMIE TILL	348
	WALKING IN THE TRACKS OF THE WOLF	351
Al Young	A Dance for Ma Rainey	354
	& brown & that basic black honey misery	354
	untitled	355
	Who I Am in Twilight	356

INTRODUCTION

Why's. . .?
—Amiri Baraka

It's Dope. . .Fire!
—Chance the Rapper

Exploding with urgency, the premier *Black Fire* anthology edited by then LeRoi Jones and Larry Neal, answered the call to fill the void left readers after seminal *The New Negro*, and Wallace Thurman's anthology *Fire!!* Those significant blasts of articulating Black literature infused further calls in such works as the *Children of the Night; Best Short Stories by Black Writers* (Gloria Naylor ed.); *Black Drama Anthology* (Woodie King, Ron Milner eds.); *(Black Writers of the Thirties, anthology (James O. Young ed.); Umbra Journal, The Black Scholar, Callaloo, African American Review, The Black Woman Anthology, (*Toni Cade Bambara & Eleanor Traylor, eds.); *The Pan African Literary Journal;* then further, Dudley Randall's *The Black Poets* anthology, Jerry Ward's *Trouble the Water* anthology, *Yardbird Reader,* even Ja A. Jahannes' *Black Gold,* anthology, and *Beyond the Frontier: African American Poetry for the 21ˢᵗ Century* (E. Ethelbert Miller ed.), and *In Search of Color Everywhere* (E. Ethelbert Miller ed). In the interim, the fire continued in Ishmael Reed's *Konch* journal, then the Charles Johnson edited *Chicago Quarterly Review, Vol 33, Anthology of Black American Literature; a*lso, more recently, there's *BLACK LIVES MATTER: A Gathering of the Tribes* journal. These remarkable works proudly hail the testimonies of the call of literature for and about Black people.

As the ancient proverb of the Akan Kingdom of West Africa states, "Unless the lion speaks, the hunter tells the tale." Therefore, it is imperative that this important work of sharing Black voices continues the goal of literature, capturing human history, just not "his" story but ours, the Black story as only those with the lived experience can articulate. Continuing this tradition enters *Black Fire This Time, Volume 1* (2022) and now *Volume II,* the acclaimed anthology series on the history and legacy of the Black Arts Movement. The theme of this series is "Black is Beautiful, Black is Powerful, Black is Home", as penned by Dr. Kim McMillon, Editor.

Following *Brown vs. the Board of Education*, the Black Power Movement, the stark violence of those times, the Black voices who articulated the angst, the art, the street talk, the elegance, the dreams, the horrors, the slashed-smashed identity issues, the "Wise…Why's" (Baraka) of who Blacks became were pronounced on the page and the stage. From the musical group the Impressions, Blacks kept on pushing forward; and the epitome of that push was no more pronounced in the election of America's first Black President Barak Hussein Obama, the 44th. Yet, since that momentous feat, so much more violence, injustice occurred and continues that it is incumbent on today's Black writers to capture their eras and to maintain the embrace of articulating Black life, love, hate, strength, inspiration, family, community, questions.

In the centuries prior, with Blacks having no control over Black stories, and the majority of the world only heard "bad news" about American Blacks, the predominant characterization toward Black Americans was negative. Certainly, even today, the truth of the Black American experience is denied in textbooks, denied in the educational system, and too often negated in life. Remember, prior to Trans-Atlantic enslavement of Africans, there was no middle class in Europe. Of course, the reality is that Blacks created so much of the wealth of America not just during enslavement but in the years hence. Whether in Art, too many inventions to name briefly from the ironing board to the computer to GPS, or in music from Blues to Jazz to Sacred Songs, Blacks in America have created more joy than grains of sand, so much so that many around the world imitate Black music, Black talk, Black style. To be hip is to be Black (Haki Madhubuti) still. Yet, the challenges endure.

Blackness today lived and articulated persists as strange, even existential. Now, there are *African* Americans, such as our 44th President, living and creating in America, who mirror those issues. One such author, Chimamanda Ngozi Adichie, explains: "In Nigeria, I had often thought about who I was—writer, dreamer, thinker—but only in America did I consider *what* I was. . . I became Black in America. It was not a choice—my chocolate-colored skin saw to that—but a revelation. I had never before thought of myself as "Black"; I did not need to, because while British colonialism in Nigeria left many cursed legacies in its wake, racial identity was not one of them" (*The Atlantic*). Adichi articulates the conundrum of American Blackness simply, starkly, profoundly. She continues:

> To be Black in America was to feel bulldozed by the weight of history and stereotypes, to know that race was always a possible reason, or cause, or explanation for the big and small interactions that make

up our fragile lives. To be Black was to realize that it was impossible for people to approach one another with the simple wonder of being human, without the specter of race lying somewhere in the shadows. To be Black was to feel, in different circumstances, frustration, anger, irritation, and wry amusement. It also brought the rare wealth of discovering African American literature, those stories full of such graceful grit. Black American writing instructed and delighted me, and I must have at some unconscious level wanted to contribute to that tradition, but obliquely, as someone standing outside American culture, a Black person without America's blighted history. (Adichi)

As Adichi writes, this forced weight Blacks carry, this negative aura of nonacceptance, this horror of American life is real, is a burden, is a constant slap-in-the-face of life; yet in spite of all of that, Black life blossoms with street life, rappers, spoken word bards, music makers, visual artists, actors, dancers, writers, now producers of movies and t.v. Such creativity can not be contained and even explodes to create lives whose contributions inspire and ignite the arts in all phases.

In this *Black Fire This Time Volume II,* find the greats on whose shoulders so many stand: Audre Lorde, bell hooks, Larry Neal, June Jordan, Jane Cortez, Ed Bullins, Carolyn Rodgers, and contemporary voices. There's "A Survey of American History" by James E. Cherry, "Mississippi Like" by C. Liegh McInnis, "Blues Women" by Joan Cartwright and "Black Magic" by Eric Andrade, all giving readers so much to hold onto, to grab, to gain, to celebrate, to contemplate, to continue this literary journey of Black human history. "To be brave, be bold, step up and make your own. . . To be cool is to be able to hang with yourself" (Prince Rogers Nelson).

These black voices, are, as Judy Juanita opens with in "We":

. . .*we* been cut in hard edged pieces. . .

. . .what do *we* have in common

besides kwanzaa cards . . .

is *we* synonymous with our glorious past. . .

. . .we speak the same language. . .

. . .we understand the subtext. . .

…calling all black people come on . . .

Thanks to Aquarius Press, Dr. Kim McMillon and Dr. Derrick Harriell, the invitation is offered. The contents call. Readers need only experience, enjoy, and share.

One request. May there be a *Black Fire This Time Volume III,* where more voices are added: Jericho Brown, Cyrus Cassells, Percival Everett, Chimamanda Ngozi Adichi, Karisma Price, Maurice Carolos Ruffin, Sarah Broom, Sunni Patterson, Charles Johnson, Skye Jackson, Ama Birch, Asia Rainey, Kelly Harris DeBerry, Chancelor Xero Skidmore, Chuck Perkins, Patricia Smith, Allison Joseph, Sha'Condria (Icon) Sibley, Evie Shockley, Pinkie Gordon Lane, and God willing more to come. Thank goodness, in spite of outside forces and minimal economic support, the sum of Black voices blossoms.

—**Dr. Mona Lisa Saloy**, 2021-2023 Poet Laureate of Louisiana

Adichi, Chimamanda Ngozi. "HOW I BECAME BLACK IN AMERICA." https://www.theatlantic.com/ideas/archive/2023/05/chimamanda-adichie-writing-americanah-reflection/674037/

Judy Juanita

At SFSU in the 1960s, Judy Juanita joined fellow student protesters to revolutionize American higher education and create the nation's first black studies department. Her semi-autobiographical debut novel, *Virgin Soul* (2013), features a young woman in the 60s who joins the Black Panther Party. Her stories appear in *Oakland Noir, Crab Orchard Review, The Female Complaint, Imagination & Place: an anthology, Tartt Six* and *Tartt Seven*. Her writing focuses on black politics, culture and art. *De Facto Feminism: Essays Straight Outta Oakland* (EquiDistance, 2016) explores key shifts and contradictions in her own artistic development as it explores black and female empowerment. In her play, *Life is a Carousel*, featured at Beyond Baroque in Venice in 2019, a black woman academic argues with the forgotten founder of Black Studies about the academy, Black Studies and the struggle. This play is included in Juanita's book *Homage to the Black Arts Movement: A Handbook* (EquiDistance, 2018). Juanita's twenty-odd plays have been produced in the Bay Area, L.A. and NYC.

we

is there a *we*

is there still a place called black america

is *we* archaic

is *we* in the dictionary of african-american slang

has *we* been cut in hard edged pieces

upperlowermiddlelowermiddleupper

what do *we* have in common

besides kwanzaa cards from walmart

is *we* synonymous with our glorious past

did *we* have a funeral and forget to come

is *we* is

or is *we* isn't

do *we* speak the same language

do *we* understand the subtext

of the language spoken about us

could the griot call out: \

all black people come in come in
calling all black people come on in

and would *we* once again
come on in?

REPARATIONS APPROVED: YESSSSSSSS

California is moving forward with its effort to compensate and apologize to Black residents for harm caused by discriminatory policies over generations after the state's reparations task force voted to approve recommendations Saturday.
—USA Today, May 10, 2023

"I can tell you from a psychological perspective that if you take $350,000 or $840,000, and you write a check to any group of people, Black, white, poor, homeless, whatever, you give any group of people that much money and say," There you go, best of luck,' you come back in six months, they're going to be broke," he said. "Whatever reparations are done, that would be an absolute disaster, as opposed to guidance and help in creating generational wealth, as opposed to income."
—Dr. Phil

Screw Dr. Phil. I will blow mine wisely

because the cancer of oppression goes deep

And furthermore, f**k Dr. Phil

who pimped out Oprah

made $20 mill off her

and pimping out people's raw emotional trauma

and has the nerve to say Blacks would go crazy

if we got reparations

NEWSFLASH: We already crazy

The idea of getting our just due

for the ancestors

is mind-boggling

for us and everyone else

because the cancer of oppression goes so deep

And further, further, furthermore,

if we spend every single penny of it

let's say 400 billion (1619-2019=400 years)
on Land Rovers, Lamborghinis, Louboutin,
diamonds and pearls, lavish weddings,
gambling in Vegas, Macau, Monte Carlo,
yachts, gold-carriage funerals, mansions,
lavish baby showers, the luxury life,
Gucci, Rolexes, trips around the world,
why should any single nonblack be upset?
It would snake its way back to their pockets

because the cancer of oppression goes that deep

Dave Chappelle

you're looking

malcolmish

dave

if only you hadn't walked

from fifty million dollars

empire wouldn't have known

if only you'd been ridiculous

you could be feted

and ignored by all

if malcolm had been mediocre

and not stood up to empire

he would be almost 100 years old

while you buck empire over and over

making your black ass

a target

empire smiles all malcolmish

giving any judas permission to kill

ask malcolm

standing in the audubon ballroom

looking malcolmish

knowing what was coming

ANEB KGOSITSILE

The literary works of Aneb Kgositsile (Gloria House, Ph.D.) have sparked imagination and action, articulating passionate and compelling ideas, and honoring the impact, sacrifices, joys, and humanity of those who have dedicated their lives to the path of freedom. Kgositsile's activism has registered people to vote, helped lift the voices of the previously unheard, and awakened people to the hypocrisy and futility of war.

Born in Tampa, Florida, Kgositsile published her first books of poetry in the 1980s, including *Blood River* (1983) and *Rainrituals* (1989), both published by

Broadside Press. In 2003, her third collection, *Shrines,* was published by Third World Press. *Medicine*, her most recent book, was published in 2017 as a joint endeavor of Broadside Lotus and University of Detroit-Mercy Press.

During the Black Arts/Black Consciousness movement, Kgositsile was among a community of artists that included poet Sonia Sanchez; poet and founder of Third World Press Haki Madhubuti; South African Poet Laureate Keorapetse Kgositsile; playwright Ron Milner; dancer-choreographer Jackie Hillsman; and poet and founder of Broadside Press Dudley Randall. Kgositsile was also active in the free speech movement while attending UC Berkeley. After leaving university to teach in a freedom school in Selma, Alabama, she worked as a field secretary in the Student Non-Violent Coordinating Committee (SNCC). She drafted SNCC's statement against the Vietnam War, the first public opposition to the war to be issued by a civil rights organization.

In Detroit, she co-founded the Detroit Coalition Against Police Brutality and the Justice for Cuba Coalition, and she participated as a teacher, administrator, and board member in the building of three African-centered schools. Active since the 1970s with Broadside Press, she was lead editor of *A Different Image: The Legacy of Broadside Press,* which won the Michigan Notable Books award in 2005.

For over 40 years, Kgositsile taught at the university level (Wayne State University, University of Michigan-Dearborn, University of Witwatersrand in South Africa), and as a volunteer in classes for elementary and high school students in Detroit's Afrocentric independent schools. She co-chaired Wayne State's Black Caucus and designed UM-Dearborn's curriculum for African American and African Studies (AAAS) and served as the program's director. Upon her retirement, Kgositsile was named Professor Emerita at UM-Dearborn (2014) and Associate Professor Emerita at WSU (1998). Her contributions to future generations of artists and activist extends beyond the classroom, as she has consistently collaborated with and mentored young Detroit writers.

Come Justice

There is a quiet perfection and sweetness in Justice.
Knowing this, we long for it.
We long for it.
We pray for it in our daily efforts to end conflict, to invite peace into our circles.
We chant for it
with the drumming of our heartbeats and our breathing,

and we hold our ear to the ground,
listening for the coming of a new world.

But there is
war in Ukraine, murderous insanity, havoc and suffering in Uvalde, San
Francisco, Haiti;
lies and evil of unprecedented magnitude
in the everyday news and rush of a crumbling culture –

but Justice, JUSTICE, never abandoning this churning field of misery,
awaits the moment of revelation,
a blaze of light in this whirlwind
of rampaging lawlessness.

Sometimes bewildered,
sometimes smothered by the gusts of cruelty engulfing us,
we persevere. We push against all the policies that would imprison us,
believing that the flame will break through – as it has in the past –
in the very moment when our will wavers
and strength is gone.

We persist, knowing there is luscious perfection, joy and peace
when Justice redeems our hope
and sets the world aright again.
Yes, there is luscious perfection, joy and peace
Whenever Justice comes.

Sacraments

They say our old uncles and aunties

would fashion their survival medicines,

roots and herbs, poems and songs,

circle dances to touch the Spirit for sustenance.

Geniuses, they were, in the arts of endurance, resilience, hope.

Thus, daily they cultivated the cotton, cane, tobacco, rice,

whatever crop; withstood the beatings and abuse,

looked forward to collards and cornbread, the communion meal

of daily resurrection; to the cool darkness of evening,

and the relief of dreams.

But there would come a day when all such knowledges

no longer served. Home hung so heavily on their hearts,

so bulging, so full and bursting,

they had only to raise their arms and they were aloft,

levitated by the longing for Africa and freedom.

There they would hang for a moment,

African saints, dissolving into air and sunlight.

"Chirren," they would whisper as they ascended,

"Today we flyin back home. You gon be alright. We see afta you."

Memories remained

of their grey, wiry beards,

their sunburnt, overworked hands and arms,

their indigo-stained fingers and palms,

their squinting eyes-so-tortured-by-the-sun,

their thread-bare trousers and tissue-thin, faded skirts,

the smell of tobacco in their shirts.

Memories

of how to fix broken tools,

cure tumors, summon joy in feasts and festivity,

mend broken hearts;

how to wait, how to be patient,

how to revive, how to love, how to laugh;

how to engender justice, how to attain peace.

Those risen saints left us chirren these *holy sacraments of endurance.*

They guide us from the place they called glory,

keep us on the righteous path,

till the world we call freedom someday will come.

For Breonna

Breonna

Louisville, Kentucky

March 13, 2020

Today the sky cried.

A torrential veil of grief

Fell on the people's hearts.

EVERETT HOAGLAND

Everett Hoagland was born and raised in Philadelphia, Pennsylvania, but has lived in New Bedford since 1973 where he was that city's first Poet Laureate, 1994-1998. He was a full-time educator for four decades and is Professor Emeritus at the nearby University of Massachusetts Dartmouth in North Dartmouth, Massachusetts where during his 30-year career there he created and sustained four different African American literature classes in addition to his poetry writing workshops.

His poetry has been published in periodicals such as THE AMERICAN POETRY REVIEW, THE MASSACHUSETTS REVIEW, THE IOWA REVIEW, THE CRISIS, THE PROGRESSIVE, THE UUA WORLD, The CAPE COD REVIEW and has been excerpted in *The Boston Globe* and *Providence Journal*. Hoagland's work has also appeared in many anthologies since 1968, including *The Jazz Poetry Anthology, Bum Rush The Page, The Best American Poetry, African American Literature* (eds. Gilyard and Wardi), *The Oxford Anthology of African American Poetry, Afro Asia, Resisting Arrest, S.O.S., Ghost Fishing: An Eco-Justice Poetry Anthology, Liberation Poetry, What Saves Us* and *Black Fire —This Time.*

He received the Gwendolyn Brooks Award, The Langston Hughes Society Award, The Boston NAACP and The Stephen Henderson Award from The African American Literature And Culture Society. Most recently, he received the 2023 Stephen Henderson Award "For Outstanding Achievement In Poetry" from the American Literature Association's African American Literature and Culture Society. He is the recipient of the 2023 American Book Award.

Hoagland has given readings all over the USA, in Ghana, in Cuba and China. Much of his life's work and some memorabilia are archived in the W.E.B. Du Bois Library at the University of Massachusetts, Amherst.

AN ELDER B.A.M. POET AT A BSU READING'S Q&A

Baba Poet, what can a poem do about anything?

Well, what did James Weldon Johnson's "Lift
Every Voice and Sing" do for us back when
sometimes that sermonette-poem-

turned-anthem, and resolve, were all we had
to collectively fuel our faith and help lift,
carry the burden of our heavy hope

chest of goals, and to unite us in the fight,
move us forward? Our choral singing
of it was the moving, group aural

hug that inspirited The Struggle,
made us one no matter our number
way before "We Shall Overcome". And

what did "Dreams", "The Dream Keeper",
"I Dream A World", "Dream Deferred"
by Langston Hughes do for Dr. King,

for the most quoted American speech of the second
half of the past century and for civil rights? What
to do? Do what we have already done in ways

that have helped us get through it all. Since
158 years before there was a U.S.A.
Do with words what we have done

with basketballs. Slam

dunk the truths about us in the U.S. the way
David Walker, Douglass, Ida Wells did,
n'do. Do with words what we have

done with dance.

Let your written poems' line-dance, on their pages, n'do.
Do with words what we have done with Double-Dutch
as in Maya Angelou's "Hopscotch", Jayne Cortez's

"Tappin' ", n'do. Rally folk at righteous protest marches
with-call-n-response rhythms. Do with words what we have
done with jazz's voicings, as in Nina Simone's and Betty Carter's

songs. Just as the Pharoah Sanders of poetry,
Askia Toure, does in his Kemetic epic, Dawn Song.
And, too, as Michael Harper does in Dear John, Dear Coltrane, n'do.

May your truth-carrying, witness-bearing words do us right,
light your generation's way forward, out of yesterday,
through today, toward tomorrow, n'do. So you, we,

remember the future the way your well-worded,
testamentary predecessors', equity-and-justice-loving,
politics-of-love-learned, revolutionary-love-loving June Jordan

and bell hooks did. Do your way what all-in revolutionary
Amiri Baraka did for us with his unsheathed, razor tongue's
weaponized truths' liberated, liberating way with language,

and inventive blues-Black takes on aspects
of cultural tradition, n'do. So act on your insights
and write, recite, righteously rap your rights. Rage

and organize, as if your, our lives depend upon it.
Because they do! Note, as a teacher-poet-sage
once wrote, "The first act of liberation is to

destroy your own cage."[1]

---

1 Michael S. Harper, "The First Act of Liberation Is to Destroy One's Cage," *The Iowa Review*, 1975.

AMIRI'S LAST SET:
SYMPHONY HALL, NEWARK, NJ, JAN. 17, 2014

There was no more,
no more, no, yes, no more
music-

al poet. You

who/who/who/who/who
bopped up onto stages
of your life griot-

like, pounded podiums,
turning them into amplified congas
nearly your size with your dis-

proportionately large worker's
hands, as you connected
the sections of your poems
by scat-

ting Monk, tuning
the silences that silhouetted
the *RAZOR* sharp truths that cut
through the bullshit. Some thought
it was about lunch time by then
(when all had dished out their praise,
whereas's, wherefore's).

But silently you reminded us

it was really "Round Midnight,"
it was all there on stage:
hot black, brown, beige, yellow, white stars
with good chops giving you your props,
stage left of your silently echoing blues-
like gallows wit,
wordlessly
telling it like it t'is of us in the u.s.

to We, The People

who/who/who/who/who
saw you there on stage
to the left of death

in what was/is

in fact the simple, evocative staged shrine,
you: a grained, brown, stand-up
wooden stand your height,
topped with your jeff,
your kente cloth

hanging

down from the wooden neck of it,
looking like age-and-work-bowed you —
who/who/who/who/who
never bowed — taking a final bow,
bowing out and saying to each of us
in silent body language poetry,

We'll be together again
at the protests, rallies,
organizing meetings,
polling places,
voting right
by voting
leftist.
Yeah,
and we'll surely
meet again, my friend,
in THE MUSIC.

KALAMU YA SALAAM

Kalamu ya Salaam is the founder of NOMMO Literary Society. NOMMO is a New Orleans-based creative writing workshop whose members are published in national anthologies such as *Dark Eros, Kente Cloth, Catch the Fire* and *360° A Revolution of Black Poets*. He is also a founder of Runagate Press, which focuses on New Orleans and African heritage cultures worldwide.

Homecoming

Characters

JUNIOR: Early twenties, walks with a cane. He has a short mustache and short afro haircut. Wears casual clothes.
YVETTE: Junior's sixteen year-old sister. Has a medium length afro haircut and is wearing a dashiki.
MOTHER: Junior's mother. Is in her mid forties.
ROBERTA: Early twenties, conservatively dressed in a blouse with ruffles and a pleaded skirt. Is wearing stockings. She is lightly and tastefully made-up.
BEA: Close friend of the Jones family. Late forties.
RAY SR.: Junior's father. Is in his mid to late forties.
FR. DONOVAN: Parish priest and long time friend of the family. He is white.

SCENE: It is the summer of 1969. The Jones household is awaiting the return from Viet Nam of Raymond Jones Jr. The front room is decorated with a large banner which says "Welcome Home Ray" and there is a large American flag on the wall beneath the banner. There is a small table off to the side with sandwiches, cookies, a punch bowl, and two bottles of wine.
(Everybody is sitting around waiting, not saying anything until Yvette enters.)

YVETTE Lord, ya'll look like ya'll at a funeral or somethin'. What's wrong? Junior, don't want to be coming home to no dead house.
(She goes over to the record player, puts on James Brown and starts dancing.)

MOTHER JONES Yvette, honey, turn it down a little bit, please. It doesn't have to be that loud.

BEA That's the way they likes it these days; so loud 'til you can't hear nothing.

MOTHER JONES Well, I don't care how they like it. I'm not going to have all of that noise in my house. Now, Yvette, you turn that noise down and sit yourself down and quit acting so wild.

YVETTE Noise. Noise!! That's James Brown. That ain't no noise. And how you gonna sit down when James Brown is on.

MOTHER JONES Yvette!

YVETTE Okay. Okay.
(She turns the music off.) Goll-lee, this sho' don't look like no welcome-home party to me.

(Yvette sits down. No one says anything for a half minute or so.)

FR. DONOVAN That's a nice dashiki, Yvette.
(Yvette pouts, looks away. Does not say anything.)

MOTHER JONES Don't you hear Father talking to you, girl? She made it herself. I think they're nice for parties and dances, but she wants to wear them all the time.

BEA They got some chillen; that's all they wear.

MOTHER JONES Yes, well, Yvette is not one of them. I see to it that she has the proper clothes befitting a young lady her age.

YVETTE The way ya'll talk, you'd think dashikis was pajamas or something.

MOTHER JONES Big Ray always calls dashikis pajamas.

YVETTE What he know?

MOTHER JONES He's your father, and he knows enough to raise you up in the way that you should go.

FR. DONOVAN The "Afro" look is the thing this year, ya know. Quite a few of the young people in the parish have, like the kids say, "gone Afro."

MOTHER JONES Well, that may be, but everything has its place. Now you take Roberta. Roberta doesn't go for all of that, and she's always dressed nice. Her dresses aren't too short and . . .

BEA Some these chillen wearin' they skirts so high 'til it's a wonder how they can sit down.

MOTHER JONES (To Bea) Some people ought to heed those words.
(Bea adjusts her dress.)

FR. DONOVAN Roberta, you don't wear dashikis?

ROBERTA No, Father.

FR. DONOVAN That's strange. Most of the young people . . .

YVETTE It ain't strange. Her mamma would kill her. It's worse than around here.

Homecoming

MOTHER JONES Which just goes to sho you how lucky you are, young lady.

ROBERTA I could wear one if I wanted to, but I don't want to.

YVETTE I bet!

MOTHER JONES You mind yourself, young lady.

ROBERTA I'm not an African, and I don't want to be one, and besides, they don›t even wear those things in Africa. It's all just fantasy.

YVETTE Is you French?

ROBERTA No, but what. . .?

YVETTE I see you wearing French ruffles.

MOTHER JONES Yvette, your ignorance is showing.

YVETTE Oh, excuse me, mother.

FR. DONOVAN Clothes are only external. It's what you are inside that counts.

BEA You so right. So many people, nothing but whitened sepulchers. They be all fine on the outside and as dirty as sin on the inside.

YVETTE Yeah, well, my Black insides won't allow me to have no white outsides.

ROBERTA You can be Black inside without wearing dashikis.

YVETTE Which is just why your head is fried right now.

ROBERTA A natural doesn't make you any Blacker.

YVETTE It sho' don't, but a fried head do make you whiter. It make you be imitating white folks and wantin' your hair to look like they hair.

FR. DONOVAN I don't think Roberta is trying to be white. She's just not doing as some of the other Black people are doing.

YVETTE Can't no Negro do like a Black people.

MOTHER JONES A Black people? Yvette, you mean a Black person. Your speech is getting worse instead of better.

YVETTE Person is singular. It denotes an individual. People is collective. It denotes a group. Negroes—think of individuals. Black people—think of groups.

BEA (Trying to change the subject.) You can't hardly tell the boys from the girls the way some of them be wearing they hair. I saw one girl the other day, from the face she look just like a boy. If you hadn't da' seen her up front, that's what you'da thought she was, 'specially since she had them ole pants on. And then, some of them wears it too long. There was one ole boy went and sat up in front of me in church, and I declare, his hair was so long 'til you couldn't even see the priest on the altar.

FR. DONOVAN Well, I think they're all right as long as you keep them up.

MOTHER JONES A person should always be well-groomed.

YVETTE Yeah. Well, what's well-groomed to me, might be sloppy to you.

MOTHER JONES
(Ignoring Yvette). May I offer anyone anything.

YVETTE I wish Junior would hurry up and get here. How long Daddy been gone?

FR. DONOVAN Sometimes the traffic from the airport is heavy.

MOTHER JONES I wonder if Junior will be wearing his uniform.

ROBERTA I hope so. He looked so good in it the last time he was home.

YVETTE He won't.

MOTHER JONES Yvette, if you can't be agreeable, you may go to your room.

YVETTE I might as well, 'cause ain't nothing going to be happening 'til Junior get here.
(She exits.)

MOTHER JONES They should be here soon. Roberta, why don't you put a

Homecoming 31

few records on before Junior gets here.
(Roberta puts on the Supremes, "Where Did Our Love Go".)

FR. DONOVAN I know all of you must be very proud and happy now that Ray has completed his military obligations.

BEA Seem just like when Big Ray was coming back from Korea. Everybody was sitting around waiting, just like we waiting now. My husband—God bless his soul—never made it home. He got killed over there. A lot of our boys got killed. . . Ann, You're so lucky. You got two men what went off to war and come back to you. You should praise the Lord he spared your husband and your child.

MOTHER JONES Yes, I know. And Junior was lucky. He was only wounded.

ROBERTA And, he got a medal for bravery.

MOTHER JONES Yes, he did get a medal for bravery.

BEA Junior got a medal for bravery, you say?

FR. DONOVAN A medal for bravery, huh? What kind of medal for bravery did he get?

ROBERTA He got a silver-star medal for bravery.

MOTHER JONES That's a high medal for bravery.

BEA He musta' killed a lot of the enemy to get that kind of medal for bravery.

FR. DONOVAN Everybody doesn't get that kind of medal for bravery.

MOTHER JONES Junior is special; that's why he got that medal for bravery.
(They sit in silence for a while, and then Ray Jones, Sr., enters.

MOTHER JONES Big Ray, where's Junior?

RAY SR. He's outside. He's coming.

ROBERTA Does he have his uniform on?

MOTHER JONES Well, what's taking him so long? Big Ray, why did you leave him?

(She sees Junior. Junior enters. Stands leaning on his walking cane. Mother runs over to embrace him.) Oh, look at you!

RAY JUNIOR (After embracing. Junior stands silently surveying the room.) What's he doing here?
(Pointing at Father Donovan).

RAY SR. Mother, your son is drunk.

RAY JUNIOR Naw, I ain't. I ain't drunk yet! Like I was saying, what is he doing here?

MOTHER JONES Well. . .well, Father is here for your homecoming party. . .

RAY JUNIOR I don't socialize with honkies.

MOTHER JONES I won't have you calling Father a honky. Not in this house. Raymond Jones, Jr. you apologize this instant.

RAY JUNIOR Mother, do you know, do you know where the word "honky" came from and what it means.
(Not waiting for an answer.) Honky is a word from up north. You see these fine, upstanding rich men use to hire poor Black women to clean, and cook, and nurse their children, and sometimes to do other things for them. Anyway, the liberal ones, (looks at Fr. Donovan) the ones who "really liked Black people" or so they would say, they would go to all of the trouble to drive out and pick up their maids. They loved us so much they would come to our houses early in the morning and sit outside and "honk" their horns so our mothers and aunts and sisters would know that it was time to go work for Mr. Charlie. And some of these "honkies" would even let you ride in the front seat with them. Yes. So, when I say honky, I don't just mean any old white man, I mean the kind of white man you would call a liberal. The kind that will come to your house. (Pause.) I'm going to my room. We can get the party on when he leaves. Call me.
(Starts to exit).

ROBERTA Ray!
(Standing in front of him). Why don't you quit acting like that!

RAY JUNIOR I thought I wrote and told you to forget it.

ROBERTA I didn't believe those letters.

Homecoming

33

RAY JUNIOR It would have been a lot better if you had. I haven't changed my mind. Like I said in the letter, it's over. We're history. Forget about me.
(He starts to exit.)

MOTHER JONES (Touching his arm). Junior, I insist. You are going to apologize to Father.

RAY JUNIOR For wh. . .

FR. DONOVAN No. No. I'll leave. It's the war. You know he's just getting back, and it will take him a while to get used to the. . .

RAY JUNIOR (Glaring). Get used to what? Get used to you praying and preaching for peace over here and over there, blessing the bombs and the guns. Ya'll would bless bullshit in Jesus' name if it served your purpose.

FR. DONOVAN (To Mother). War does horrible things to a young man's mind. (To Junior). Son, I understand what you're going. . .

RAY JUNIOR You damn right you do. I know you understand what I'm going through because you and your kind helped send me "through" it. You just as much a part of the game as them generals and politicians. Shit, man. You the man too! And ya›ll got him sitting up here like he cares about Black people.

MOTHER JONES Now that's enough! I don't care how much war you been through; that's no reason to insult people who care about you.

RAY JUNIOR Yeah, him and Hallmark. They care enough to send the very best. So, there we went, every young, Black man they could find. The very best. Sent to the jungles of Vietnam.

BEA Son, nobody wants war. We all want peace, but sometimes you got to fight for . . .

RAY JUNIOR Mr. Donovan, just answer one question for me. Answer it simply "yes" or "no." Are you part of the Peace Movement? Did you demonstrated to stop the war?

FR. DONOVAN My son. . .

RAY JUNIOR I'm not your son!

FR. DONOVAN No, I didn't demonstrate. I prayed, and I worked in my own way. . .

RAY JUNIOR Your "own way." Yeah, I know your way, what you mean is the American way. Well, let me tell you, everybody got to take a stand—me, you, everybody; you dig? They got priest and preachers out in the streets trying to stop this war, and they got priest and preachers sitting down with the generals trying to keep it going. They got white folks and they got Black folks out there trying to deal with stopping this war, and then they got people like you. People who hide behind a collar and soft words. Yeah. What did you do when they blew King away? King was against the war. He was a preacher, but he wasn't faking. He was for real. I make myself clear?

FR. DONOVAN Perhaps, it's just that we see things differently.

RAY JUNIOR No, we don't. We both looking at the same reality! I went to war. You sent me to war. At least now I know I was wrong. Do you know you were wrong? Huh, Mr. Donovan. Do you know that you were wrong?

FR. DONOVAN My conscience is clear. . .

RAY JUNIOR Hey, like I said, I did wrong. I killed a lot of people and messed up a lot of people's land. I'm sorry, and I won't do it again. Your Jesus could come down to sign me up, wouldn't make no difference. I ain't going again. Not again. I won't be wrong twice. You know like the first time it was shame on them for sending me. But the second time, it would be shame on me for going. Once you know the truth you suppose to accept the truth and follow the truth. Now ain't that the truth, Mr. Donovan? (They look at each other). Well, like I said, when he leaves, we can get the party on.

BEA Why, because Father's white?

RAY JUNIOR Hey, where you been. Didn't you just hear me run it down. Wake up; this is a new day. Naw, it's not just because he's white. He's white and he's wrong, and I don't deal with nobody like that.

ROBERTA You don't know what Father has done. He. . .

RAY JUNIOR (Turning away). Where's Yvette?

MOTHER JONES She's in her room.

RAY JUNIOR (Hollering). Hey, Yvette. Yvette!

(He exits.)

MOTHER JONES Father, I'm so embarrassed that this could happen in our home. I want you to know that you're welcome here anytime.

FR. DONOVAN I understand. I understand. You see, the war does funny things to people. It twists them all up inside, and it takes them a while to readjust. I'll stop by later to see you, and I'll pray for Ray. God be with all of you.

(He exits.)

MOTHER JONES Let me show you to the door.
(Mother exits.)

BEA (To Ray, Sr.) Big Ray, you didn't act this way when you came back. I don't understand; why is Junior acting like. . .

RAY JUNIOR (Entering with Yvette). Hey, he gone yet.
(Looking around). Yeah, well good. Now we can get the party on. Where's the drink.

(He goes over to the table where the food and drinks are and pours himself a paper cup of wine. Mother re-enters. Watches him. He looks at her, raising the cup.) To us.

(Drinks the cup in one swallow.)

BEA We thought you might have your uniform on.

RAY JUNIOR I ain't got no more uniforms. Uniform! You want to know what I did with my uniform when I got out? I threw it away. Threw it in a dimpsy dumpster. You know what a dimpsy dumpster is? Well, that's like a great big trash bin. And, they throw all kinds of trash in 'em. Well, after I signed out, I took my uniform off and threw it in right along with all the other trash. Uniform, ha!

BEA Junior, that wasn't the right thing to do. It wasn't at all like you—in fact, I don't hardly believe you is acting like you.

RAY JUNIOR Yeah, well, it's me. Me. Yeah, it's me. It is me, Sister Bea. Ole Sister Bea, you remember me? You remember me, Sister Bea? Remember how you use to take care of me, Sister Bea. And sometimes you would even spank me. Ole Sister Bea, am I like I used to be or is me not like me used to be? How do I seem to thee, Sister Bea?

BEA (Getting up, smoothing out her dress.) Son, you ain't nothing like the boy I used to take care of, and you ain't acting like nobody I'd care to know. I don't know what kind of evil done got into you, but the devil done got hold to you; that's for sure. When you left, you wasn't nothing like you is now.

RAY JUNIOR Yeah, when I left, I sure wasn't nothing like I am now, but you see, old woman, I couldn't stay like that forever. No matter how much you tried, I couldn›t be like that. And, I know what it was you was trying to do. You was trying to make me out the son you never had.

MOTHER JONES Junior, now you've gone entirely too far with this foolish talk of yours.

BEA No, let him go ahead on. He knows what he's talking about You're right, Junior, I did used to treat you like my son, and there were times I wished you were my son, but as God is my witness, if this is the way my child would have turned out, I'm glad the Lord never gave me a child.

RAY JUNIOR God don't give you no child. A man give you a child. If you'da had a man, you'da had a child, Sister Bea.

BEA The man I had, God bless his soul, was more man than you'll ever be, son.

RAY JUNIOR Why, 'cause he died fighting for honkies?

BEA He was glad to have the opportunity to serve his country. And as much as he suffered in Korea, and yes, even as much as he suffered here, he never had a bad word for nobody. He hated nobody, but you, son, you're all twisted up with hate inside.

RAY JUNIOR But, I'm alive. And this world going to have to deal with me as I am, not as they want me to be, but the way I am—like it or not.

BEA Well son, I feel sorry for your parents, for the people who invested so much love and caring into raising you. I've known your people all my life and I've loved them all my life. I remember when you were born and I thank God for the opportunity I had to help raise you and your sister. I don't know what this world is coming to but thank God I don't have to deal with you the way you are now. Thank God I can go home and shut my door. I will pray for you

Homecoming

son, pray for you to have a speedy recover, and pray that the Lord give your father and mother the strength it's going to take to deal with you in the state your in. Junior, I don't like the way you are and I refuse to stand here and suffer any more of your insults to me and to everybody else.
(Pause). I'll be seeing the rest of ya'll; I'm going home.

(She exits.)

MOTHER JONES Wait Bea.
(Bea keeps going. Mother walks with her to the door.)

RAY JUNIOR (Staring toward the door). Ya'll think ya'll can just send us off somewhere, have us kill up a bunch of people, and then come back here and play like ain't nothing changed. Ya'll think we're going to act like everything is cool. Ya'll think ya'll can ignore us. But, I got news for you. Junior's home, and I don't like what I saw. I don't like what I did. I don't like it. I was on the front line, right? Well, I'm back now, and I ain't going to let nobody ignore me. I ain't. . .

ROBERTA Ray, who are you talking to? What are you talking about?

RAY JUNIOR (Turning to Roberta). Hey, look. Why don't you go on home too.

RAY SR. You and me going to have a talk tomorrow, boy.

RAY JUNIOR We can talk now.

RAY SR. No, now ain't the time. We'll talk tomorrow. Night ya'll.
(He exits.)

RAY JUNIOR (Goes over to the table, pours and drinks more wine.) The opportunity to serve his country. Ain't that a joke. The nigger ain't never had no country.
(Mother re-enters.) All they want you to do is die and kill. Kill who they say kill and die when they say die. That's all it was—killing and dying. That's all our people ever been doing—killing and dying.

YVETTE Ray, if you keep drinking that fast, you're going to get. . .

RAY JUNIOR I don't need you to. . .

YVETTE (Mimicking his voice). Tell me what to do?

RAY JUNIOR Yeah, you right. Come on, little sister, let's dance. Let me see if you still remember them steps we used to do. Put on some sounds—some jump sounds.
(Yvette puts James Brown on, and she and Junior begin to dance.) My leg is still a little messed up from getting shot, but I can still step. Watch me now. Ooohhh weeee!

MOTHER JONES (After watching them for a minute. Shouting.) Junior! Junior! Will you sit down a minute, please.

RAY JUNIOR (Over his shoulder, still dancing.) Yeah, what you want?

MOTHER JONES Yvette, will you please turn that off.

YVETTE Aw mother, we suppose to be having a party.

MOTHER JONES Yvette, do as I say!
(Yvette cuts the box of and angrily sits down.) Now young man, what is going on with you?

RAY JUNIOR What you mean, what's going on?

MOTHER JONES You know what I mean. Raymond Jones, Jr., don't you play with me!

RAY JUNIOR Well, Ι'll tell you what's been going on. The white man been messing over us, and we don't even realize it. I'll tell you what's been going on, the whole war ain't nothing but a white man's war being fought by Black men against yellow men. I'll tell you what's been going on. The army is treating Black men like they dirt. Black men always getting the shit details. I'll tell you what's been going on. Them honkies over there trying to teach them Vietnamese how to call us nigger! That's what's been going on. You want to hear some more?

MOTHER JONES All of that may be true, but that's still no reason for you to act the way you're acting.

RAY JUNIOR Well, how you want me to act? What you want me to do?

MOTHER JONES I want you to act like a civilized human being.

RAY JUNIOR A civilized human being. Oh yeah, you mean like I should go

Homecoming

to Africa and enslave people. I should come here and commit genocide on the Indians. I should drop the atomic bomb on Japanese civilians. I should destroy Vietnam. A civilized human being. I should be like that? Well, like I ain't gonna do that. I ain't going to act civilized 'cause I ain't civilized. What we got to be civilized about? We ain't got no land of our own, no money of our own. What do we own? Do we own a civilization? What we got to be civilized about?

YVETTE Rap brother! Tell it to her. Run it down!

MOTHER JONES If you want to remain here, I would suggest you be quiet, young lady.
(To Junior who is getting another drink.) And what kind of civilization are you going to replace this one with? It is going to be better than this one, or is it just going to be the same thing only with the Negroes on top?

RAY JUNIOR Aw, come on, mother. We can talk about this some other time.

MOTHER JONES Son, you're making yourself out to be just like the white people you talking about killing.

RAY JUNIOR No, I ain't. Can't no Black people be like no white people. First place, there ain't enough white people for us to kill as many of them as they done killed of us. Then, there ain't enough of them that's fit to be slaves, like we was.

MOTHER JONES Ray, is killing all you know now?

RAY JUNIOR For the last two years, yeah. That's all I been taught recently. That's all I been doing. What, you think I was going to come back here talking about, "love!"?

MOTHER JONES No. I didn't think that. But I don't think you're being fair to yourself.

RAY JUNIOR I got news for you, mother. Ain't nothing fair about the world.

MOTHER JONES And I've got news for you. That's no reason to feel sorry for yourself and wallow in your own self-pity.

RAY JUNIOR Shittt. If you'd been over there, I wonder if you would be talking like you're talking.

MOTHER JONES Don't forget your father was in the war. I was here when he came back. I know how you hurt, but I know being a man means dealing with hurt and not throwing tantrums like a child. Don›t you think I know something about war?

RAY JUNIOR Korea was different.

MOTHER JONES No son. All wars are the same. Korea wasn't different. It's peace that is different—peace! War is different from peace, Ray. What men do in war, well that's why war is so horrible.

RAY JUNIOR Yeah, the old double standard. It's all right to kill as long as you're at war. But, who's to say when it's okay to go to war? Why ain't it okay to make war on these rich sons of bitches sitting over here, sending everybody over there?

MOTHER JONES It's not okay, because you can't win. When your father came back, he wanted to fight them too. He was so angry, you just can't imagine. . . I don't want to go through this again. God, help me. I saved one Black man, and now my son wants to destroy the world.

RAY JUNIOR No mother, I don't want to destroy the world. I want to save the world. I want to save the world from what white men are doing to it.

MOTHER JONES (She cries silently.) Ray, don't you understand? I'm tired of war. I'm glad you're home. I'm glad you're safe. Let's just live our lives now. The war is over. (She embraces Junior. He stiffens.)

RAY JUNIOR (Softly, turning away from her.) No mother. I'm back, (facing her) but I'm not safe. For me, the war ain't over. It ain't over. I'm a Black man, and every breath I breathe, I breathe it on one frontline or another. There ain't no peace for me, not now. Not in these times. I come back here and I see what they've done to our community. When we were coming back from the airport, I was looking at everything and it was just making me sad all over. We're at war right here and we don't even see it. We don't even see it. Home. Home, this is. . .

MOTHER JONES Ray, at least be glad you have a home to return to.

RAY JUNIOR I got ya'll, but I can't call this land home. A white man's heaven, is a Black m. . .

MOTHER JONES Stop the rhetoric! Stop it! That's how war begins! Just like that, just like what you're doing now. Stop it. All this talk of hate. What can you

Homecoming

41

build with hate. Nothing, but walls to separate people. Nothing but prisons
to keep people locked up. Don't perpetuate the same hate that you accuse the
white man of.

RAY JUNIOR Yeah, all right.
(Turns away form her. Faces the flag on the wall, gives clenched fist, Black
Power salute). I pledge allegiance to Black people and to our struggle to free
ourselves from the injustice and oppression of America.

MOTHER JONES You can make fun if you want to, but you just remember,
whether you like it or not, this is your country, and we'll all be better off when
young men like you stand up and help straighten out whatever may be wrong
with our country.

RAY JUNIOR It's not our country. It's the white man's country, and I don't like
it. In fact, that shouldn't even be on our wall. I think I'm going to take that rag
off the wall.

MOTHER JONES (Moving directly in front of him). Now, you just wait one
minute, young man. When you get your own home, you can put whatever you
like on the walls, but in this house, your father and I will decide what goes.

RAY JUNIOR Yeah; okay.
(Walking away from her and then turning to face her.) It's funny though how
they got you, Negroes, ready to protect something that ain't never meant
nothing but death to you.

MOTHER JONES America has meant more than death to us. It has also
meant life to us, and it can mean freedom if we're strong enough to deal with it.
(Pause). Yvette, say good-night.

YVETTE But mother, it's only. . .

MOTHER JONES Won't you at least let your brother be alone with Roberta
for a little while. You can see him all day tomorrow.

YVETTE Okay. Good-night.
(Yvette and mother exit).

RAY JUNIOR (Walks over to the table and takes another drink of wine). You
still here, huh?

ROBERTA Yes, I'm still here.

RAY JUNIOR You kind of slow on understanding. How many different ways I got to tell you we through?

ROBERTA I don't believe that.
(She walks over to him. Touches his arm).

RAY JUNIOR (Moves away). Suit yourself.
(He goes over to the record box and puts on Ray Charles, "Drown In My Own Tears." Looks at Roberta. Walks out of the room. Roberta stands listening to the music, to the words, to the memories inside her head. Resolves she will not cry, and she will not let Ray walk away without explaining himself. She faces where he walked off, covers her face briefly, composes herself, and waits.)

RAY JUNIOR (Re-enters, walks around Roberta, gets another drink, sips but does not drink it all. Moves directly in front of Roberta and looks into her face.) You a jive woman, you know that?

ROBERTA Ray, I love you.

RAY JUNIOR (Mimicking her voice). Ray, I love you.

ROBERTA Ray, don't do this to me. Please, Ray.

RAY JUNIOR Ray, don't do this to me. Please, Ray.

ROBERTA The whole time you were away, I was waiting for you, thinking about you. Most nights, I sat home and I wrote to you. Just for you, and. . . and now you want to tell me we're through. Just forget about us. Forget about how we were before you left. Well, It's not like that. I'm not going to let you do that to me.

RAY JUNIOR You ain't, huh? Well, how you gonna stop me?
(He turns from her and sips from the cup of wine.)

ROBERTA Ray, stop that.
(Roberta grabs Ray's arm, and he pulls away from her.)

RAY JUNIOR Leave go of me. Get off my back. Just get off my goddamn back. Damn woman. Why don't you leave me alone.
(He paces back and forth, leaning heavily on his walking cane. The wine is getting to him.)

Homecoming

ROBERTA (She pauses, motions to reach out to him. Stops. Starts to reach out again, but catches herself. Turns away briefly, then refaces him. Softly.) Ray, can I remind you of the promises you made to me? Should I repeat all the vows you said you'd never break . . .

RAY JUNIOR Oh, please don't start that shit. . .

ROBERTA I'm not making it up. It's words you said to me. Roberta, I will always love you. Roberta, I'm not going to do you like all those other guys do to girls. Trust me, Roberta. Remember, Ray?
(Ray does not answer.) Ray, answer me. Do you remember the promises you made to me? I didn't ask you for them, you promised me. Do you remember?

RAY JUNIOR Roberta. . .

ROBERTA That's the first time you said my name since you've been back.

RAY JUNIOR (Hangs his head, looks at the floor). Hey, look. You're right. I said those things a long time ago, but look, you got eyes, you can see. Look, I've changed. The man who said those things ain't here no more. I've changed.

ROBERTA (She waits until he looks up at her.) Ray. . .
(Moves to embrace him).

RAY JUNIOR
(Moves away. Softly.) Stop. It won't work. I don't think the same thoughts. I don't act the same way. I don't like what I used to like. . .

ROBERTA What about love?

RAY JUNIOR (Turns, answers her quickly). I don't love you in the same way.
(Watches her reaction. She is hurt.) I mean, I respect you. You're good people and all that, and you gon'be real good for somebody, but that somebody ain't me. It's over.

ROBERTA Ray, please.

RAY JUNIOR Please, my ass! Don't you understand English. It's over. Through. Finis. Ka-put.
(They look at each other). I can't deal with you . . .

ROBERTA Why?

RAY JUNIOR Oh, let's stop this soap opera shit. Look, why don't you go home. I don't want to hurt you any more. We're just on different wavelengths now.

ROBERTA Ray, I want to understand. I'm stronger than you think. Why won't you give me a chance? Ray, please, Ray let me try to help you?

RAY JUNIOR It's not me who needs the help.
(Silence.) Roberta, if you really understood, we wouldn't be having this conversation. You would be a different person, I would know it and you would know it. I used to be like you. I used to believe in all this. It's not my job to change you into somebody like me. I mean I don't know.
(Rubs his face.) For you the world is what it was. For me the world is what it is. Tomorrow, tomorrow, who knows.

ROBERTA Ray. . .

RAY JUNIOR (Screaming). Go home. It's over.

ROBERTA (Shaking her head). Over! Over! What are you talking about? Just like that, because you say so? What about me? I got feelings. You act like it's just you and you can do whatever you want. I hope you don't think you can just walk in here and tell me to get out of your life, just like that. What you take me for, a fool? You think I'm a damn yo-yo or something you got at your beckon call. You can say it's over if you want to, but everywhere you go, you're going to see me. Every time you're somewhere, I'm going to be there. I'll be damn if I'm going to let you drop me just like that. (Snaps her fingers) Who do you think you are?

(Junior is still pacing back and forth. Roberta becomes very angry, and when he raises the cup to take another drink, she pulls his arm down. He is too intoxicated to keep his balance. When he tries to jerk free from her, the cane slips, and he falls.)

RAY JUNIOR Shit!

ROBERTA Ray, Ray, I'm sorry. I'm sorry. I forgot about. . .
(Roberta tries to help Junior to his feet, but he pulls away from her and slowly rises on his own.)

RAY JUNIOR I told you to leave me alone.

ROBERTA Ray, please. (Roberta moves to put her arms around him.)

Homecoming

RAY JUNIOR I told you to leave me alone.

ROBERTA Let›s sit down and talk.

RAY JUNIOR (Shakes free from her). NOOOOOOOOO!

ROBERTA Ray, I'm begging you. Ray.

RAY JUNIOR Oh, go fuck yo›self!
(Roberta slaps Junior very hard, and he slaps her back, almost as quickly as she slapped him. She stands there holding her face and looking at Ray, not believing that he has hit her.)

RAY JUNIOR Now, why don't you go home. (Roberta exits very slowly. Junior turns his back to her as she walks away. She stops and looks back at him. He half looks over his shoulder.) I ain't no more good for you. Just go on home, please. (Roberta exits. Ray breathes deeply. Looks at the flag on the wall.) And Goddamn this motherfucking flag.
(He rips the flag off the wall and then goes over to the record player and starts "Drown In My Own Tears" over again. He then picks up the wine bottle and drinks from it. Sings along with the record for a little while, then sits down on the floor putting the wine bottle beside him.) I shot that mother right in the back of his head. I told him I was going to get him. Wasn't nothing but a punk-ass second lieutenant. Always was riding our back. I shot him. Jones, do this. Jones, do that. Jones, your equipment ain't straight. Jones your weapon is filthy. Jones—Jones—Jones, and you people and ya'll boys this and ya'll boys that. Ya'll colored fellows got to do this, you boys need to learn how to do that. And had cheek enough to have a confederate flag in his tent. I told him not to mess with me. I told him. I told him, said "sir, you keep messing with me, and I'ma kill yo' ass". And he just put me on point on another patrol. And then he told me take them pictures down, and I didn't, and he gave me a Article Fifteen, but I told him, and twice, he liked to got all us killed with his dumb ass, but I got him. I shot him dead in the back of his old, ugly head. And I'ma shoot a whole bunch more them ole, ugly crackers before it's over. Yeah, I'ma do it. Fuck the army. Look at me. . .marching through all that mud and rain. . . and. . .
(Junior mumbles the rest.)

YVETTE (Yvette has entered while Junior is on the floor mumbling.) Junior? Junior?

RAY JUNIOR Yeah, what?
(Junior rolls over, stretched flat out on his back.)

YVETTE Some homecoming. You done went and got drunk. Now, look at you laying all over the floor.

RAY JUNIOR Yeah, it's a bitch; ain't it? You know, I done figured it out. I mean, I figured out why we was in Vietnam. It musta' been 'cause it was one of them Vietnamese what killed Kennedy. Oswald must of been Vietnamese. (Junior laughs, but Yvette doesn't laugh with him.) And you watch, after Vietnam, they might have us going down there to South America, and next, we gon' be over there messing with all that oil and them Arabs, and if we go for that, before you know it, they'll have us in Africa. Ain't it a bitch. They took us from Africa on a slaveship, and now, they liable to try to send us back there on a troop ship and tell us to shoot'em up over there.

YVETTE Junior, get up.

RAY JUNIOR Okay. Okay. I'm getting up.
(He tries to get up, but he has to struggle just to sit up. He remains sitting and looking around. He looks at Yvette. She is in her slip and has a robe on, but the robe is open. She sees that he is looking at her. She closes her robe.)

YVETTE Don't stop now. Ain't no man suppose to be sitting on the floor all drunk?

RAY JUNIOR 'Vette, I'm going to get up, but wait a minute. I got to ask you something.

YVETTE Junior, get up.
(She starts to reach out to help him. He grabs her arm and then pushes her away gently.)

RAY JUNIOR You still a virgin?

YVETTE (The question catches her off guard. She doesn't know how to answer.) Why, Junior? Why you asking me that? Yes. . .

RAY JUNIOR 'Vette, you know what I did?

YVETTE (She senses that he is serious.) What you did, Junior?

RAY JUNIOR You, what, you fifteen now, huh?

YVETTE Sixteen. I just made sixteen.

RAY JUNIOR Sixteen. Shit. 'Vette, I bought a girl was sixteen when I was in Nam.

YVETTE Come on Junior, get up. You ain't got to talk about that.

RAY JUNIOR Yes, I do. Yeah, I got to talk about it. I got to tell somebody. Her little brother was pimping her. Bought her for for five dollars. Five dollars, and she did whatever I told her to do. She kissed me wherever I told her to kiss me. . .

YVETTE Junior, it's over now. It's all over now.

RAY JUNIOR No, it ain't. It ain›t over. It's still in my head. I don't even know why I did it. You wrote me a letter once talking about how proud you were that me and the guys were standing up for Black people over there in Nam, and you sent me this picture with you standing by the Black Liberation Flag. I was so proud of you. I carried that picture everywhere. (Pauses. Chokes.) 'Vette, everytime I look at that picture now, I see that lil girl I fucked over.

YVETTE Junior, come on. Get up, you're talking crazy.

RAY JUNIOR No, lil sister, I'm talking truth. It wasn't just I fucked her, it was, there's, I mean.

YVETTE (Yvette is afraid. She doesn't understand what's happening.) Junior, get up. Please, get up.

RAY JUNIOR 'Vette, what's worse than a big old, grown man fucking a little girl? Huh?

YVETTE Junior, I don't know. Get up. Come on. . .

RAY JUNIOR I'll tell you, 'Vette. What's worse is killing them. (Junior looks at Yvette.) And, I did that too. Yvette, you understand? (She covers her mouth and takes one small step backward.) I was shooting little girls. Girls your age, Yvette. I'm looking at you but I'm seeing that girl I killed. I shot her. When you over there and your buddies are getting shot, and the only enemy you can find are old men and little girls. 'Vette, your brother is a killer.

YVETTE Junior, I don't know what to . . .Oh, get up, please get up. You're a Black man. Get up!

RAY JUNIOR Yeah. Yeah, you're right. I want to be a Black man, but sometimes, I just don't know what to do about all the things I've already done. (He moans a hurt moan and struggles to get up.) Give me a hand.

YVETTE No. Get up on your own. You can do it. You don't need somebody always helping you up after you get yourself messed up.

RAY JUNIOR Aug, 'Vette. Come on.

YVETTE Ray, get up and quit begging. Be a man, Ray.
(Yvette kneels next to him.) Come on, get up.

RAY JUNIOR My leg is hurting. It's hurting where I got shot, and I can't push up on it.

YVETTE Damn your leg. Get up. If you can shoot women, you can push on that leg.
(They look at each other. He struggles to rise, gets up on one knee).

RAY JUNIOR 'Vette, I. . .

YVETTE I'm sorry, Ray. I shouldn't have said that. I'm sorry. I won't say it again. Come on.
(She moves to help him. He pushes her away, and in the process falls back down.) What am I suppose to do, let you stay down there. Let you pass out on the floor so mother or daddy can find you in the morning?

RAY JUNIOR I don't care.

YVETTE Well, I care.
(Very dejected). Aw, Ray, why you always got to fail? Why for once, just once, you can't do it all the way, just get up. I don't care about those girls. I mean, I care but what's done is done. I want you to get up now. Ray. . .

RAY SR. (Entering slowly). What's going on in here? Boy, what you doing on the floor?

YVETTE Nothing. Junior fell down on account his leg, but he's all right.

RAY SR. Well, help him up, girl.
(Yvette bends to help Junior, but he refuses.)

Homecoming

49

RAY JUNIOR Naw, leave me alone. I can make it on my own. I ain't invalid.

RAY SR. Well, get up, boy!

RAY JUNIOR Daddy, don't call me that. I ain't no boy.

RAY SR. Boy, get up!

RAY JUNIOR (Hollering). I ain't no boy!

RAY SR. You a boy as long as you acting like you acting. You a boy long as you laying there on the floor too drunk to stand up on your feet like a man.

RAY JUNIOR I ain't no boy. Don't call me that. I killed a honky for calling me that. Don›t call me no boy!

RAY SR. And you think that make you a man? You think killing somebody white gon make you a man?

RAY JUNIOR Just don't call me no boy.

RAY SR. Boy, let me tell you somethin'.
(Takes a deep breath.) I believe you. I believe you shot one of them white boys over there in Nam. Probably made you mad or something and you went off and shot him to get even. But, you listen here, I'ma tell you something. Don't you never be bragging about killing nobody. Ain't no honor in killing, all the honor is in figuring out how to live.

RAY JUNIOR I knew you wouldn›t understand.

RAY SR. I understand a lot more than you think I do and more than that, the really deep thing is that you understand a lot less than you think you do.
(Gets a chair and pulls it near to Junior, sits down.) How old you think I am, boy? (Junior doesn't answer.) You know I was in World War II. Yeah, you know that already. You ever hear me talk about it? You ever hear me talk about how they treated us in that war? You ever hear me talk about the time in Australia we, and I'm talking about a bunch of Black men, we got together, loaded up our guns and went to war against them white soldiers? Naw, most people don't know a thing about any of that, but it happened. What I'm telling you son is that the real battle ain't in war time, our real battle is when we get back home. We got back here in 1946 and everything was still messed up. Why you think I let Yvette talk all that Africa talk, hang with a lot of boys talking about revolution and ain't never been to war. Why you think I ain't never said

nothing to you when I picked you up and you were talking all that mess, and today. I want yall to fight. I want you to be a fighter. But I don't want to see you fail, and I sure don't want to see you wallowing in your own self pity. Whatever you do to stand tall and reach as high as you want to reach. I'ma stand with you, and that go for your sister too. Both of yall, whatever you want to be, whatever road you want to run. But I'll be goddamn if I let either one of yall end up be sniveling, lil snotty nose, cry babies who can't keep going when the going gets rough.

(Ray, Sr., gets up, picks up Junior's walking cane. Holds it. Looks at Junior. Grips the cane with both hands—a hand at either end. Spreads his legs and holds the cane parallel to the floor in front of Junior.) Now, get up. Pull yourself up like a man.

(Junior looks at the cane. Hesitates. Grips it with one hand, and then with the other. Struggles mightily and finally slowly rises to his feet. Ray, Sr., gives the cane to Junior.) Now you remember that and don't you ever be bending down low less you sho' you can stand back up straight again. You remember that. A man can make hisself low all different kinds of ways. It's easy to go low, but it's hard to stand tall, and getting up is always hard. Now you go on in there and get some sleep.

RAY JUNIOR (Humbly.) Yes, sir.
(Starts out very slowly.)

RAY SR. (To Yvette.) Girl you go on to bed, too.

YVETTE Yes, sir.
(She exits, passing by Junior.)

RAY SR. Junior.
(Junior stops and turns to face Ray, Sr., who walks slowly over to Junior.) You a man now, son. You can't be blaming your actions on nobody else. Not on the white man or nobody. You responsible for what you do and don't do. And as long as you my son, I'm not going to let you be any less than you can be. You understand that? If you want to act like a boy, well then you can just count on me knocking you down to the ground where all boys belong. But, you be a man, and I'll walk with you all the way. You understand?

RAY JUNIOR Yes, sir.

RAY SR. Good. Now go on and get yourself some sleep.
(Junior starts to exit again.) Junior.
(Standing close).

RAY JUNIOR Yeah.

RAY SR. Welcome home, son.
(They embrace.)
(LIGHTS.)
(CURTAIN)

Val Gray Ward

Val Gray Ward was an internationally acclaimed dramatist-historian, producer, director, educator, cultural activist, and "HistoryMaker" who is known throughout the world as "The Voice of the Black Writer." Ward was born in one of the oldest all-Black towns in the U.S., Mound Bayou, Mississippi. She is renowned for her ritual and staged theatre productions; one-woman shows, Harriet Tubman and My Soul is a Witness; and popularizing the works of celebrated and lesser-known prolific black writers through her sensitive interpretations. In 1968, Ward founded Chicago's pioneering Black theatre, Kuumba Theatre with the active support of her husband veteran journalist, professor emeritus of journalism, and co-founder of The National Association of Black Journalists (NABJ) Francis Ward, their children, and the community. In 1969, Ward opened the door as the inaugural director of the Afro-American Cultural Center at the University of Illinois Champaign-Urbana. Ward is the recipient of over 200 awards including several lifetime-achievement awards, 21 Emmys for her edu-tainment film Precious Memories: Strolling 47th Street, and a Grammy nomination for her tribute CD rhapsody in Hughes 101 honoring the life and legacy of Langston Hughes. You may recall that Val and her husband co-authored "The Black Artist—His Role in the Struggle," which is published in the first volume of BFTT as well as earlier publications. The nonagenarian is still giving stirring lectures and performances, virtually. Inspired by her life's work, the course "Val Gray Ward: The Power of Black Arts, Theatre, and Movement" is presently taught at Wellesley College, MA.

Talking Drum

(For Sister Sonia)

you ancient drum

bold spirit of the ancestors

shaking our Black skins and limbs loose

into freedom morning marches through the fiery streets of Alabama, Harlem,

California, Philadelphia, Chicago, and Soweto…

with your, with your, with your your your your click…

I say with your your your clicking incantations and oracular orikis

for Black love, yes Black love, I say Black love, love, love, love, life, love, life, love,

life, love…Black life, Black mother, Black child womannnn, I say Black

womannnnn……..Black womennnnn…

sister, sister, sister, sisters,

walking and talking in struggle,

walking and talking in power,

walking and talking in truth,

walking and talking in Blackness…

you, Nikki, and me, 3 sisters

how do we count the ways, how do we count the days, and how do we

count 50 plus years, by decades, by scores by lifetimes, tell us how do we….

Black black black….

ebay eyah ebay eyah it will get better ebay eyah betterrrrr

Blackerrrr…blackerrrrr betterrrr blackerrrrr betterrrr…ancient drummer…

Ancient Black sister…Sonia…

It will get betterrrrrr…

September 13, 2022

RAYMOND NAT TURNER

"The Town Crier," Raymond Nat Turner, is a NYC poet privileged to have read at the Harriet Tubman Centennial Symposium. He is Artistic Director of the stalwart JazzPoetry Ensemble UpSurge!NYC and has appeared at numerous festivals and venues including the Monterey Jazz Festival and Panafest in Ghana West Africa. He currently is Poet-in-Residence at Black Agenda Report. He's also Co-Chair of the New York Chapter of the National Writers Union (NWU).

Just Ms. Brooks and Me
A Moment with Gwendolyn Brooks

I met Gwendolyn Brooks at a San Francisco Press Club event for master poets in the 1980s. Admission was $10 plus transportation and my money was tight. I remember at the BART station (Bay Area Rapid Transit) I apparently was taking too long to figure out how to pay for my ticket because the 'brother' behind me got angry and started threatening me to hurry up, using a gun to emphasize his point.

Uh-oh, how is this going to end? I wondered.

Making it to the event alive, my heart rate went down. Ms. Brooks gave a stellar reading to a packed house. All the bigwigs from the city were there, honoring her. She received tons of accolades, awards and flowers. And she was surrounded after the reading!
And then everyone left ...

Suddenly, it was just the Sister-Elder-Queen-Mother, all her awards and bouquets ... and me. The event was held in the hotel in which she was staying. Maybe folks assumed that she had assistants to help her, but she traveled simply, by train, solo. I was working in warehousing back then; I was really strong. I helped her get her stuff up to her room, making two or three trips.

Excited to be in her presence and have this limited time with her, I launched into my questions.

"How do you write — longhand or type?" I asked her. *"When do you write, late at night or in the morning?"*

She was generous in talking about her process. She told me that she woke at 5:00, did her exercises, ate, and then started writing. I think she told me she typed but I'm not sure if I remember that correctly. I asked if I could send her some work, and she gave me her address.

I sent her some of my work, and she wrote back:
"Thank you for sharing your lively work."

"LIVELY!"

For years, I used that as a one-word quote from this renowned poet and godmother of the Black Arts Movement.

GIDEON YOUNG

Gideon Young is a member of the Carolina African American Writers' Collective and Carrboro Poets Council. Find recent and forthcoming work in Journal of Black Mountain College Studies, Modern Haiku, North Carolina Literary Review, Our State, and WALTER. His debut haiku collection *my hands full of light* was published by Backbone Press, April 2021. Two books for young readers, *Prince Rivers: A Leader for Justice* and *Art for Change* are forthcoming from Gibbs Smith Education. Gideon is co-author of *One Window's Light: A Collection of Haiku,* published by Unicorn Press, 2017, winner of the Haiku Society of America Merit Award for Best Anthology. Gideon's 2021 film, *A Curious Honeybee*, a celebration of multiple literacies, was premiered by the Arts Education Partnership and the Education Commission of the States. He is a Fellow for A+ Schools of North Carolina, a K-12 Literacy Specialist, and stay-at-home Dad. Discover more at www.gideonyoung.com.

kwansaba crown

this country says you were born flying
in the face of its oldest rule—
brown and loved. we lift you up
cradle your warm face to our faces
the murmur and spark of your skin
your blood crossed over ocean and swung
the lash. your wings gold and fire

kwansaba crown 55

······

lash your wings with gold and fire
invent fine knots that have no names
tie them snug around your green bones
this world wants to watch you fray
won't warn you the term for loop
is *eye*. an eye that slips is
called *noose*. you keep you in view

······

our name anew, keep you in view
pray the spirits of our spiral cells
their hope tall drums' tight deep boom
battle dance of spun blood toward light
each jitter red drop an elder's eye
under your skin their buzz a blue
ancient chorus hums power in your moves

······

ancient chorus hums power in your moves
i know from the clatter how elegant
your elbows bend to cast rainbow blocks
across our ash floors you unbuild towers
we made of selves before you sparked
your small fingers offer us bright bricks
more again, you say without saying, *here*

······

more again, you say without saying, here
watch me sway but stand toes curled
press my bones' weight into ash floors
yet of bones into ash into dust
i know nothing of winter except winter:
an absence of wild geese, early evening
sun on silver limbs, your lifted gaze

...

sun on silver limbs, your lifted gaze
burns away all of me but memory
how your skull above your ears fit
in the cradle of my spread fingers
your soft spot exact to the center
of my palm our pulse same rhythm
spring breeze charms the air with lilac

...

spring breeze charms the air with lilac
you ignore the grass between your toes
new word *more* a wren takes wing
out from the crayon in your fist
acorn filled with earth hear my yearn
my blood near yours forever i know
this world sings you were born flying

the river

- remix of The Swing *by Robert Louis Stevenson*

so brown up in the air
a child swings

the air
so blue

all over the country
the air so blue

we sing
the pleasantest things

we sing
a child can do anything

up over the wall
child

look on the garden green
child

how do you like the river
child

the river deep down
blue

you
flying child

you
green child

you
brown child

look wide
see the country

how to till the garden
child

how to till
the river

child
look up

see how
all over the country

brown bodies
swing

what is it i hide from myself

when i say *the bright side of slavery*[1]
to avoid sweeping all southerners into the muck
i both deny myself and excuse myself—
i am black and must rail against the dark
i am black and must *hasten the glad day of deliverance*[2]
i am white and see my face in the crowds
i am white and do not want to call myself devil
i am brown and a bug under America's boot
i am brown and the hope of what might be
i am brown and loved and spread my arms to the sun
i am brown and black and white and slave and free
i am so new upon this earth my voice is one of creation
i am swirling up from the ether
i must make my own way

[1] Preface excerpt from *Behind the Scenes*, the autobiography of Elizabeth Keckley, 1818-1907. A mixed-race former slave, who purchased her freedom for $1200, Elizabeth philosophized that slavery must run its course before being destroyed, describing slavery as "a curse" and "evil".

[2] Appendix excerpt from Frederick Douglass's *Narrative of the Life of Frederick Douglass*, 1818-1895. An escaped slave, Frederick was entirely opposed to slavery and slaveholders, citing "No Compromise!" and declaring abolishment a "sacred cause".

GERARDO DEL GUERCIO

Interview with Karina Griffith

Karina Griffith is Canadian-Caribbean filmmaker and actress as well as a Research and Teaching Assistant at University of Toronto. Her research into cinematic movements, identity and belonging informs her installations and work with the moving image. Using super-8 film, video, crochet and sound, Karina Griffith's recent works are representations of fear and fantasy, often focussing on how they relate to the immigrant perspective. In sum, Karina is Griffith interested in creating contrasts that explore personal phobias to expose the universality of alienation.

Tell us a bit about your recent projects. Are there any recurring themes? Do you have a particular scene or line? Are they any different from your other projects?

Griffith: The themes I often grapple with in my films are identity and immigration. My parents immigrated to Canada from Guyana in the sixties (my sister and I were born in Toronto), and now I live in Germany. The more I tell stories, the more I recognize that my experiences with migration informs my unique point of view on the world.

For instance, I am currently editing a short documentary about blackface in Germany. I think most North Americans would be surprised that is a part of contemporary German culture - but we must always remember that they have a different history than us. *DER SCHWIMMUNTERRICHT*(Swimming Lessons) is a documentary about adults with a fear of deep water learning how to swim. On the surface, one would not think this has anything to do with these themes, but I found through making this film that our phobias are also a part of who we are, even if we would rather not define ourselves that way.

I recently created an installation with crochet and satellite dishes-that was new for me, working in three dimensions. Although, I like to think of film as a three-dimensional medium—the third dimension being the audience.

What films by someone else would you recommend that you admire and why?

I am most interested in the place where fact and fiction intersect, so both of my recommendations play with documentary and drama. I saw an unforgettable Canadian film at the Berlinale last year, *FRANCINE*, that I have been talking about ever since. The story is about a woman who is released from prison and has a hard time integrating in society, but finds solace in her relationship with animals. The filmmakers cast people that were very much like the characters they wrote. They also worked from a 10 page script, which left a lot of room for improvisation. The result was a film that feels incredible real.

PUTTY HILL is a great experiment that feels like a regular film. The filmmaker came up with a loose plot (a young man commits suicide in a small town), and the story unfolds through informal interviews with various characters speaking directly into the camera. The characters are essentially playing themselves, so when the filmmaker asks them what they did that day, they answer honestly. But when he asked them about the fictional character who took his life, they return to the loose plot points in the script. It's a must see.

Are the 21st century and films well matched and in what ways?

I feel I should make some comment about how no one has time to read anymore, and that we are so focussed on the senses of sight and sound (although Apple has re-integrated "touch" into our experience of storytelling). But I feel film fits to this century because it is of this century. I am excited about the documentary residencies and interactive projects coming out of the National Film Board of Canada - they seem very "now".

Tell us about your interest in film

My Caribbean-Canadian family loves telling inevitably funny, long, stories, so maybe that's where it comes from. But then, I should be in radio, right? Perhaps it is the communal aspect of filmmaking - you need a lot of people to make a film and then, you hope many people will watch it together.

What is your favourite thinking spot?

I recently acquired a "Schrebergarten" here in Germany, which is something like a cross between an allotment garden and a cabin. Between the World Wars, it was decided that people who live in the cities have a worse chance of surviving because they die of hunger. So land was set aside (mostly near the railway tracks) for city-dwellers to have gardens. The rule is you are supposed to grow food on 30% of the land. This is my absolute favourite thinking and writing spot. Gardening is absolutely complimentary to the creative process.

What film genre do you believe is the best? What makes it the best?

Do you count independent film as a genre? If so, these are usually my favourites. I love nothing more than watching a short film or a feature from a first-time filmmaker who has a fresh perspective on a genre. These films are usually a labour of love, made by any means necessary, because the story just had to be told. This is why the atmosphere at film festivals is so wonderful—the opportunity for discovery. In this era of sequels and remakes, how often can you say you have seen something truly new?

What are your future plans?

I am currently writing a feature film about plants who manipulate humans for their own ends. I challenge the idea that plants are passive and merely exist for animals to use. The story is set in the Caribbean and loosely based on my great Aunt Hectorine who was a bush healer in Guyana. My present and future are all about making this

AUDRE LORDE

Poet, essayist, and novelist Audre Lorde was born Audrey Geraldine Lorde on February 18, 1934, in New York City. Her parents were immigrants from Grenada. The youngest of three sisters, she was raised in Manhattan and attended Catholic school. While she was still in high school, her first poem appeared in *Seventeen* magazine. Lorde received her BA from Hunter College and an MLS from Columbia University. She served as a librarian in New York public schools from 1961 through 1968. In 1962, Lorde married Edward Rollins. They had two children, Elizabeth and Jonathon, before divorcing in 1970.

Her first volume of poems, *The First Cities* (Poets Press), was published in 1968. In the same year, she became the writer-in-residence at Tougaloo College in Mississippi, where she discovered a love of teaching. At Tougaloo, she also met her long-term partner, Frances Clayton. *The First Cities* was quickly followed with *Cables to Rage* (Paul Breman, 1970) and *From a Land Where Other People Live* (Broadside Press, 1973), which was nominated for a National Book Award. In 1974, she published *New York Head Shot and Museum* (Broadside Press). Whereas much of her earlier work focused on the transience of love, this book marked her most political work to date.

In 1976, W. W. Norton released her collection *Coal* and, shortly thereafter, published *The Black Unicorn* (1995). Poet Adrienne Rich said of *The Black Unicorn* that "Lorde writes as a Black woman, a mother, a daughter, a Lesbian, a feminist, a visionary; poems of elemental wildness and healing, nightmare and lucidity." Her other volumes include *Chosen Poems Old and New* (1982) and *Our Dead Behind Us* (1986), both published by W. W. Norton.

Poetry Is Not a Luxury

The quality of light by which we scrutinize our lives has direct bearing upon the product which we live, and upon the changes which we hope to bring about through those lives. It is within this light that we form those ideas by which we pursue our magic and make it realized. This is poetry as illumination, for it is through poetry that we give name to those ideas which are, until the poem, nameless and formless-about to be birthed, but already felt. That distillation of experience from which true poetry springs births thought as dream births concept, as feeling births idea, as knowledge births (precedes) understanding.

As we learn to bear the intimacy of scrutiny, and to flourish within it, as we learn to use the products of that scrutiny for power within our living, those fears which rule our lives and form our silences begin to lose their control over us.

For each of us as women, there is a dark place within where hidden and growing our true spirit rises, "Beautiful and tough as chestnut/ stanchions against our nightmare of weakness" and of impotence.

These places of possibility within ourselves are dark because they are ancient and hidden; they have survived and grown strong through darkness. Within these deep places, each one of us holds an incredible reserve of creativity and power, of unexamined and unrecorded emotion

Poetry Is Not a Luxury

and feeling. The woman's place of power within each of us is neither white nor surface; it is dark, it is ancient, and it is deep.

When we view living, in the european mode, only as a problem to be solved, we then rely solely upon our ideas to make us free, for these were what the white fathers told us were precious.

But as we become more in touch with our own ancient, black, non-european view of living as a situation to be experienced and interacted with, we learn more and more to cherish our feelings, and to respect those hidden sources of our power from where true knowledge and therefore lasting action comes.

At this point in time, I believe that women carry within ourselves the possibility for fusion of these two approaches as keystone for survival, and we come closest to this combination in our poetry. I speak here of poetry as the revelation or distillation of experience, not the sterile word play that, too often, the white fathers distorted the word poetry to mean — in order to cover their desperate wish for imagination without insight.

For women, then, poetry is not a luxury. It is a vital necessity of our existence. It forms the quality of the light within which we predicate our hopes and dreams toward survival and change, first made into language, then into idea, then into more tangible action. Poetry is the way we help give name to the nameless so it can be thought. The farthest external horizons of our hopes and fears are cobbled by our poems, carved from the rock experiences of our daily lives.

As they become known and accepted to ourselves, our feelings, and the honest exploration of them, become sanctuaries and fortresses and spawning grounds for the most radical and daring of ideas, the house of difference so necessary to change and the conceptualization of any meaningful action. Right now, I could name at least ten ideas I would have once found intolerable or incomprehensible and frightening, except as they came after dreams and poems. This is not idle fantasy, but the true meaning of "it feels right to me." We can train ourselves to respect our feelings, and to discipline (transpose) them into a language that matches those feelings so they can be shared. And where that language does not yet exist, it is our poetry which helps to fashion it. Poetry is not only dream or vision, it is the skeleton architecture of our lives.

Possibility is neither forever nor instant. It is also not easy to sustain belief in its efficacy. We can sometimes work long and hard to establish one beachhead of real resistance to the deaths we are expected to live, only to have that beachhead assaulted or threatened by canards we have been socialized to fear, or by the withdrawal of those approvals that we have been warned to seek for safety. We see ourselves diminished or softened by the falsely benign accusations of childishness, of non-universality, of self-centeredness, of sensuality. And who asks the question: am I altering your aura, your ideas, your dreams, or am I merely moving you to temporary and reactive action? (Even the latter is no mean task, but one that must be rather seen within the context of a true alteration of the texture of our lives.)

The white fathers told us, I think therefore I am; and the black mothers in each of us-the poet- whispers in our dreams, I feel therefore I can be free. Poetry coins the language to express and charter this revolutionary awareness and demand, the implementation of that freedom. However, experience has taught us that the action in the now is also always necessary. Our children cannot dream unless they live, they cannot live unless they are nourished, and who else will feed them the real food without which their dreams will be no different from ours?

Sometimes we drug ourselves with dreams of new ideas. The head will save us. The brain alone will set us free. But there are no new ideas still waiting in the wings to save us as women, as human. There are only old and forgotten ones, new combinations, extrapolations and recognitions from within ourselves, along with the renewed courage to try them out. And we must constantly encourage ourselves and each other to attempt the heretical actions our dreams imply and some of our old ideas disparage. In the forefront of our move toward change, there is only our poetry to hint at possibility made real. Our poems formulate the implications of ourselves, what we feel within and dare make real (or bring action into accordance with), our fears, our hopes, our most cherished terrors.

For within structures defined by profit, by linear power, by institutional dehumanization, our feelings were not meant to survive. Kept around as unavoidable adjuncts or pleasant pastimes, feelings were meant to kneel to thought as we were meant to kneel to men. But women have survived. As poets. And there are no new pains. We have felt them all already. We have hidden that fact in the same place where we have hidden our power. They lie in our dreams, and it is our dreams that point the way to freedom. They are made realizable through our poems that give us the strength and courage to see, to feel, to speak, and to dare.

If what we need to dream, to move our spirits most deeply and directly toward and through promise, is a luxury, then we have given up the core-the fountain-of our power, our womanness; we have give up the future of our worlds.

For there are no new ideas. There are only new ways of making them felt, of examining what our ideas really mean (feel like) on Sunday morning at 7 AM, after brunch, during wild love, making war, giving birth; while we suffer the old longings, battle the old warnings and fears of being silent and impotent and alone, while tasting our new possibilities and strengths.

Power

The difference between poetry and rhetoric
is being ready to kill
yourself
instead of your children.

I am trapped on a desert of raw gunshot wounds
and a dead child dragging his shattered black
face off the edge of my sleep
blood from his punctured cheeks and shoulders
is the only liquid for miles
and my stomach
churns at the imagined taste while
my mouth splits into dry lips
without loyalty or reason
thirsting for the wetness of his blood
as it sinks into the whiteness
of the desert where I am lost
without imagery or magic
trying to make power out of hatred and destruction
trying to heal my dying son with kisses
only the sun will bleach his bones quicker.

A policeman who shot down a ten year old in Queens
stood over the boy with his cop shoes in childish blood
and a voice said "Die you little motherfucker" and
there are tapes to prove it. At his trial
this policeman said in his own defense
"I didn't notice the size nor nothing else

only the color". And
there are tapes to prove that, too.

Today that 37 year old white man
with 13 years of police forcing
was set free
by eleven white men who said they were satisfied
justice had been done
and one Black Woman who said
"They convinced me" meaning
they had dragged her 4'10" black Woman's frame
over the hot coals
of four centuries of white male approval
until she let go
the first real power she ever had
and lined her own womb with cement
to make a graveyard for our children.

I have not been able to touch the destruction
within me.
But unless I learn to use
the difference between poetry and rhetoric
my power too will run corrupt as poisonous mold
or lie limp and useless as an unconnected wire
and one day I will take my teenaged plug
and connect it to the nearest socket
raping an 85 year old white woman
who is somebody's mother
and as I beat her senseless and set a torch to her bed
a greek chorus will be singing in 3/4 time
"Poor thing. She never hurt a soul. What beasts they are."

Michael S. Harper

Poet and teacher Michael S. Harper was born in 1938, in Brooklyn, New York. He earned his BA and MA from California State University and his MFA from the Iowa Writers' Workshop. Known for his innovative use of jazz rhythms, cultural allusion, historical referent, and personal narrative, Harper was distinctive in that he often sought to bridge the traditional separation between black America and white America, writing poems that speak across the divide and draw upon elements of the racial, historical, and personal past of all Americans.

Harper's interest in history pervaded his poetry. Using stories from both his family's past and from events in black history in general, he builds a sophisticated vision of racial encounter and experience.

Harper's use of jazz and blues in his poems is also remarkable. Through syncopation, rhyme, and rhythm, Harper alluded to musical forms that were born out of the African-American experience.

In his first volume, the National Book Award-nominated *Dear John, Dear Coltrane* (1970), Harper used the legendary jazz pioneer John Coltrane as a character and cribs his style. Coltrane became a link for Harper to connect the historical with his own personal family history.

Harper's later collections of poetry included *Honorable Amendments* (1995) and *Songlines in Michaeltree: New and Collected Poems* (2000). As a professor at Brown University from 1970 to 2016, Harper helped shape generations of poets, writers, and scholars. The first poet laureate of Rhode Island (1988-1993), he received fellowships from the National Endowment for the Arts and the Guggenheim Foundation, among others. In 2008 he won the prestigious Frost Medal for Lifetime Achievement from the Poetry Society of America.

Dear John, Dear Coltrane

a love supreme, a love supreme

a love supreme, a love supreme

Sex fingers toes

in the marketplace

near your father's church

in Hamlet, North Carolina—

witness to this love

in this calm fallow

of these minds,

there is no substitute for pain:

genitals gone or going,

seed burned out,

you tuck the roots in the earth,

turn back, and move

by river through the swamps,

singing: a love supreme, a love supreme;

what does it all mean?

Loss, so great each black

woman expects your failure

in mute change, the seed gone.

You plod up into the electric city—

your song now crystal and

the blues. You pick up the horn

with some will and blow

into the freezing night:

a love supreme, a love supreme—

Dawn comes and you cook

up the thick sin 'tween

impotence and death, fuel

the tenor sax cannibal

heart, genitals, and sweat

that makes you clean—

a love supreme, a love supreme—

Why you so black?

cause I am

why you so funky?

cause I am

why you so black?

cause I am

why you so sweet?

cause I am

why you so black?

cause I am

a love supreme, a love supreme:

So sick

you couldn't play Naima,

so flat we ached

for song you'd concealed

with your own blood,

your diseased liver gave

out its purity,

the inflated heart

pumps out, the tenor kiss,

tenor love:

a love supreme, a love supreme—

a love supreme, a love supreme—

bell hooks

Activist and writer bell hooks was born in Hopkinsville, Kentucky as Gloria Jean Watkins. As a child, hooks performed poetry readings of work by Gwendolyn Brooks, Langston Hughes, and Elizabeth Barrett Browning. She earned a BA from Stanford University, an MA from the University of Wisconsin-Madison, and a PhD from the University of California-Santa Cruz.

hooks was the author of over 30 books, including *Ain't I a Woman: Black Women and Feminism* (1981), named by Publisher's Weekly as one of the 20 most influential books published in 20 years; *Feminist Theory: From Margin to Center* (1984); *Yearning: Race, Gender, and Cultural Politics* (1991), winner of the American Book Award/Before Columbus Foundation Award and the poetry collections *And There We Wept* (1978) and *When Angels Speak of Love* (2005), and *Appalachian Elegy: Poetry and Place* (2012), winner of the Black Caucus of the American Library Association's Best Poetry Award.

Throughout her life, hooks explored the relationship between sexism, racism, and economic disparity in books aimed at scholars and at the public.

hooks was the winner of the Writer's Award from the Lila-Wallace—Reader's Digest Fund, and has been named one of our nation's leading public intellectuals by the Atlantic. She taught at USC, Yale University, Oberlin College, the City College of New York, and Berea College.

hooks died in late 2021 at the age of 69.

Appalachian Elegy (Sections 1-6)

1.

hear them cry

the long dead

the long gone

speak to us

from beyond the grave

guide us

that we may learn

all the ways

to hold tender this land

hard clay direct

rock upon rock

charred earth

in time

strong green growth

will rise here

trees back to life

native flowers

pushing the fragrance of hope

the promise of resurrection

2.

such then is beauty

surrendered

against all hope

you are here again

turning slowly

nature as chameleon

all life change

and changing again

awakening hearts

steady moving from

unnamed loss

into fierce deep grief

that can bear all burdens

even the long passage

into a shadowy dark

where no light enters

3.

night moves

through the thick dark

a heavy silence outside

near the front window

a black bear

stamps down plants

pushing back brush

fleeing manmade

confinement

roaming unfettered

confident

any place can become home

strutting down

a steep hill

as though freedom

is all

in the now

no past

no present

4.

earth works

thick brown mud

clinging pulling

a body down

heard wounded earth cry

bequeath to me

the hoe the hope

ancestral rights

to turn the ground over

to shovel and sift

until history

rewritten resurrected

returns to its rightful owners

a past to claim

yet another stone lifted to

throw against the enemy

making way for new endings

random seeds

spreading over the hillside

wild roses

come by fierce wind and hard rain

unleashed furies

here in this touched wood

a dirge a lamentation

for earth to live again

earth that is all at once a grave

a resting place a bed of new beginnings

avalanche of splendor

5.

small horses ride me

carry my dreams

of prairies and frontiers

where once

the first people roamed

claimed union with the earth

no right to own or possess

no sense of territory

all boundaries

placed by unseen ones

here I will give you thunder

shatter your hearts with rain

let snow soothe you

make your healing water

clear sweet

a sacred spring

where the thirsty

may drink

animals all

6.

listen little sister

angels make their hope here

in these hills

follow me

I will guide you

careful now

no trespass

I will guide you

word for word

mouth for mouth

all the holy ones

embracing us

all our kin

making home here

renegade marooned

lawless fugitives

grace these mountains

we have earth to bind us

the covenant

between us

can never be broken

vows to live and let live

CAROLYN RODGERS

Born in Chicago in 1940, Carolyn Marie Rodgers was born to Clarence Rodgers, a welder, and his wife, Bazella. The last born of four children, her family had moved from Little Rock, Arkansas to Chicago's South Side, where Rodgers grew up. She earned her BA from Roosevelt University in 1965 and an MA in English from the University of Chicago in 1980. Early in her career, Rodgers was associated with the Black Arts Movement, attending writing workshops led by

Gwendolyn Brooks and through the Organization of Black American Culture. Rodgers's poetry collections include Paper Soul (1968); Songs of a Black Bird (1969), which won the Poet Laureate Award of the Society of Midland Authors; her best-known book, how i got ovah: New and Selected Poems (1975), a finalist for the National Book Award in 1976; The Heart as Ever Green: Poems (1978); and Morning Glory: Poems (1989).

Rodgers's poetry addresses feminist issues, including the role of Black women in society, though her work evolved over time from a militant stance to one more focused on the individual and Christianity. Other themes she explored in her poetry include mother-daughter relationships, relationships between Black men and Black women, street life, and love. In addition to poetry, Rodgers wrote plays, short stories, and essays. She worked as a book critic for the Chicago Daily News and as a columnist for the Milwaukee Courier.

Rodgers founded Third World Press in 1967 with Haki Madhubuti, Johari Amini, and Roschell Rich and began Eden Press with a grant from the Illinois Arts Council. She was as a social worker through the YMCA and taught at various colleges, including Columbia College, Malcolm X Community College, Albany State University, and Harold Washington College.

Rodgers received awards from the Conrad Kent River Memorial Fund and the National Endowment for the Arts. She was inducted into the International Literary Hall of Fame for Writers of African Descent in 2009 on the campus of Chicago State University.

Rodgers died in 2010 in Chicago at the age of 69.

Translation
(Thinking of Enoch) for Black People

The spirits
we are
live like leaves bowing trees
curtsying, breaking & fencing
into winds.
brushing, bruising & mingling
with each other.

I say,
we will live.
no death is a
singular unregenerating
event.
we will continue to be

constant
to flux
into each other
and surmount
the itinerant style of
the incalculable storms.

U Name This One

let uh revolution come, uh
state of peace is not known to me
anyway
since I grew uhround in chi town
where
howlin wolf howled in the tavern on 47th st.
and muddy waters made us cry the salty nigger blues
   where pee wee cut lonnell fuh messin wid
   his sistuh and blood baptized the street
   at least twice ev'ry week and judy got
   kicked outa grammar school fuh bein pregnant
   and died tryin to ungrow the seed
we was all up in there and
just living was guerilla warfare, yeah.

let uh revolution come.
Couldn't be no action like what
I dun already seen

ED BULLINS

Award-winning playwright Ed Bullins was a force in American theater for more than thirty-five years. Born on July 2, 1935 in Philadelphia, Pennsylvania, Bullins earned his B.A. degree in English and playwriting from Antioch University in San Francisco, California. He then received his M.F.A. degree from San Francisco State University in 1994.

In 1958, Bullins moved to Los Angeles, earned his general education diploma, and attended Los Angeles City College. Moving to San Francisco in 1964, Bullins entered a college writing program. In 1965, his plays *How Do*

You Do, Dialect Determinism and *Clara's Ole Man* were staged at the Firehouse Repertory Theatre in San Francisco. With poet Amiri Baraka, Bobby Seale, Huey Newton and Eldridge Cleaver, Bullins founded the cultural and political organization Black House and worked as its cultural director. Later, he served as minister of culture for the Black Panther Party.

In 1967, Bullins started his six-year association with Robert McBeth's New Lafayette Theatre in New York City and he became its playwright-in-residence. Also the editor of *Black Theatre* magazine, Bullins wrote and produced many plays during his time at the Lafayette.

Winner of the 1968 Vernon Rice Drama Desk Award for plays performed at the American Place Theatre in New York, Bullins also won the 1971 Obie Award for distinguished playwriting and the Black Arts Alliance Award for his plays *The Fabulous Miss Marie* and *In New England Winter*. Bullins earned Guggenheim Fellowships for playwriting in 1971 and 1976 and grants from the Rockefeller Foundation and the National Endowment for the Arts. In 1995, Bullins was appointed as a professor of theater and a distinguished artist-in-residence at Northeastern University.

Bullins passed away on November 13, 2021.

Clara's Ole Man

THE PEOPLE

CLARA, *a light brown girl of 18, well-built with long, dark hair. A blond streak runs down the middle of her head, and she affects a pony tail. She is pensive, slow in speech but feline. Her eyes are heavy-lidded and brown; she smiles—rather, blushes—often.*

BIG GIRL, *a stocky woman wearing jeans and tennis shoes and a tight-fitting blouse which accents her prominent breasts. She is of an indeterminable age, 25-40, and is loud and jolly, frequently breaking out in laughter from her own jokes.*

JACK, *20 years old, wears a corduroy Ivy League suit and vest. At first, JACK's speech is modulated and too eloquent for the surroundings but as he drinks his words become slurred and mumbled.*

BABY GIRL, BIG GIRL'S *mentally retarded teenage sister. The girl has the same hairdo as CLARA. Her face is made up with mascara, eye shadow, and she has black arching eyebrows penciled darkly, the same as CLARA.*

MISS FAMIE, *a drunken neighbor.*

STOOGIE, *a local street-fighter and gang leader. His hair is processed.*[1]

BAMA, *one of* STOOGIE'S *boys.*

HOSS *another of* STOOGIE'S *boys.*

C.C., *a young wino.*

TIME: *Early spring, the mid-1950s.*

SCENE: *A slum kitchen on a rainy afternoon in South Philadelphia. The room is very clean, wax glosses the linoleum and old wooden furniture; a cheap but clean red checkered oilcloth covers the table. If the room could speak it would say, "I'm cheap but clean."*

A cheap AM radio plays rhythm 'n' blues music throughout the play. The furniture is made up of a wide kitchen table where a gallon jug of red wine sits. Also upon the table is an oatmeal box, cups, mugs plates and spoons, ashtrays and packs of cigarettes. Four chairs circle the table, and two sit against the wall back-stage. An old-fashioned wood-and-coal-burning stove takes up a corner of the room, and a gas range of 1935 vintage is backstage next to the door to the yard. A large, smoking frying pan is on one of the burners.

JACK and BIG GIRL *are seated at opposite ends of the table;* CLARA *stands at the stove fanning the fumes toward the door.* BABY GIRL *plays upon the floor with a homemade toy.*

CLARA [*fans, fumes*] Uummm uummm . . . well, there goes the lunch. I wonder how I was dumb enough to burn the bacon?

BIG GIRL Just comes natural with you, honey, all looks and no brains . . . now with me and my looks, anybody in South Philly can tell I'm a person that naturally takes care of business . . . hee hee . . . ain't that right, Clara?

CLARA Awww girl, go on. You's the worst messer—upper I knows. You didn't even go to work this morn'. What kind of business is that?

BIG GIRL It's all part of my master plan, baby. Don't you worry none . . . Big Girl knows what she's doin'. You better believe that!

CLARA Yeah, you may know what you're doin' but I'm the one who's got to call in for you and like that you're sick.

BIG GIRL Well, it ain't a lie. You know I got this cough and stopped up feeling. [*Looking at* JACK] You believe that, don't you, young blood?

JACK Most certainly. You could very well have a respiratory condition and also have all the appearances of a extremely capable person.

BIG GIRL [*slapping table*] HEE HEE . . . SEE CLARA . . . SEE? Listen

Clara's Ole Man

to that, Clara. I told you anybody could tell it. Even ole hot lips here can tell.

CLARA [*pours out grease and wipes stove*] Awww . . . he just says that to be nice . . . he's always sayin' things like that.

BIG GIRL Is that how he talked when he met you the other day out to your aunt's house?

CLARA [*hesitating*] Nawh . . . nawh he didn't talk like that.

BIG GIRL Well, how did he talk, huh?

CLARA Awww . . . Big Girl. I don't know.

BIG GIRL Well, who else does? You know what kind of line a guy gives ya. You been pitched at enough times, haven't ya? By the looks of him I bet he gave ya the ole smooth college boy approach . . .[*To JACK*] C'mon, man, drink up. We got a whole lot mo' ta kill. Don't you know this is my day off and I'm celebratin'?

JACK [*takes a drink*] Thanks . . . this is certainly nice of you to go to all this trouble for me. I never expected it.

BIG GIRL What did you expect, young blood?

JACK [*takes another sip*] Ohhh, well . . . I . . .

CLARA [*to BABY GIRL on floor*] Don't put that dirty thing in your mouf, gal! [She walks around the table to BABY GIRL and tugs her arm.] Now, keep that out of your mouf!

BABY GIRL [*holds to toy sullenly*] NO!

CLARA You keep quiet, you hear, gal!

BABY GIRL NO!

CLARA If you keep tellin' me no I'm goin' ta take you upstairs ta Aunt Toohey.

BABY GIRL [*throws back head and drums feet on floor*] NO! NO! SHIT! DAMN! NO! SHIT!

CLARA [disturbed] NOW STOP THAT! We got company.

BIG GIRL [*laughs hard and leans elbows upon table*] HAW HAW HAW . . . I guess she told you, Clara. Hee hee . . . that little dirty mouf biitch, [*pointing to BABY GIRL and becoming choked*] . . . that little . . . [*cough cough*] . . . hooee boy!

CLARA You shouldn't have taught her all them nasty words, Big Girl. Now we can't do anything with her. [*turns to JACK*] What do you think of that?

JACK Yes, it does seem a problem. But with proper guidance she'll more than likely be conditioned out of it when she gets into a learning situation among her peer group.

BIG GIRL [takes a drink and scowls] BULLSHIT!
CLARA Aww . . . B.G.
JACK I beg your pardon, Miss?
BIG GIRL I said bullshit! Whatta ya mean with proper guidance . . .
    points. I taught that little bitch myself . . . the best cuss words I
    know before she ever climb out of her crib . . . whatta yam mean
    when she gets among her "peer" group?
JACK I didn't exactly say that. I said when . . .
BIG GIRL [cuts him off] Don't tell me what you said, boy. I got ears.
    I know all them big horseshit doctor words . . . tell him, Clara . . .
    tell him what I do. Where do I work, Clara?
CLARA Awww . . . B.G., please.
BIG GIRL Do like I say! Do like big wants you to!
CLARA [surrenders] She works out at the state nut farm.
BIG GIRL [triumphant] And tell mister smart and proper what I do.
CLARA [automatically] She's a technician.
JACK Oh, that's nice. I didn't mean to suggest there was anything
    wrong with how you raised your sister.
BIG GIRL [jolly again] Haw haw haw . . . Nawh, ya didn't I know you
    didn't even know what you were sayin', young blood. Do you know
    why I taught her to cuss?
JACK Why no, I have no idea. Why did you?
BIG GIRL Well, it was to give her freedom, ya know? [JACK shakes his
    head.] Ya see, workin' in the hospital with all the nuts and fruits
    and crazies and weirdos I get ideas 'bout things. I saw how when
    they get these kids in who have cracked up and even with older
    people who come in out of their skulls they all mostly cuss. Mostly
    all of them, all the time they out of their heads, they cuss all the
    time and do other wild things, and boy do some of them really
    get into it and let out all of that filthy shit that's been stored up all
    them years. But when the docs start shockin' them puttin' them on
    insulin they quiets down, that's when the docs think their getting'
    better, but really they ain't. They're just learn'n like before to hold it
    in . . .just like before, that's one reason most of them come back or
    are always on the verge afterwards of goin' psycho again.
JACK [enthusiastic] Wow, I never thought of that! That ritual action of
    purging and catharsis can open up new avenues in therapy and in
    learning theory and conditioning subjects . . .
BIG GIRL Saaay whaaa . . . ? What did you have for breakfast, man?

CLARA [*struck*] That sounds so wonderful . . .

JACK [*still excited*] But, I agree with you. You have an intuitive grasp of very abstract concepts!

BIG GIRL [*beaming*] Yeah, yeah . . . I got a lot of it figured out . . . [to JACK] Here, fill up your glass again, man.

JACK [*to CLARA*] Aren't you drinking with us?

CLARA Later. Big Girl doesn't allow me to start in drinking too early

JACK [*confused*] She doesn't?

BIG GIRL [*cuts in*] Well, in Baby Girl's case I said to myself that I'm teach'n her how in front and lettin' her use what she knows whenever it builds up inside. And it's really good for her, gives her spirit and everything.

CLARA That's what probably warped her brain.

BIG GIRL Hush up! You knows it was the fuckin' disease. All the doctors said so.

CLARA You don't believe no doctors 'bout nothin' else!

BIG GIRL [*glares at CLARA*] Are you showin' out, Clara? Are you showin' out to your little boyfriend?

CLARA He ain't mah boyfriend.

JACK [*interrupts*] How do you know she might not have spirit if she wasn't allowed to curse?

BIG GIRL [*sullen*] I don't know anything, young blood. But I can take a look at myself and see the two of us. Look at me! [*Stares at JACK*] LOOK AT ME!

JACK Yes, yes, I'm looking.

BIG GIRL Well, what do you see?

CLARA B.G. . . . PLEASE!

BIG GIRL [*ignores*] Well, what do you see?

JACK [*worried*] Well, I don't really know . . . I . . .

BIG GIRL Well, let me tell you what you see. You see a fat bitch who's 20 pounds overweight and looks ten years older than she is. You want to know how I got this way and been this way most of my life and would be worse off if I didn't let off some steam drinkin' this rotgut and speakin' my mind?

JACK [*to Big Girl who doesn't listen but drinks*] Yes, I would like to hear.

> [*CLARA finishes the stove and takes a seat between the two. BABY GIRL goes to the yard door but does not go out into the rain she sits down and looks out the door at an angle.*]

BIG GIRL Ya see, when I was a little runt of a kid my mother found out she
   couldn't keep me or Baby Girl any longer cause she had TB, so I got
   shipped out somewheres and Baby Girl got shipped out somewheres
   else. People that Baby Girl went to exposed her to the disease. She as
   lucky, I ended up with some fuckin' Christians . . .
CLARA Ohhh, B.G. you shouldn't say that!
BIG GIRL Well, I sho as hell just did! . . . Damned kristers! I spent 12 years
   with those people, can you imagine? A dozen years in hell. Christians
   . . . HAAA . . . always preachin' 'bout some heaven over yonder and
   building a bigger hell here den any devil have imagination for.
CLARA You shouldn't go round sayin' things like dat.
BIG GIRL I shouldn't! Well what did your Christian mammy and pot-gutted
   pappy teach you? When I met you you didn't even know how to take a
   douche.
CLARA YOU GOT NO RIGHT!!! [*She momentarily rises as if she's going to
   launch herself on Big Girl.*]
BIG GIRL [*condescending*] Awww . . . forget it sweetie . . . don't make no
   never mind, but you remember how you us'ta smell when you got ready
   fo bed . . . like a dead hoss or a baby skunk . . . [*To JACK, explaining*]
   That damned Christian mamma and pappa of hers didn't tell her a
   thing 'bout herself . . . ha ha ha . . . thought if she ever found out her
   little thing was used fo anything else 'cept squattin' she'd fall backwards
   right up in it . . . ZaaaBOOMM . . . STRAIGHHT TA HELL . . .ha ha . . .
   didn't know that lil Clara had already found her heaven and on the same
   trail.
CLARA [*ashamed*] Sometimes . . . sometimes . . . I just want to die for bein'
   here.
BIG GIRL [*enjoying herself*] Ha ha ha . . . that wouldn't do no good. Would
   it? Just remember what shape you were in when I met you, kid. Ha ha
   ha. [*to JACK*] Hey, boy, can you imagine this pretty little trick here had
   her stomach seven months in the wind, waitin' on a dead baby who died
   from the same disease that Baby Girl had . . .
CLARA He didn't have any nasty disease like Baby Girl!
BABY GIRL [*hears her name but looks out door*] NO! NO! SHIT! DAMN!
   SHIT! SHIT!
BIG GIRL HAW HAW HAW . . . now we got her started . . .
   [*She laughs for over a minute; JACK waits patiently, sipping; CLARA is
   grim. BAAY GIRL has quieted.*]
BIG GIRL She . . . she . . . ha ha . . . was walkin' round with a dead baby in

Clara's Ole Man   85

her and had no place to go.

CLARA [*fills a glass*] I just can't understand you, B.G. You know my baby died after he was born. Somedays you just get besides yourself.

BIG GIRL I'm only helpin' ya entertain your guest.

CLARA Awww . . . B.G. It wasn't his fault. I invited him.

JACK [*dismayed*] Well, I asked really. If there's anything wrong I can go.

BIG GIRL Take it easy, young blood. I'm just havin' a little fun. Now lets get back to the Clara Saga . . . ya hear that word, junior? . . . S-A-G-A, SUCKER! You college boys don't know it all. Yeah, her folks had kicked her out and the little punk she was big for what had tried to put her out on the block and when that didn't work out . . . [*mocking and making pretend blushes*] . . . because our sweet little thing here was soooo modest and sedate . . . the nigger split! . . . HAW HAW HAW . . . HE MADE IT TO NEW YORK!
> [*She goes into a laughing, choking and crying fit. BABY GIRL rushes over to her and on tip toes pats her back.*]

BABY GIRL Big Girl! Big Girl [*A knocking sounds and CLARA exits to answer the door.*]

BIG GIRL [*catches her breath*] Whatcha want, little sister?

BABY GIRL The cat. The cat. Cat got kittens. Cat got kittens.

BIG GIRL [*still coughing and choking*] Awww, go on. You know there ain't no cat under there with no kittens. [*To JACK*] She's been makin' that story up for two months now about how some cat crawls up under the steps and has kittens. She can't fool me none. She just wants a cat but I ain't gonna get none.

JACK Why not, cats aren't so bad. My mother has one and he's quite a pleasure to her.

BIG GIRL For your mammy maybe, but all they mean round here . . . [*singsong*] . . . is fleas and mo mouths to feed. With an invalid aunt upstairs we don't need anymo expenses.

JACK [gestures toward Baby Girl] It shows that she has a very vivid imagination to make up that story about the kittens.

BIG GIRL Yeah, her big sister ain't the biggest liar in the family.
> [*CLARA returns with MISS FAMIE staggering behind her, a thin middle-aged woman in a long seamen's raincoat, dripping wet, and wearing house slippers that are soaked and squish water about the kitchen floor.*]

BIG GIRL Hi, Miss Famie. I see you're dressed in your rainy glad rags today.

MISS FAMIE [*slurred speech of the drunk*] Hello, B.G. Yeah, I couldn't pass up seein' Aunt Toohey, so I put on my weather coat. You know that don't a day pass that I don't stop up to see her.

BIG GIRL Yeah, I know, Miss Famie. Every day you go up there with that quart of gin under your dress and you two ole lushes put it away.

MISS FAMIE Why, B.G. You should know better than that . . .

CLARA [*re-seated*] B.G., you shouldn't say that . . .

BIG GIRL Why shouldn't I? I'm payin' for over half of that juice and I don't git to see none of it 'cept the empty bottles.

BABY GIRL CAT! CAT! CAT!

MISS FAMIE Oh, the baby still sees them there cats.

CLARA You should be ashamed to talk to Miss Famie like that.

BIG GIRL [*to JACK*] Why you so quiet? Can't you speak to folks when they come in?

JACK I'm sorry. [*to MISS FAMIE*] Hello, mam.

MISS FAMIE Why howdie, son.

CLARA Would you like a glass of wine, Miss Famie?

MISS FAMIE Don't mind if I do, sister.

BIG GIRL Better watch it, Miss Famie. Wine and gin will rust your gizzard.

CLARA Ohh . . . [pours a glass of wine] . . . Here, Miss Famie.

BABY GIRL CAT! CAT!

BIG GIRL [*singsong, lifting her glass*] Mus' I tell . . . muscatel . . . jitterbug champagne. [Reminisces] Remember, Clara, the first time I got you to take a drink? [to MISS FAMIE] You should have seen her. Some of this same cheap rotgut here. She's never had a drink before but she wanted to show me how game she was. She was a bright little smart thing, just out of high school and didn't know her butt from a doorknob.

MISS FAMIE Yes, indeed, that was Clara all right.

BIG GIRL She drank three water glasses down and got so damned sick I had to put my finger down her throat and make her heave it up . . . HAW HAW . . . babbled her fool head off all night . . . said she'd be my friend always . . . that we'd always be together . . .

MISS FAMIE [*gulps down her drink*] Wine will make you do that the first time you get good'n high on it.

JACK [*takes drink*] I don't know. You know . . . I've never really been wasted and I've been drinkin' for quite some time now.

BIG GIRL Quite some time, huh? Six months?

JACK Nawh. My mother used to let me drink at home. I've been drinkin' since 15. And I drank all the time I was in the service.

BIG GIRL Just because you been slippin' some drinks out of ya mammy's bottle and you slipped a few under ya belt with the punks in the barracks don't make ya a drinker, boy!

CLARA B.G. . . . do you have to?

> [*MISS FAMIE finishes her second drink as BIG GIRL and CLARA stare at each other.*]

MISS FAMIE Well, I guess I better get up and go see Aunt Toohey. [*She leaves.*]

JACK Nice to have me you, mam.

MISS FAMIE Well good-bye, son.

BIG GIRL [*before MISS FAMIE reaches top of stairs*] The ole ginhead tracked water all over your floor, Clara.

CLARA Makes no never mind to me. This place stays to clean I like when someone comes so it gets a little messy so I have somethin' ta do.

BIG GIRL Is that why Jackie boy is here? So he can do some messiin' 'round?

CLARA Nawh, B.G.

JACK [*stands*] Well, I'll be going. I see that . . .

BIG GIRL [rises and tugs his sleeve] Sit down an' drink up, young blood. [pushes him back in his seat] There's wine here . . . [*slow and suggestive*] . . . there's a pretty girl here . . . you go for that, don't you?

JACK It's not that . . .

BIG GIRL You go for little Clara, don't you?

JACK Well, yes, I do . . .

BIG GIRL HAW HAW HAW . . . [*slams the table and sloshes wine*] HAW HAW HAW . . . [*slow and suggestive*] . . . What I tell ya, Clara? You're a winner. First time I laid eyes on you I said to myself that you're a winner.

CLARA [*takes a drink*] Drink up, B.G.

BIG GIRL [*to JACK*] You sho you like what you see, young blood?

JACK [*becomes bold*] Why sure. Do you think I'd come out on a day like this for anybody?

BIG GIRL HAW HAW HAW . . . [*peels of laughter and more coughs*] . . .

JACK [*to CLARA*] I was going to ask you to go to the matinee 'roound Pep's but I guess it's too late now.

CLARA [*hesitates*] I never been.

BIG GIRL [*sobers*] That's right. You never been to Pep's and it's only 'round the corner. What you mean it's too late, young blood? It don't start getting good till 'round four.

JACK I thought she might have ta start gettin' supper.

BIG GIRL She'd only burn it the fuck up too if she did. [*to CLARA*] I'm goin' ta take you to Pep's this afternoon.

CLARA You don't have ta, B.G.

BIG GIRL It's my day off, ain't it?

CLARA But it costs so much, don't it?

BIG GIRL Nawh, not much . . . you'll like it. Soon as C.C. comes over ta watch Baby Girl we can go.

CLARA [*brightens*] O.K.!

JACK I don't know who's there now, but they always have a good show. Sometimes Ahmad Jamal . . .

BABY GIRL [*cuts speech*] CAT! CAT! CAT!

BIG GIRL Let's toast to that . . . [*raising her glass . . .*] To Pep's on a rainy day.

JACK HEAR! HEAR! [*He drains his glass. A tumbling sound is heard from the backyard as they drink and BABY GIRL claps hands as STOOGIE, BAMA and HOSS appear in yard doorway. The three boys are no more than 16. They are soaked but wear only thin jackets, caps and pants. Under STOOGIE's cap he wears a bandanna to keep his processed hair dry.*]

BIG GIRL What the hell is this?

STOOGIE [*goes to BIG GIRL and pats her shoulder*] The heat, B.G. The man was on our asses so we had to come on in out of the rain, baby, dig?

BIG GIRL Well tell me something' I don't know, baby. Why you got to pick mah back door? I ain't never ready for any more heat than I gets already.

STOOGIE It just happened that way, B.G. We didn't have any choice.

BAMA That's right, Big Girl. You know we ain't lame 'nuf to be usin' yo pad for no highway.

HOSS Yeah, baby, you know how it is when the man is there.

BIG GIRL Well, that makes a difference. [*Smiles*] Hey, what'cha standin'

Clara's Ole Man 89

there with your faces hangin' out for? Get yourselves a drink.
    [*HOSS goes to the sink to get glasses for the trio; STOOGIE looks
    JACK over and nods to BAMA, then turns to CLARA.*]
STOOGIE How ya doin' Clara? Ya lookin' fine as ever.
CLARA I'm okay, Stoogie. I don't have to ask 'bout you none. Bad news
sho travels fast.
STOOGIE [*holds arms apart in innocence*] What'cha mean, baby?
What'cha been hearin' 'bout Papa Stoogie?
CLARA Just the regular. That your gang's fightin' the Peaceful Valley
guys up in North Philly.
STOOGIE Awww . . . dat's old stuff. Sheet . . . you way behind, baby.
BAMA Yeah, sweetcake, dat's over.
CLARA Already?
HOSS Yeah, we just finished sign'n a peace treaty with Peaceful Valley.
BAMA Yeah, we out ta cool the War Lords now from ov'va on
Powelton Avenue.
HOSS Ole Stoogie here is settin' up the war council now we got a pact
with Peaceful Valley and, man, when we come down on those punk
War Lords . . . baby . . . it's just gonna be all ov'va.
BIG GIRL Yeah, it's always one thing ta another with you punks.
STOOGIE Hey, B.G., cool it! We can't help it if people always
spreadin' rumors 'bout us. Things just happen an' people talk and don't
understand and get it all wrong, dat's all.
BIG GIRL Yeah, all of it just happens, huh? It's just natural . . . you's
growin' boys.
STOOGIE That's what happen'n, baby. Now take for instance Peaceful
Valley. Las' week we went up there . . . ya know, only five of us in
Crook's Buick.
CLARA I guess ya was just lookin at the scenery?
HOSS Yeah, baby, dat's it. We we lookin' . . . fo' some jive half-ass
niggers.
    [*The boys laugh and giggle as STOOGIE enacts the story.*]
STOOGIE Yeah, we got Specs from off 'a Jefferson and Gratz walkin'
with them bad foots down Master . . . ha ha ha . . .
BAMA Tell them what happened to Specs, man.
HOSS Awww, man, ya ain't gonna drag mah man Bama again?
    [*They laugh more, slapping and punching each other,
    taking off their caps and cracking each other with them,
    gulping their wine and performing for the girls and*

JACK.]

[*STOOGIE has his hair exposed.*]

STOOGIE Bama here . . . ha ha ha . . . Bama burnt dat four—eyed mathafukker in the leg.

HOSS Baby, you should'a seen it!

CLARA Yeah, that's what I heard.

STOOGIE Yeah, but listen, baby. [*points to BAMA*] He was holding the only heat we had . . . ha ho ho . . . and dis jive sucker was aimin at Spec's bad foots . . . ha ha . . . while that blind mathafukker was blastin' from 'round the corner straight through the car window . . .

> [*They become nearly hysterical with laughter and stagger and stumble around the table.*]

HOSS Yeah . . . ha ha . . . mathafukkin' glass was flyin' all over us . . . ha ha . . . we almost got sliced ta death and dis stupid mathafukker was shootin' at the man's bad foots . . . ha ha . . .

BAMA [*scratching his head*] Well, man. Well, man . . . I didn't know what kind of rumble we was in.

> [*CLARA and BIG GIRL laugh as they refill their glasses, nearly emptying the jug. BIG GIRL gets up and pulls another gallon out of the refrigerator as laughter subsides.*]

BIG GIRL [*sits down*] What's the heat doin' after ya?

STOOGIE Nothin'.

CLARA I bet!

STOOGIE [*sneer*] That's right, baby. They just singled us out to make examples out of.

> [*This gets a laugh from his friends.*]

BIG GIRL What did you get?

HOSS Get?

BIG GIRL [*turns on him*] You tryin' to get wise, punk?

STOOGIE [*patronizing*] Awww, B.G. You not goin' ta take us serious, are ya?

> [*Silence*]

Well, ya see. We were walkin' down Broad Street by the State Store, see? And we see this old rumdum come out and stagger down the street carryin' this heavy package . . .

CLARA And?

STOOGIE And he's stumblin', see. Like he's gonna fall. So good ole Hoss here says, "Why don't we help that pore man out?" So Bama walks

Clara's Ole Man

up and helps the man carry his package, and do you know what?
BIG GIRL Yeah, the mathafukker "slips" down and screams and some
cops think you some wrong doin' studs . . . yeah, I know . . . of course
you didn't have time to explain.
STOOGIE That's right, B.G. So to get our breath so we could tell our
side of it we just stepped in here, dig?
BIG GIRL Yeah, I dig. [*Menacing*] Where is it?
HOSS Where's what?
         [*Silence*]
STOOGIE If you had just give me another minute, B.G. [Pulls out
a quart of vodka] Well, no use savin' it anyway. Who wants some
100-proof tiger piss?
BAMA [*to STOOGIE*] Hey, man, how much was in dat mathafukker's
wallet?
STOOGIE [*nods toward JACK*] Cool it, sucker.
HOSS [*to STOOGIE*] But man, you holdin' the watch and ring too!
STOOGIE [*advancing on them*] What's wrong with you jive-ass
mathafukkers?
BIG GIRL Okay, cool it? There's only one person gets out of hand
'round here, ya understand?
STOOGIE Okay B.G. Let it slide . . .
BABY GIRL CAT! CAT! CAT!
BAMA [*to HOSS*] Hey, man, dis chick's still chasin' dose cats.
STOOGIE [*to JACK*] Drink up, man. Not everyday ya get dis stuff.
[BAMA picks up the beat of the music and begins a shuffling dance.
BABY GIRL begins bouncing in time to the music.]
HOSS C'mon, Baby Girl; let me see ya do the slide.
BABY GIRL NO! NO! [*She claps and bounces.*]
HOSS [*demonstrates his steps, trying to out-dance BAMA*] C'mon, Baby
Girl, shake that thing!
CLARA No, stop that, Hoss. She don't know what she's doin!
BIG GIRL That's okay, Clara. Go on, Baby Girl, do the thing.
         [*STOOGIE grabs salt from the table and shakes it upon the floor,
         under the feet of the dancers.*]
STOOGIE DO THE SLIDE, MAN! SLIDE
         [*BABY GIRL lumbers up and begins a grotesque maneuver while
         grunting out strained sounds.*]
BAB GIRL Uuuhhh . . . sheeeeee . . . waaa . . . uuhhh . . .
BIG GIRL [*standing, toasting*] DO THE THING, BABY!!!

CLARA Awww . . . B.G. Why don't you stop all dat?

STOOGIE [*to JACK*] C'mon, man, git with it.

> [*JACK shakes his head and STOOGIE goes over to CLARA and holds out his hand.*]

STOOGIE Let's go, Baby.

CLARA Nawh . . . I don't dance no mo . . .

STOOGIE C'mon, pretty mama . . . watch this step . . . [*He cuts a fancy step.*]

BIG GIRL Go on and dance, sister.

> [*STOOGIE moves off and the three boys dance.*]

CLARA Nawh . . . B.G., you know that I don't go for the kind of stuff no mo.

BIG GIRL Go on, baby!

CLARA No!

BIG GIRL I want you to dance, Clara.

CLARA Nawh . . . I just can't.

BIG GIRL DO LIKE I SAY! DO LIKE BIG WANTS!

> [*The dancers stop momentarily but begin again when CLARA joins them. BABY GIRL halts and resumes her place upon the floor, fondling her toy. The others dance until the record stops.*]

STOOGIE [*to JACK*] Where you from, man?

JACK Oh, I live over in West Philly now, but I come from up around Master.

STOOGIE Oh? Do you know Hector?

JACK [*trying to capture an old voice and mannerism*] Yeah, man. I know the cat.

STOOGIE What's your name, man?

JACK Jack, man, maybe you know me by Tookie.

STOOGIE [*ritually*] Tookie . . . Tookie . . . yeah, man, I think I heard about you. You us'ta be in the ole Jet Cobras!

JACK Well, I us'ta know some of the guys then. I been away for a while.

BAMA [*matter-of-factly*] Where you been, man? Jail?

JACK I was in the Marines for three years.

STOOGIE Hey, man. That must'a been a gas.

JACK It was okay. I seen a lot . . . went to a lot of places.

BIG GIRL Yeah, you must'a seen it all.

STOOGIE Did you get to go anywhere overseas, man?

JACK Yeah, I was aboard ship most of the time.

HOSS Wow, man. That sounds cool.

BAMA You really was overseas, man?

JACK Yeah. I went to Europe and North Africa and the Caribbean.

STOOGIE What kind of a boat were you on, man?

JACK A ship.

BIG GIRL A boat!

JACK No, a ship.

STOOGIE [*rising, BAMA and HOSS surrounding JACK*] Yeah, man, dat's what she said . . . a boat!

CLARA STOP IT!!!

BABY GIRL NO! NO! NO! SHIT! SHIT! SHIT! DAMN! SHIT!

MISS FAMIE [*voice from upstairs*] Your Aunt don't like all that noise.

BIG GIRL You and my aunt better mind ya fukkin' ginhead business or I'll come up there and ram those empty bottles up where it counts!

BAMA [*sniggling*] Oh, baby. We forgot your aunt was up dere sick.

STOOGIE Yeah, baby. Have another drink.

> [*He fills all glasses except CLARA's. She pulls hers away.*]

CLARA Nawh, I don't want any more. Me and BIG GIRL are goin' out after a while.

BAMA Can I go too?

BIG GIRL There's always have to be one wise mathafukker.

BAMA I didn't mean nuttin' B.G., honest.

STOOGIE [to JACK] What did you do in the Army, man?

JACK [feigns a dialect] Ohhh, man. I told you already I was in the Marines!

HOSS [to CLARA] Where you goin'?

CLARA B.G.'s takin' me to Pep's.

BAMA Wow . . . dat's nice, baby.

BIG GIRL [gesturing towards JACK] Ole smoothie here suggesting takin' Clara but it seems he backed out, so I thought we might step around there anyway.

JACK [annoyed] I didn't back out!

STOOGIE [to JACK] Did you screw any of them foreign

bitches when you were in Japan, man?

JACK Yeah, man. I couldn't help it. They was all over, ya know?

BIG GIRL He couldn't beat them off.

STOOGIE Yeah, man. I dig.

JACK Especially in France and Italy. Course, the Spanish girls are the best, but the ones in France and Italy ain't so bad either.

HOSS You mean those French girls ain't as good as those Spanish girls?

JACK Nawh, man, the Spanish girls are the best.

BAMA I never did dig no Mexican nor Rican spic bitches. Too tough, man.

JACK They ain't Mexican or Puerto Rican. They Spanish . . . from Spain . . . Spain is different from Mexican. In Spain . . .

STOOGIE What'cha do now, man?

JACK Ohhh . . . I'm goin' ta college prep on the G.I. Bill now . . . and workin' a little.

STOOGIE Is that why you sound like you got a load of shit in your mouth?

JACK What do you mean!

STOOGIE I thought you talked like you had shit in your mouth because you had been ta college, man.

JACK I don't understand what you're tryin' to say, man.

STOOGIE It's nothin', man. You just talk funny sometimes . . . ya know what I mean. Hey, man, where do you work?

JACK [visibly feeling his drinks] Nawh, man, I don't know what ya mean and I don't go to college man, it's called prep.

STOOGIE Thanks, man.

JACK And I work at the P.O.

BAMA Pee-who?

JACK The post office, man.

BAMA No shit, baby.

STOOGIE Thanks, George. I always like to know things I don't know anything about. [He turns back on JACK.]

JACK [to BIG GIRL] Hey, what time ya goin' round to Pep's?

BIG GIRL Soon . . . are in a hurry, young blood? You don't have to wait for us.

JACK [now drunk] That's okay . . . it's just getting' late, ya know, man . . . and I was wonderin' what time Clara's ole man gets home . . .

BIG GIRL Clara's ole man? . . . Whad do you mean, man? . . .
[The trio begins snickering, holding their laughter back; JACK
is too drunk to notice.]
JACK Well, Clara said for me to come by today in the
afternoon when her ole man would be at work . . . and I was
wonderin' what time he got home . . .
[BIG GIRL stands, tilting over her chair to crash backwards on
the floor. Her bust juts out; she is controlled but furious.]
BIG GIRL Clara's ole man is home now . . .
[A noise is heard outside as C.C. comes in the front door.
The trio are laughing louder but with restraint; CLARA looks
stunned.]
C.C. It's just Me . . . just ole C.C.
HOSS Shss . . . shut up, man.
JACK [starts up and feels drunk for the first time] What . . .
you mean he's been upstairs all this time?
BIG GIRL [staring] Nawh, man, I don't mean that!
JACK [looks at BIG GIRL, then at the laughing boys and
finally to CLARA] Ohhh . . . jezzus! [He staggers to the
backyard door, past BABY GIRL, and becomes sick.]
BIG GIRL [to CLARA] Didn't you tell him? Didn't you tell
him a fukkin' thing?
[C.C. comes in. He is drunk and weaves and says nothing. He
sees the wine, searches for a glass, bumps into one of the boys,
is shoved into another, and get booted in the rear before he
reaches wine and seat.]
BIG GIRL Didn't you tell him?
CLARA I only wanted to talk, B.G. I only wanted to talk to
somebody. I don't have anybody to talk to . . . [crying] I don't
have anyone . . .
BIG GIRL It's time for the matinee. [to STOOGIE] Before you
go, escort my friend out, will ya?
CLARA Ohhh . . . B.G. I'll do anything but please . . . ohhh Big
. . . I won't forget my promise.
BIG GIRL Let's go. We don't want to miss the show, do we?
CLARA Please, B.G., please. Not that. It's not his fault! Please!
BIG GIRL DO LIKE I SAY! DO LIKE I WANT YOU TO DO!
[CLARA drops her head and rises and exxxits stage right
followed by BIG GIRL. STOOGIE and his boys finish their

drinks, stalk and swagger about. BAMA opens the refrigerator and HOSS takes one long last guzzle.]
BAMA Hey Stoogie babe, what about the split?
STOOGIE [drunk] Later, you square-ass, lame-ass mathafukker!

[HOSS giggles.]

BABY GIRL CAT! CAT! CAT!
C.C. [seated drinking] Shut up, Baby Girl. Ain't no cats out dere.
MISS FAMIE [staggers from upstairs, calls back] Good night Toohey. See ya tomorrow.

[With a nod from STOOGIE, BAMA and HOSS take JACK's arms and wrestle him into the yard. The sounds of JACK's beating are heard. MISS FAMIE wanders to the yard door, looks out but staggers back from what she sees and continues sprawling toward the exit, stage right.]

BABY GIRL CAT! CAT! CAT!
C.C. SHUT UP! SHUT ON UP, BABY GIRL! I TOLE YA . . . DERE AIN'T NO CATS OUT DERE!!!
BABY GIRL NO! DAMN! SHIT! SHIT! DAMN! NO! NO!

[STOOGIE looks over the scene and downs his drink, then saunters outside. Lights dim out until there is a single soft spot on BABY GIRL's head, turned wistfully toward the yard, then blackness. Curtain.]

JAYNE CORTEZ

Poet Jayne Cortez was born in Fort Huachuca, Arizona, and grew up in California. In addition to publishing a number of collections, including *Somewhere in Advance of Nowhere* (1996) and *Mouth on Paper* (1977), she released several recordings, many of which feature her band, the Firespitters. She has been described as a lyrically innovative and visceral poet, and her work has been presented at universities, festivals, and museums, including the Museum of Modern Art in New York City. Widely anthologized, her work has been translated into 28 languages and featured in publications such as *Poems for the Millennium* and *Postmodern American Poetry*. Cortez was the recipient of a fellowship from the National Endowment for the Arts as well as awards such as the International African Festival Award and the American Book Award. She was also the founder of the Watts Repertory Company and her own publishing company. She lived in New York City until her death in 2012.

The Oppressionists

Art
what do the art
suppressors
care about art
they jump on bandwagons
wallow in press clips
& stink up the planet
with their
pornographic oppression
Art
what do they care about art
they go from being
contemporary baby kissers to
old time corrupt politicians
to self-appointed censorship clerks
who won't support art
but will support war
poverty
lung cancer
racism
colonialism
and toxic sludge
that's their morality
that's their religious conviction
that's their protection of the public
& contribution to family entertainment
what do they care about art

JUNE JORDAN

One of the most widely-published and highly-acclaimed Jamaican American writers of her generation, poet, playwright and essayist June Jordan was known for her fierce commitment to human rights and political activism. Over a career that produced twenty-seven volumes of poems, essays, libretti, and work for children, Jordan engaged the fundamental struggles of her era: for civil rights, women's rights, and sexual freedom. A prolific writer across genres, Jordan's poetry is known for its immediacy and accessibility as well as its interest in identity and the representation of personal, lived experience—her poetry is often deeply autobiographical. Jordan's work also frequently imagines a radical, globalized notion of solidarity amongst the world's marginalized and oppressed. In volumes like *Some Changes* (1971), *Living Room* (1985) and *Kissing God Goodbye: Poems 1991-1997* (1997), Jordan uses conversational, often vernacular English to address topics ranging from family, bisexuality, political oppression, racial identity and racial inequality, and memory. Regarded as one of the key figures in the mid-century American social, political and artistic milieu, Jordan also taught at many of the country's most prestigious universities including Yale, State University of New York-Stony Brook, and the University of California-Berkeley, where she founded Poetry for the People. Her honors and awards included fellowships from the National Endowment for the Arts, the Massachusetts Council on the Arts, and the New York Foundation for the Arts, a Rockefeller Foundation grant, and the National Association of Black Journalists Award.

1977: Poem for Mrs. Fannie Lou Hamer

You used to say, "June?
Honey when you come down here you
supposed to stay with me. Where
else?"
Meanin home
against the beer the shotguns and the
point of view of whitemen don'
never see Black anybodies without
some violent itch start up.
                         The ones who
said, "No Nigga's Votin in This Town . . .
lessen it be feet first to the booth"
Then jailed you
beat you brutal

1977: Poem for Mrs. Fannie Lou Hamer

bloody/battered/beat
you blue beyond the feeling
of the terrible

And failed to stop you.
Only God could but He
wouldn't stop
you
fortress from self-
pity

Humble as a woman anywhere
I remember finding you inside the laundromat
in Ruleville
        lion spine relaxed/hell
        what's the point to courage
        when you washin clothes?

But that took courage

        just to sit there/target
        to the killers lookin
        for your singin face
        perspirey through the rinse
        and spin

and later
you stood mighty in the door on James Street
loud callin:

        "BULLETS OR NO BULLETS!
        THE FOOD IS COOKED
        AN' GETTIN COLD!"

We ate
A family tremulous but fortified
by turnips/okra/handpicked
like the lilies

filled to the very living
full
one solid gospel
         (sanctified)

one gospel
      (peace)

one full Black lily
luminescent
in a homemade field

of love

LARRY NEAL

Larry Neal or Lawrence Neal (September 5, 1937 – January 6, 1981), co-editor of the original Black Fire (1968) with Amiri Baraka, was an American writer, poet, critic and academic. He was a notable scholar of African-American theater, well known for his contributions to the Black Arts Movement of the 1960s and 1970s. He was a major influence in pushing for black culture to focus less on integration with White culture, rather than celebrating its differences within an equally important and meaningful artistic and political field, thus celebrating Black heritage.

The Black Arts Movement
Drama Review, Summer 1968
1.

The Black Arts Movement is radically opposed to any concept of the artist that alienates him from his community. This movement is the aesthetic and spiritual sister of the Black Power concept. As such, it envisions an art that speaks directly to the needs and aspirations of Black America. In order to perform this task, the Black Arts Movement proposes a radical reordering of the western cultural aesthetic. It proposes a separate symbolism, mythology, critique, and iconology. The Black Arts and the Black Power concept both relate broadly to the Afro-American's desire for self- determination and nationhood. Both concepts are nationalistic. One is concerned with the relationship between art and politics; the other with the art of politics.

Recently, these two movements have begun to merge: the political values inherent in the Black Power concept are now finding concrete expression in the aesthetics of

The Black Arts Movement

Afro-American dramatists, poets, choreographers, musicians, and novelists. A main tenet of Black Power is the necessity for Black people to define the world in their own terms. The Black artist has made the same point in the context of aesthetics. The two movements postulate that there are in fact and in spirit two Americas — one black, one white. The Black artist takes this to mean that his primary duty is to speak to the spiritual and cultural needs of Black people. Therefore, the main thrust of this new breed of contemporary writers is to confront the contradictions arising out of the Black man's experience in the racist West. Currently, these writers are re-evaluating western aesthetic, the traditional role of the writer, and the social function of art. Implicit in this re-evaluation is the need to develop a "black aesthetic." It is the opinion of many Black writers, I among them, that the Western aesthetic has run its course: it is impossible to construct anything meaningful within its decaying structure. We advocate a cultural revolution in art and ideas. The cultural values inherent in western history must either be radicalized or destroyed, and we will probably find that even radicalization is impossible. In fact, what is needed is a whole new system of ideas. Poet Don L. Lee[1] expresses it:

> . . . We must destroy Faulkner, dick, jane,[2] and other perpetrators of evil. It's time for DuBois, Nat Turner, and Kwame Nkrumah.[3] As Frantz Fanon[4] points out: destroy the culture and you destroy the people. This must not happen. Black artists are culture stabilizers; bringing back old values, and introducing new ones. Black art will talk to the people and with the will of the people stop impending "protective custody."

The Black Arts Movement eschews "protest" literature. It speaks directly to black people. Implicit in the concept of 'protest" literature, as Brother Etheridge Knight[5] has made clear, is an appeal to white morality:

> Now any Black man who masters the technique of his particular art form, who adheres to the white aesthetic, and who directs his work toward a white audience is, in one sense, protesting. And implicit in the act of protest is the belief that a change will be forthcoming once the masters are aware of the protestor's "grievance" (the very word connotes begging, supplications to the gods). Only when that belief has faded and protestings end, will Black art begin.

Brother Knight also has some interesting statements about the development of a "Black aesthetic":

National Humanities Center, 2007: nationalhumanitiescenter.org/pds/. Presented as originally published in *Drama Review* 12 (Summer 1968),
pp. 29-39. Reprinted in Larry Neal, *Visions of a Liberated Future: Black Arts Movement Writings*, ed., Michael Schwartz (New York: Thunder's Mouth Press, 1989). Reprinted by permission of the Avalon Publishing Group. Footnotes and images added by NHC. Complete image credits at nationalhumanitiescenter.org/pds/maai3/imagecredits.htm.
[1] Donald Luther Lee (1942-): African American poet who later took the name Haki Madhubuti.
[2] Dick and Jane were characters in the widely used primary reading instruction series of the 1950s and 1960s.

> Unless the Black artist establishes a "Black aesthetic" he will have no future at all. To accept the white aesthetic is to accept and validate a society that will not allow him to live. The Black artist must create new forms and new values, sing new songs (or purify old ones); and along with other Black authorities, he must create a new history, new symbols, myths, and legends (and purify old ones by fire). And the Black artist, in creating his own aesthetic, must be accountable for it only to the Black people. Further, he must hasten his own dissolution as an individual (in the Western sense) — painful though the process may be, having been breast-fed the poison of "individual experience."

When we speak of a "Black aesthetic" several things are meant. First, we assume that there is already in existence the basis for such an aesthetic. Essentially, it consists of an African-American cultural tradition. But this aesthetic is finally, by implication, broader than that tradition. It encompasses most of the usable elements of Third World culture. The motive behind the Black aesthetic is the destruction of the white thing, the destruction of white ideas, and white ways of looking at the world. The new aesthetic is mostly predicated on an Ethics which asks the question: whose vision of the world is finally more meaningful, ours or the white oppressors'? What is truth? Or more precisely, whose truth shall we express, that of the oppressed or of the oppressors? These are basic questions. Black intellectuals of previous decades failed to ask them. Further, national and international affairs demand that we appraise the world in terms of our own interests. It is clear that the question of human survival is at the core of contemporary experience. The Black artist must address himself to this reality in the strongest terms possible. In a context of world upheaval, ethics and aesthetics must interact positively and be consistent with the demands for a more spiritual world. Consequently, the Black Arts Movement is an ethical movement. Ethical, that is, from the viewpoint of the oppressed. And much of the oppression confronting the Third World and Black America is directly traceable to the Euro-American cultural sensibility. This sensibility, antihuman in nature, has, until recently, dominated the psyches of most Black artists and intellectuals. It must be destroyed before the Black creative artists can have a meaningful role in the transformation of society.

It is this natural reaction to an alien sensibility that informs the cultural attitudes of the Black Arts and the Black Power movement. It is a profound ethical sense that makes a Black artist question a society in which art is one thing and the actions of men another. The Black Arts Movement believes that your ethics and your aesthetics are one. That the contradictions between ethics and aesthetics in western society is symptomatic of a dying culture.

[3] Kwame Nkrumah (1909-1972): anti-colonialist and first president of Ghana (Gold Coast until independence from Britain in 1957).

[4] Frantz-Fanon (1925-1961): black psychiatrist, social philosopher and essayist (born in Martinique, West Indies; educated in France) who supported anti-colonial activism.

[5] Etheridge Knight (1931-1991): African American poet of the Black Arts Movement.
National Humanities Center

devorah major

devorah major is a California-born "granddaughter of immigrants, documented and undocumented who works as a writer, editor, writing coach, spoken word performer, recording artist, and poetry professor." The Poet-in-Residence of the Fine Arts Museums of San Francisco, major has toured internationally in places such as Italy, Bosnia, Jamaica, Venezuela, Belgium, England, and throughout the United States both performing her poetry and serving on panels speaking on African-American poetry, Beat Poetry, and poetry of resistance. Her most recent poetry collection is *califia's daughter* (Willow Books).

valued colors

whenever
our circle gathered
on eleuthera island
we were a ring of embracing colors
sandy white to glowing mahogany

my golden daughter leaned close to the buttermilk
my pecan son angled near the auburn
each of us a polished hue of brown in the summer sun

love was immediate when meeting
cheek kisses lingering hugs and
no one spoke of shades or hair texture

only sought to braid the cords of our attachment
all four generations born of the same great-great great grandmother
stolen from Yoruba land over two centuries before

and as for paper bags they were of limited value
always less sturdy than the hand-woven ones
easily bought at the straw marketplace

but in the states when I was young
a spirited burnt-umber sistah

wanted to capture me and cut off my curly hair
because it was long and my skin wore a hue
of fresh baked cornbread

while I was sad because I could not sport
an afro crown like my brother's girlfriend
or style in red with her elegance

colorful copy we were all crowded under
an umbrella newly named black
living in a box called colored
tied with a negro ribbon

then in rebellion we broke loose
and grew into a kaleidoscope
of variegated blackness
that reflects a radiant legacy
of resilience

salt water crossings

did our waters of salt breathe
as we birthed our young
did we swim in those laughing waves
before the wrenching
before the tearing
before the theft

did we harvest the bounty
of her fish to feed our families
and with thankfulness did we
offer her fresh flower songs
that were swallowed by her crests
we did do we did do

did we cleanse our wounds
in her seas and discover our dreams
under those glistening midnight waves

did we listen to the ancestors' guidance
as the surf met the sand
did we know and relish
the waters of salt
before their arrivals
before our crossings
we did do we did do

before we were packed
into strange ship hulls
chained, naked, and trapped
in an evil we had never imagined

we did not know these waters as venom
then we learned their sting as they were
poured in buckets over
our bruised and torn bodies
to wash away the stench of
blood, feces, and razor tears
its salt bite was bitter
as our homes turned to memory
turned to myth and then
were forgotten

all was salt and moan
soaking through our skin
to live forever
in the marrow of our bones

we did not see the stars change
did not know when
the moon was hungry
and fierce or full and satiated

but we knew salt

we ate its curses
we savored its healing
we learned its lessons

Liseli A. Fitzpatrick

Liseli A. Fitzpatrick, Ph.D. is a Trinidadian poet and professor of African Cosmologies and Sacred Ontologies in the Africana Studies Department at Wellesley College, MA. Her penchant for poetry is driven by her deep-rooted desire to effect emancipatory change in the co-creation of an equitable, compassionate, just, and breathable world. Love, ancestral reverence, embodied wisdom, nature and liberation are central themes in her work. In 2018, Fitzpatrick made history as the first Ph.D. in African American and African Studies at The Ohio State University. She is a 2019 Furious Flower Poetry Center fellow, and a member of the Wintergreen Women Writers' Collective. Fitzpatrick's writings, which she dubs "poetry for the people's sake" is fueled by her resolute spirit and unshakable love for life.

Tell Me at 90!
For Baba Useni Eugene Perkins

In the beginning was the word and the word was with Africa and the word was African

And the word was in You And the word was
You And the word is You Iridescent Black

  "Black Fairy"

The wished-for child

    "Hey, Black Child!"

Born of earth and water

Of Marion and Eva

Tell Me, "The well-born Man" The 3rd of three

Robert, Toussaint, and Eugene "The Star of the Sea"

    and "Breath of Life" him-herself

Roots and rocks of clay…

What do you expect to get from

a master sculptor and a sweeping domestic

Black magic

Black radicalism

Black art

Black power

Black pride

Black life

Black liberation

Black love

You are the greatest long-distance runner alive

You are the breathing embodiment of

"if you want to go fast go alone but if you want to go far go with others"
Together we strive…

A milestone…

From South Side Chicago to worldwide

From Mississippi to Malawi

You firmly affirm our Blackness our Pan-
Africaness

In praise song,

      in lyric, in journals,

in picture books,

in community centers, in homes, in
schools,

in prisons,

in churches,

in libraries,

in rainbows…

moving across time and space painting murals with
words

to show and tell us who we are

who we really, really are

Lifting mirrors and Souls

  From *A Cry of the Ghetto* to Kuumba's *Image Makers* back to *Black is
  Beautiful* and *Harvesting New Generations*

Empowering our youth

Now, Tell Me, what does 90 feel like?

Another decade

of living and giving your life to us

for us

For FREE-

       dom's…sake!

For Love's sake,

For Heaven's sake,

For Goodness's sake…

Tell Me…what does it really, really feel like to be 90…to be alive and be

You, Useni!

Tell Me II/African brothers like you don't die they fly…
(For Baba Useni)

Black Triumphant Spirit,

Tell Me,

where do Black bodies

and spirits go after they have given us

Heaven on Earth and *Black Fairies*

and *Midnight Blues in the Afternoon*

and liberation?

Is there a resting place peaceful enough for a gentle GIANT and generous

GENIUS to lay down his heart and head?

Is there a burial ground or monument

big enough, sanctified enough, worthy enough, or imperishable to

immortalize Black African brothers like you?

Or a sky limitless enough for your legendary

Moko Jumbie stilt-walking limbs?

Tell Me, Tell Me, Tell Me...

RAYMOND PATTERSON

Born in Harlem in 1929, poet and writer Raymond R. Patterson received an education from the New York City Public School System. At Lincoln University in Pennsylvania, he was elected class poet and won the Boretone Mountain Poetry Award. Serving in the United States Army (1951-53), he later received a MA in English from NYU and married Boydice Alice Cooke in 1957. Working at Benedict College, Patterson later became an emeritus professor of English at City College of the City University of New York.

From an unpublished book-length poem on the life of Phillis Wheatley to the librettist for Hale Smith's operas *David Walker* and *Goree*, Patterson's collection is diverse, plentiful, and inspiring. He is also the author of *26 Ways of Looking at a Black Man and Other Poems* (1969) and *Elemental Blues* (1983), and his poetry has been set by Smith in *Three Patterson Lyrics* (1986). Patterson's work has additionally been published in the *Transatlantic Review, Ohio Review, Beloit Poetry Journal*, along with anthologies including *The Poetry of the Negro, New Black Voices, The Norton Introduction to Literature* as well as *The Best American Poetry of 1996*.

Receiving a National Endowment for the Arts Award and a Creative Artists Public Service fellowship, Patterson has read his works everywhere from local venues to the Library of Congress in Washington, D.C., and the 60th Birthday Celebration of Chinua Achebe at the University of Nigeria. An Umbra Poet, he served on the executive boards of the Poetry Society of America, the PEN American Center, and the Walt Whitman Birthplace. Finally, Patterson was the founder of the Langston Hughes Festival, which he directed from 1973 to 1993.

To A Weathercock

I am moved by passing winds,
Spun mockingly upon one stand
Where all flight ends where it begins.

Strange breezes, from a distant land
Have called me,, too, and I have turned
And turned and could not understand.

Beneath each season's sun I've burned
With you, and watched freed wings depart
For dreamed-of-places where I've yearned

To go. Do these things touch your heart?
I've seen you fret on windless days,
Felt more than a metal in your art.

And I have pondered on the ways
Of wind and God that so confound,
And I have heard your turning round
Sounding the grief I could not phrase...

ETHERIDGE KNIGHT

Etheridge Knight was born in Corinth, Mississippi. He dropped out of high school while still a teenager and joined the army to serve in the Korea war. Wounded by shrapnel during the conflict, he returned to civilian life with an injury that led to drug addiction. Knight was convicted of robbery in 1960 and served eight years in the Indiana State Prison. While in prison, Knight began to write poetry, and he corresponded with, and received visits from, Black literary luminaries such as Dudley Randall and Gwendolyn Brooks. His first collection was *Poems from Prison* (1968).

Knight was married to poet <u>Sonia Sanchez</u>, and both were important members of the poets and artists connected to the <u>Black Arts Movement</u>. Knights honors and awards included fellowships and prizes from the Guggenheim Foundation, the National Endowment for the Arts, and the Poetry Society of America. Etheridge Knight died in 1991.

The Bones of My Father

1
There are no dry bones
here in this valley. The skull
of my father grins
at the Mississippi moon
from the bottom
of the Tallahatchie,
the bones of my father
are buried in the mud
of these creeks and brooks that twist
and flow their secrets to the sea.
but the wind sings to me
here the sun speaks to me
of the dry bones of my father.

2
There are no dry bones
in the northern valleys, in the Harlem alleys
young / black / men with knees bent
nod on the stoops of the tenements
and dream
of the dry bones of my father.

And young white longhairs who flee
their homes, and bend their minds
and sing their songs of brotherhood
and no more wars are searching for
my father's bones.

3

There are no dry bones here.
We hide from the sun.
No more do we take the long straight strides.
Our steps have been shaped by the cages
that kept us. We glide sideways
like crabs across the sand.
We perch on green lilies, we search
beneath white rocks...
THERE ARE NO DRY BONES HERE

The skull of my father
grins at the Mississippi moon
from the bottom
of the Tallahatchie.

For Malcolm, A Year After

Compose for Red a proper verse;
Adhere to foot and strict iamb;
Control the burst of angry words
Or they might boil and break the dam.
Or they might boil and overflow
And drench me, drown me, drive me mad.
So swear no oath, so shed no tear,
And sing no song blue Baptist sad.
Evoke no image, stir no flame,
And spin no yarn across the air.
Make empty anglo tea lace words—
Make them dead white and dry bone bare.

Compose a verse for Malcolm man,
And make it rime and make it prim.
The verse will die—as all men do—
but not the memory of him!
Death might come singing sweet like C,
Or knocking like the old folk say,
The moon and stars may pass away,
But not the anger of that day.

MARI EVANS

Born and raised in Toledo, Ohio, Black Arts poet, playwright, and children's writer Mari Evans was educated at the University of Toledo, where she studied fashion design. She was influenced by <u>Langston Hughes</u>, who was an early supporter of her writing. Evans explored the nature of community and the power of language to name and reframe. Her best-known poems include "Speak the Truth to the People," "To Be Born Black," and "I Am a Black Woman."

Evans's poetry collections include *Continuum: New and Selected Poems* (2007; 2015); *A Dark and Splendid Mass* (1992); *Nightstar: 1973–1978* (1981); *I Am a Black Woman* (1970), which won the Black Academy of Arts and Letters poetry award; and *Where Is All the Music?* (1968). Evans also published the essay collection *Clarity as Concept: A Poet's Perspective* (2006). Evans's critical works include *Black Women Writers (1950–1980): A Critical Evaluation* (1984) and *Black Women Writers: Arguments and Interviews* (1983). Her work featured in numerous anthologies, including *Black Voices: An Anthology of Afro-American Literature* (1968) and *Black Out Loud: An Anthology of Modern Poems by Black Americans* (1970).

The recipient of fellowships from the National Endowment for the Arts, MacDowell Colony, Yaddo, and the John Hay Whitney Foundation, Evans also received an honorary doctorate from Marian College and was featured on a Ugandan postage stamp. She taught at Spelman College, Purdue University, and Cornell University. Evans lived in Indianapolis for nearly 70 years, before her death in 2017.

I Am A Black Woman

I am a black woman

the music of my song

some sweet arpeggio of tears

is written in a minor key

and I

can be heard humming in the night

Can be heard

humming

in the night

I saw my mate leap screaming to the sea
and I/with these hands/cupped the lifebreath
from my issue in the canebrake
I lost Nat's swinging body in a rain of tears
and heard my son scream all the way from Anzio
for Peace he never knew....I
learned Da Nang and Pork Chop Hill
in anguish
Now my nostrils know the gas
and these trigger tire/d fingers
seek the softness in my warrior's beard

I am a black woman
tall as a cypress
strong
beyond all definition still
defying place
and time
and circumstance
assailed
impervious
indestructible
Look
on me and be
renewed

Who Can Be Born Black?

Who

can be born black

and not

sing

the wonder of it

the joy

the

challenge

And/to come together

in a coming togetherness

vibrating with the fires of pure knowing

reeling with power

ringing with the sound above sound above sound

to explode/in the majesty of our oneness

our comingtogether

in a comingtogetherness

Who

can be born

black

and not exult!

MAYA ANGELOU

An acclaimed American poet, storyteller, activist, and autobiographer, Maya Angelou was born Marguerite Johnson in St. Louis, Missouri. Angelou had a broad career as a singer, dancer, actress, composer, and Hollywood's first female black director, but became most famous as a writer, editor, essayist, playwright, and poet. As a civil rights activist, Angelou worked for Dr. Martin Luther King Jr. and Malcolm X. She was also an educator and served as the Reynolds professor of American Studies at Wake Forest University. By 1975, wrote Carol E. Neubauer in *Southern Women Writers: The New Generation,* Angelou was recognized "as a spokesperson for... all people who are committed to raising the moral standards of living in the United States." She served on two presidential committees, for Gerald Ford in 1975 and for Jimmy Carter in 1977. In 2000, Angelou was awarded the National Medal of Arts by President Bill Clinton. In 2010, she was awarded the Presidential Medal of Freedom, the highest civilian honor in the U.S., by President Barack Obama. Angelou was awarded over 50 honorary degrees before her death.

The Mothering Blackness

She came home running
    back to the mothering blackness
    deep in the smothering blackness
white tears icicle gold plains of her face
    She came home running

She came down creeping
    here to the black arms waiting
    now to the warm heart waiting
rime of alien dreams befrosts her rich brown face
    She came down creeping

She came home blameless
    black yet as Hagar's daughter
    tall as was Sheba's daughter
threats of northern winds die on the desert's face
    She came home blameless

Caged Bird

A free bird leaps
on the back of the wind
and floats downstream
till the current ends
and dips his wing
in the orange sun rays
and dares to claim the sky.

But a bird that stalks
down his narrow cage
can seldom see through
his bars of rage
his wings are clipped and
his feet are tied
so he opens his throat to sing.

The caged bird sings
with a fearful trill
of things unknown
but longed for still
and his tune is heard
on the distant hill
for the caged bird
sings of freedom.

The free bird thinks of another breeze
and the trade winds soft through the sighing trees
and the fat worms waiting on a dawn bright lawn
and he names the sky his own.

But a caged bird stands on the grave of dreams
his shadow shouts on a nightmare scream
his wings are clipped and his feet are tied
so he opens his throat to sing.

The caged bird sings
with a fearful trill

of things unknown
but longed for still
and his tune is heard
on the distant hill
for the caged bird
sings of freedom.

SARAH WEBSTER FABIO

Poet, performer, scholar, and educator Sarah Webster Fabio is considered a foundational member of the West Coast Black Arts Movement. Born in Nashville, Tennessee, Fabio was educated at Spelman College, Fisk University, and San Francisco State College, where she earned an MA in language arts. In 1966, Fabio attended the Festival of Negro Arts in Dakar, Senegal, reading with <u>Langston Hughes</u>, <u>Gwendolyn Brooks</u>, and other luminaries of the Black Arts scene. In the late 1960s, Fabio taught at Merritt College and helped establish the first black studies departments at the California College of the Arts and the University of California-Berkeley. In the 1970s, Fabio pursued work toward a PhD in American studies and African American studies at the University of Iowa. She taught at the University of Iowa, the University of Wisconsin, and Oberlin College before her death from colon cancer.

Fabio published numerous collections of poetry and four recordings with Folkways Records. In her poetry, she explored the personal, political, and cultural dimensions of African American experience and utilized metaphor alongside realistic portrayals of African American life. Her collections of poetry include *Saga of a Black Man* (1968); *Mirror, a Soul* (1969); *Black Talk: Shield and Sword* (1973); and her seven-volume masterpiece, *Rainbow Signs* (1973). Other books by Fabio include *Dark Debut: Three Black Women Coming* (1966), *Return of Margaret Walker* (1966), the anthology *Double Dozens: An Anthology of Poets from Sterling Brown to Kali* (1966), and *No Crystal Stair: A Socio-Drama of the History of Black Women in the U.S.A.* (1967). Fabio was a pioneer of spoken word, and her work as a performer braided together multiple registers of speech, instrumentation, and jazz percussion.

The Hand That Rocks (lyrics)

The hand that rocks the cradle
rocks the boat.
Baby, last night when you called me
feelin' smug and safe because

you were 2,000 miles away
giving me that old line about
"Wish you were here."
Jesus, you forgot
I'm of the order of that bad New Orleans
Sister Marie
and I've been known to have the power.
I mean, I reach out
touch,
turn a boat around in mid-sea
and pile up,
here brimming over
like a sinking ship with memories
of my tender lovin' care.
My man,
as he decides to come
right on back home to me…

ANGELA JACKSON

Angela Jackson is a Chicago poet, playwright, and novelist. She has received numerous honors for both fiction and poetry, including the 2022 Ruth Lilly Poetry Prize, the Pushcart Prize, the Poetry Society of America's Shelley Memorial Award, and fellowships from the National Endowment for the Arts and the Illinois Arts Council. Her poetry collection *All These Roads Be Luminous* (1998) was nominated for the National Book Award, and her debut novel, *Where I Must Go* (2009), won the American Book Award. In addition to *Comfort Stew*, Jackson has written several other plays: *Witness!* (1978), *Shango Diaspora: An African-American Myth of Womanhood and Love* (1980), and *Lightfoot: The Crystal Stair.*

Miz Rosa Rides the Bus

That day in December I sat down
by Miss Muffet of Montgomery.
I was myriad-weary. Feets swole
from sewing seams on a filthy fabric;
tired-sore a pedalin' the rusty Singer;

Miz Rosa Rides the Bus

dingy cotton thread jammed in the eye.
All lifelong I'd slide through century-reams
loathsome with tears. Dreaming my own
silk-self.

It was not like they all say. Miss Liberty Muffet
she didn't
jump at the sight of me.
Not exactly.
They hauled me
away—a thousand kicking legs pinned down.

The rest of me I tell you—a cloud.
Beautiful trouble on the dead December
horizon. Come to sit in judgment.

How many miles as the Jim Crow flies?
Over oceans and some. I rumbled.
They couldn't hold me down. Long.
No.

My feets were tired. My eyes were
sore. My heart was raw from hemming
dirty edges of Miss L. Muffet's garment.
I rode again.

A thousand bloody miles after the Crow flies
that day in December long remembered when I sat down
beside Miss Muffet of Montgomery.
I said—like the joke say—What's in the bowl, Thief?
I said—That's your curse.
I said—This my way.
She slipped her frock, disembarked,
settled in the suburbs, deaf, mute, lewd, and blind.
The bowl she left behind. The empty bowl mine.
The spoiled dress.

Jim Crow dies and ravens come with crumbs.
They say—Eat and be satisfied.
I fast and pray and ride.

ALVIN AUBERT

Alvin Bernard Aubert (March 12, 1930-January 7, 2014) was born in Lutcher, LA. He left school early and worked until joining the U.S. Army in 1947. He earned his GED, progressed to the rank of master sergeant, and started reading poetry seriously. Aubert earned a BA from Southern University in Baton Rouge and an MA from the University of Michigan, Ann Arbor, where he was a Woodrow Wilson National Fellow. He pursued postgraduate work at the University of Illinois.

Aubert is the author of the poetry collections *Against the Blues* (1972), *Feeling Through* (1975), *A Noisesome Music* (1979), *South Louisiana: New and Selected Poems* (1985), *If Winter Come: Collected Poems 1967–1992 (1994)*, and *Harlem Wrestler and Other Poems* (1995). His poetry draws on his personal experience of growing up in a small Mississippi River town as well as his interest in African American cultural figures.

A career in teaching took Aubert back to Southern University, where he taught for ten years, to SUNY Fredonia and then to Wayne State University in Michigan, where he was professor and director of the Center for Black Studies as well as chair of Africana Studies. In 1975, he founded the journal Obsidian: Black Literature in Review, which was an early forum for African American literature and literary criticism.

Auberts's honors include fellowships from the National Endowment for the Arts, the Callaloo Award, and the Xavier Activist for the Humanities Award.

The Revolutionary

He is bound to make something happen
he is not quite sure what
but he is determined
he flits from flower to flower
he has more legs than a hive of bees
he takes everything out of them leaving them for dead.

It will be a long time before anything happen.
In the meantime he plies his adversary's craft
on whomever is at hand and is useful to him
in that way, being bound as he is
to making something happen
something worthy of himself almost anything.....

Nat Turner in the Clearing

Ashes, Lord—
But warm still from the fire that cheered us,
Lighted us in this clearing where it seems
Scarcely an hour ago we feasted on
Burnt pig from our tormentors' in willing
Bounty and charted the high purpose you
Word had launched us on, And now, my comrades
Dead, or taken; your servant, pressed by the
Blood-drenched yelps of hounds, forsaken, save for
The stillness of the word that persist quivering
And breath-moist on his tongue; and these faint coals
Soon to be rushed to dying glow by the
Indifferent winds of miscarriage-What now,
My Lord? A priestess once, they say, could write
On leaves, unlock the time-bound spell of deeds
Undone. I let fall upon these pale remains
Your breath-moist word, preempt the winds, and give
Them now their one last glow, that some dark child
In time to come might pass this way and, in
This clearing, read and know....

HEATHER BUCHANAN & KIM MCMILLON

Heather Buchanan is an award-winning writer, publisher and producer. Her press, Aquarius Press, is the publisher of the Black Fire This Time series. Kim McMillon, Ph.D., is a contributor to the anthology *Some Other Blues: New Perspectives on Amiri Baraka* (Ohio University Press). McMillon produced the Dillard University-Harvard's Hutchins Center Black Arts Movement Conference in New Orleans (2016). She was a guest editor for *The Journal of PAN African Studies*' special edition on the Black Arts Movement . She was the editor of *Black Fire This Time, Vol. 1.*

"We're Bringing You Black Theatre": Remembering Ed Bullins
Ishmael Reed, Askia Touré, Eugene B. Redmond and Sonia Sanchez in Conversation

On November 13, 2021, the world lost one of its last great black dramatists. Edward Artie Bullins (b. 7/2/35) was a brash experimental playwright who unabashedly held up a large mirror for Black America to see itself magnified in a way that few black playwrights have achieved since. The New York Drama Critics' Circle and Obie Award winner was associated with the Black Arts Movement and served as the Minister of Culture for the Black Panther Party in San Francisco in the 1960s. Born in Philadelphia, Bullins joined the creative writing program at San Francisco State College, where he pursued playwriting. His play *Clara's Ole Man* premiered on August 5, 1965, at San Francisco›s Firehouse Repertory Theatre. After seeing Amiri Baraka›s play *Dutchman*, Bullins felt inspired to join him at Black House, the cultural center of the Black Arts Movement. As a result, Bullins helped found Black Arts/West in San Francisco.

Four poets and writers who knew Ed well—Ishmael Reed, Askia Touré, Eugene B. Redmond, and Sonia Sanchez—remember the prolific playwright as a friend and teacher.

Ishmael Reed, Playwright, Black Arts Movement Founder and MacArthur Fellow

I see somebody who didn't write for the 71% of people who buy tickets. Ed almost had a play on Broadway about Joanne Little, the Black woman who killed a prison guard who'd made advances on her. Broadway wanted to make changes, but he wouldn't compromise. So that was Ed's first experience with the great white way.

But out here [in California], my students and I were his apprentices. Ed worked with the Black Repertory Theater and directed one of my plays, *Savage Wilds,* which at that time was a work-in-progress, and my students were part of the crew. There was a memorable anecdote involving one of my students and Ed. On the blackboard was "Dinner at 5:30 with Professor Reed," the student wrote, "bring your own watermelon."

So these were kids from suburban areas, and they'd had minimal contact with Blacks. I told the student either I could report him to the Dean or he could do an apprenticeship with Ed Bullins. He chose that. For ten weeks, he worked with Ed and Mona Vaughn Scott, the Black Rep's producer. Mona's parents had a theater in the south but were run out of town by the Klan, who had fired shots into their home, nearly wounding Mona, an infant at the time. They started a theater in Berkeley and eventually occupied a theater on Adeline. I thought my student would be a crew member, but Ed cast him in one of his plays. I don't know where that guy is now, but I know that he will never forget that experience.

That's the kind of openness that Ed Bullins showed. He lived not too far from me while in Oakland in 1989. Bullins built a theater on San Pablo, the Bullins Memorial Theater, the "BMT"; it was named after a son of his who had been killed. He not only produced plays but acted. I saw him perform in Ed's *In The Wine Time*. His son performed in my play, *Hubba City*, which didn't just cover the mule end of the drug trade, the kind of stuff you get from *The Wire* and its clones. *Hubba City* concentrated not only on the Black street distributors but the banks, real estate interests, and the suburban gun dealers who benefitted.

The place was shabby, but Ed renovated it to hold about 50 people. And there, he directed my play *Savage Wilds,* which is about the entrapment of the late Marion Barry, the mayor of Washington. A'lelia Bundles and some other Black women sponsored a reading of the play in DC. *The Washington Post* called the play "paranoid" because it reported that government and media people were using cocaine all over Washington, and Barry had been singled out. The FBI entrapment of Barry cost the government $4 million. The assistant to Richard Thornburgh, who prosecuted Barry, was indicted for cocaine use, "the highest official ever prosecuted for the crime." Thornburgh's son was accused of selling cocaine. I wasn't paranoid; I'd done more research than the reviewer.

We worked with Ed for maybe two years. He went back to New York, but I think those two years—1989 and 1990—were when Ed showed independence and established his theater instead of auditioning for the mainstream and becoming a token (not threatening middle-class audiences). I went to see one of his plays in midtown Manhattan. People came down from Harlem, some pushing baby carriages. You could tell that this was the first time some of them had seen a play because when the lights dimmed, indicating that the play was about to start, people shouted, "What happened to the lights?"

Askia Touré, Black Arts Movement Founder, Poet, Editor, Playwright, Activist, 2022 Sam Cornish Poetry Award Winner and Poet Laureate of Boston, Massachusetts

I don't recall when I first met Ed, he was just always there. He and Amiri were very tight. We were having meetings with activists getting together. I'd heard that Ed was a great radical playwright and a good friend of Amiri's.

In a sense, Ed and Amiri were like big brothers to me, role models. I told them, "I want to be like you guys." They told me, "No—you be *better* than us." Ed and Amiri were cultural activists. They embodied the stance of African American writers at the time, taking on the Establishment. They never allowed fame to separate them from their people. I was awed by them both. I saw Ed and Amiri's plays in Harlem. It was the norm for us upcoming writers to check out Ed and Amiri's plays. I'd tell other young writers and artists that Ed and Amiri were gentlemen, not punks; they didn't let anybody run over them. We took notes. After the plays, they'd both take time to talk with us. They never acted like "stars."

Amiri set such an example. He was an articulate firebrand. He would take the dictionary and beat the hell out of it, taking on arrogant and racist people. Amiri told me, "You've got to learn how to deal with these guys." I'd never experienced a guy like that; I'd only seen guys who try to take a punch, but Amiri was different. He was really sharp and used humor as a weapon. He kind of got that I admired him.

In contrast to Amiri, Ed didn't talk much; rather, he demonstrated through his work. One thing interesting about Ed was his more sly sense of humor. He didn't like blowhards and pompous people. He was humble. He said, "You can't let blowhards dominate you." He talked about the independence of the black artist. Despite his sense of humor, however, Ed was a serious business-oriented dramatist. He didn't screw around. When we witnessed Ed's work, we young writers would say to each other, "Did you hear what he said?" and write it all down. Ed would hear us and give us a wink.

Eugene B. Redmond, Emeritus Professor, English and Black Studies and Poet Laureate of East St. Louis

I knew Ed since the 1960s. During the 60s/70s, there were boatloads of conferences, workshops and rallies all over the country and elsewhere. With comrades, fellow teachers, friend-poets and organizers, I traveled to many of them: Los Angeles, Oakland, San Francisco, Sacramento, Atlanta, New York/Newark, Philly, D.C., West Indies, West Africa, England, France, The Netherlands, then back this way to East/St. Louis Chicago, Detroit ... New Orleans. There was one big conference I didn't make: Fisk University Black Writers '66; I really regret it because that was

"We're Bringing You Black Theatre": Remembering Ed Bullins 127

a major pivotal one. I saw Ed at many of the confabs.

In my mind, Ed was quiet. We always shook hands and hugged, but he didn't say a lot. There were lots of Black Theatre Confabs in New York. In 1976, Ed came to see one of my plays there at the Frank Silvera Playwrights Workshop. Everybody was there—Amiri Baraka, Jayne Cortez, sculptor Mel Edwards, Joan Sandler, Louise Merriweather, Raymond Patterson. Many of the top playwrights and critics—including Larry Neal—were there.

There was a vigorous discussion after my play. Some people decimated it—that was what it was all about—critical feedback in a workshop setting—so some of it was helpful to me. I was developing as a playwright. I didn't abandon it [playwriting] but it wasn't my main focus. The play, *Will I Still Be Here Tomorrow?*, was about a junior Olympian in Sacramento who had been shot to death by the police. The title was influenced by Diana Ross's "Will You Still Love Me Tomorrow?" I played on that title, that idea. One teenager was shot by the police and another young man picked him up, put him on his back and started running away, trying to get some help. Police riddled the already wounded one with bullets and killed him. That was a real big thing in Sacramento in the 1970s. Joan Sandler worked out production of my play; she was big in Black theatre in New York at the time. Not everybody decimated the play—people gave their comments just as they would for any play.

I remember that Ed came up to greet me and shake my hand. He then gave me a real bear hug and said, "You've got a lot of talent, brother, keep writing. Don't let some of what was said today get you down." I told him that I understood. I, too, was a critic; my book, *Drumvoices,* a critical history of Black poetry, had just come out. That's all Ed said. We had similar backgrounds; I understood the violence he had seen in his youth. Ed knew who I was because, like him, I was publishing and being mentioned in *Negro Digest, Black World, The Journal of Black Poetry* … I was also publishing in some of the radical, mostly-white publications like everybody at the time. Ed was guest editor of The *Drama Review,* a prestigious white publication. He edited their "Black" issue. Larry Neal was in there, Baraka, a whole bunch of people. I had edited a special issue of *Negro American Literature Forum* that came out of Indiana. I put 20 Black poets in there. So we were all in the "mix."

I saw Ed off and on after that. I saw him at a Black Arts and Poetry conference at San Francisco State College. The last time I saw him was in 2009 at Baraka's 75th birthday at the Schomburg Center for

Research in Black Culture in New York. I asked Ed to sign a copy of the commemorative anthology that Amiri's friends had compiled. Ed and I had some stuff in there. Sadly, Ed sent someone over to me who said, "He wants to know your name." I said, "*My* name?" It was then that I realized Ed didn't remember who I was. He'd told me it was good to see me but maybe he was faking it; a lot of people do that when they lose their memory. I remember going to Maya's [Angelou] and I told her what happened. I always kept her abreast of everything.

Ed Bullins was one of the foremost thinkers. Ed was one of the most prolific playwrights, too, something like 50 plays. Baraka's *Dutchman* was somewhat ahead of the Black Arts Movement. He "knew" experimental theatre—you can be black and still be experimental. That's why I liked *Dutchman*. Meanwhile, Ed's influence on my own work was the imagination—How can you imagine an act, a voice or a sound? We knew that being black can put you in a box but we wanted to be black without being put in a box. I thought Ed did a good job of that. Baraka did a good job, too—he stayed in the "way out there"; he had a basketball player going to the moon.

Ed's Black Social Realism influenced me. He was writing that stuff in the 1960s. I was coming out of grad school, out of a white classical/ modern literature. Where was the understanding of black people, the psychology, the nuances?

Ed knew how to write about black people. We sat in a circle at a workshop at San Francisco State College. We had some wonderful exchanges. Ed had his own mind within the Black Arts Movement. He would not just latch on and follow somebody—he'd question things. I remember discussions we had about black characters; they were good talks. How to develop a black character who had been raised to be black and white, working with that character onstage, the nuances. We had a discussion at a Black Power Conference in New York in the 1970s. I saw/ heard him talk about characterization with Ron Milner in Detroit.

During breaks at conferences, Ed seemed to have two thoughts within: He wanted to find a home for black theatre and he wanted to make sure we didn't "over-white" our work. It took Ed a while to find a home for what he wanted to do. He argued for black theatre through his publications and plays—and days.

Sonia Sanchez, Black Arts Movement Founder, Poet, Professor and 2022 MacDowell Medal Recipient

We were at San Francisco State College to begin teaching Black Studies. Ed was there on campus. He was always collecting new plays for the black theatre. Every time he did an anthology, he brought more and more people from all over to work together. Ed got on the phone, calling people together from various places. He called upon not only Baraka, but also Charles Fuller from Philadelphia, N.R. Davison from New Orleans, Kensey Babbs from Detroit, me, and Marvin X from California.

Ed was with us at the Black House, which had been established by Brother Eldridge Cleaver and the people who worked with him, including Baraka and me. Ed became the Minister of Culture for the Black Panther Party. He published my poems and Baraka's poems in their newspaper. At San Francisco State College, Baraka was brought in specifically to teach theatre, and I taught creative writing and Black literature. We were following the tradition of what Baraka had been doing in Harlem, one-act plays and poetry for the people. We served food and drinks. Ed had started that process of "20-cycle plays." Ed experimented with plays; *Malcolm '71* was only one and-a-half pages.

Ed published women. He published people we never heard of before, new people that were not in the *Black Fire* [1968] anthology, new people. It was a wonderful thing.

Ed was a great teacher of plays. He shared what was being shared with him, and there was a joy. Ed did one of the first workshops in New York City, teaching primarily young white playwrights. Ed's joy was teaching these young people who wanted to be playwrights. Most of the writers that came out of that workshop would have plays that were being produced in New York City. It shows what a fantastic person he was in sharing his knowledge. I remember thinking this is a young playwright in love with plays. Ed Bullins continued to produce plays. He took his genius up to Harlem to the New Lafayette Theatre. This was a resurrection of the Lafayette Theatre, now called the New Lafayette Theatre, to show that African Americans have always done theatre and been community-based with our theatre. We had a sense of herstory and history with the New Lafayette Theatre. He turned out journals about what they were doing in the New Lafayette Theatre. His was a historical place for Black theatre. We learned so much from the workshops he gave and from his willingness to showcase his plays and the plays of other African American playwrights. He brought in playwrights like J.E. Gaines, Richard Wesley, and others. Ed would say, "Do you write plays?" "Can you send me a play?" He taught them how to be promising playwrights. I loved him very much for what he did.

He did a two-part issue of *Drama Review*. There were two divisions: The Black Revolutionary Theatre—Larry Neal, Ben Caldwell, Sonia Sanchez, LeRoi Jones (Amiri Baraka), Ron Milner, Eddie Keynes, Jr. and the Theatre of the Black Experience—Bill Gunn, Dorothy Ahmed, and Joseph "Joe" White. He also explained that he situated himself in the Theatre of Black Experience and explained that there were two distinct arenas of Black Theatre. The theatre he was producing is what was happening in Black lives and what mattered.

When Baraka came to Oakland, we traveled to the black areas, bringing the black experience to Oakland. One humorous story was our 8 a.m. program. We marched through the neighborhood drumming and singing. We were so exuberant, not realizing how early morning it was! All we knew was, "We're bringing you black theatre." Finally, a resident told us, "I want to hear you, but come back at 12, and we'll be ready for it." So we came back around 12/12:30 p.m.

Two-page short plays were all you needed to get people's attention. We had a night of Black Poetry at the Filmore with Marvin X, Baraka, Ed, Sarah Fabio, and myself. As each one performed, the audience became more and more involved and intense in their responses to each poet. When Baraka ended the session, the Fillmore exploded with people standing up, stomping their feet, and chanting.

Ed was always a playwright and a teacher. He was always writing a play. You knew he was doing that 20-cycle work, doing what he loved. That is his legacy. He would say, "I'm a playwright...I'm writing." And "If you're a writer, write!" Ed wasn't competitive. He opened up a space for everyone.

Ed impacted August Wilson and American Theatre in a significant way. It was about *how* he wrote about the black experience. Ed didn't shy away from controversial subjects. He wasn't ashamed to show us ourselves as we are. However, critics would look at him through the lens of whiteness. I considered Ed a warrior playwright. It was how he looked at his people; he gave them a chance to resurrect themselves.

I taught Ed's plays for 40 years. I was blessed to know him. He was living in Boston and told me he had a new book coming out and invited me to the launch. The book sold out. It was an unforgettable experience. I was proud to be there with him and see how the city responded to him. I felt connected to him.

Ed will be remembered as one of the great black playwrights of our time.

Ishmael Reed is the winner of the prestigious MacArthur Fellowship, the renowned L.A. Times Robert Kirsch Lifetime Achievement Award and the Lila Wallace-Reader's Digest Award. He has been nominated for a Pulitzer and finalist for two National Book Awards and is Professor Emeritus at the University of California at Berkeley and founder of the Before Columbus Foundation, which promotes multicultural American writing. He also founded PEN Oakland which issues the Josephine Miles Literary Awards. Reed is the author of more than thirty titles including the acclaimed novel *Mumbo Jumbo*, as well as nonfiction, poetry and nine plays .He recently premiered a new play, *The Conductor*, in New York. Reed penned the Introduction to *Black Fire This Time, Vol. 1* (2022).

Askia Muhammad Abu Bakr el Touré is one of the founding members of the Black Arts Movement of the 1960s and 1970s. As a poet, editor, and activist, Touré helped define a new generation of black consciousness that sought to affirm through the arts the community's African heritage as a means to create an uplifting and triumphal identity for the modern black experience. Touré is the author of several books of poetry and has been published in numerous anthologies.

Upon his discharge from military service, Touré headed to New York, and from 1960 to 1962 he studied visual arts at the Art Students League of New York. In 1963 Touré, working with illustrator Tom Feeling and artist Elombe Brath, helped produce a brief, privately published illustrated history of Samory Touré, who resisted French colonialism in Guinea in the 1800s and was the grandfather of Sékou Touré, former president of Guinea who successfully led his country's struggle for independence from the French in the 1950s. This publication marked the beginning of his life-long interest in the history of Africa.

In 1962, Touré began providing illustrations to *Umbra* magazine, whose staff included several prominent poets, authors, and activists. Here, in this company he began to focus on his poetry and to develop his own poetic style. Turning first to W.E.B. De Bois for inspiration, Touré's influences eventually came from a broad range of writers, including Irish poet William Butler Yeats, Chilean poet Pablo Neruda, and Harlem Renaissance writer Langston Hughes, among others. Ultimately, Touré found his poetic home in the rhythm, phrasing, and tonality of black music, with particular homage paid to the jazz saxophone of John Coltrane.

During the early 1960s, Touré solidified his growing role as a leader of the emerging

Black Arts Movement by working with several new black arts publications. From 1963 to 1965 he served on the editorial board of Black America, the literary arm of the black nationalist Revolutionary Action Movement (RAM). For the following two years he was on the staff of *Liberator Magazine*, and then he served as an associate editor on the staff of *Black Dialogue*, which had begun publication in the spring of 1965. Eventually, the *Journal of Black Poetry* (now *Kitabu Cha Juai*) emerged from *Black Dialogue* and Touré was named editor-in-chief. Through all these forums, Touré sought to redefine black identity and strengthen the movement against racial injustice and oppression.

Touré was deeply affected by the assassination of Malcolm X on February 21, 1965. In response he joined with influential scholar Larry Neal to founded the newspaper *Afro World*, which went to press just one week after Malcolm X's death. That spring Touré, again partnering with Neal and took the Black Arts Movement to the streets of Harlem by organizing the Harlem Uptown Youth Conference. They invited artists from the Black Arts Repertoire Theatre School to perform music, poetry, and plays in the blocked-off streets of Harlem. Among the many Harlem-based artists, Touré performed some of his own poetry in this massive block party. This event spawned the creation of Harlem's Black Arts School. He is the inaugural recipient of the Sam Cornish Poetry Award. He is the Poet Laureate of Boston, Massachusetts.

Eugene B. Redmond is Emeritus Professor of English and Black Studies at Southern Illinois University Edwardsville. He was named Poet Laureate of East St. Louis in 1976. That same year, Doubleday released his "critical history," *Drumvoices: The Mission of Afro-American Poetry*. In the late 1960s, he taught with Katherine Dunham and writer Henry Dumas (1934-1968) at SIU's Experiment in Higher Education. He also helped found Black Studies Programs and weekly newspapers, including the *East St. Louis Monitor*, where he wrote weekly columns and editorials. As literary executor of Dumas's estate, and with assistance from Toni Morrison, Maya Angelou, Quincy Troupe and Amiri Baraka, Redmond edited several volumes of his late friend's writings. These included *Ark of Bones* (short fiction), *Knees of a Natural Man* (poetry), *Jonoah and the Green Stone* (novel) and *Echo Tree* (short fiction). While/after serving as Professor of English and Poet-in-Residence in Pan African/Ethnic Studies at CSU-Sacramento (70's-80's), Redmond won an NEA Fellowship, a Pushcart Prize, an Outstanding Faculty Research/Teaching Award, and two American Book Awards. He also co-directed CSUS's Annual Third World Writers and Thinkers Symposium. Third World Press published his *Arkansippi Memwars* in 2012.

Sonia Sanchez is a poet, professor and international lecturer on Black Culture and literature, women's liberation, peace and racial justice. She is the author of over 20 books including *Homecoming, We a BaddDDD People, Love Poems, I've Been a Woman, A Sound Investment and Other Stories, Homegirls and Handgrenades, Under a Soprano Sky, Wounded in the House of a Friend* (Beacon Press 1995), *Does Your House Have Lions?* (Beacon Press, 1997), *Like the Singing Coming off the Drums* (Beacon Press, 1998), *Shake Loose My Skin* (Beacon Press, 1999), *Morning Haiku* (Beacon Press, 2010), and most recently, *Collected Poems* (Beacon Press, 2021). In addition to being a contributing editor to *Black Scholar* and T*he Journal of African Studies*, she has edited an anthology, *We Be Word Sorcerers: 25 Stories by Black Americans. BMA: The Sonia Sanchez Literary Review* is the first African American journal that discusses the work of Sonia Sanchez and the Black Arts Movement. A recipient of a National Endowment for the Arts, the Lucretia Mott Award for 1984, the Outstanding Arts Award from the Pennsylvania Coalition of 100 Black Women, the Community Service Award from the National Black Caucus of State Legislators, she is a winner of the 1985 American Book Award for *Homegirls and Handgrenades,* the Governor's Award for Excellence in the Humanities for 1988, the Peace and Freedom Award from Women International League for Peace and Freedom (W.I.L.P.F.) for 1989, a PEW Fellowship in the Arts for 1992-1993 and the recipient of Langston Hughes Poetry Award for 1999. *Does Your House Have Lions?* was a finalist for the National Book Critics Circle Award. She is the Poetry Society of America's 2001 Robert Frost Medalist and a Ford Freedom Scholar from the Charles H. Wright Museum of African American History. Sanchez has lectured at over 500 universities and colleges in the United States and has traveled extensively, reading her poetry in Africa, Cuba, England, the Caribbean, Australia, Europe, Nicaragua, the People's Republic of China, Norway, and Canada. She was the first Presidential Fellow at Temple University and she held the Laura Carnell Chair in English at Temple University. She is the recipient of the Harper Lee Award, 2004, Alabama Distinguished Writer, and the National Visionary Leadership Award for 2006. She is the recipient of the 2005 Leeway Foundation Transformational Award and the 2009 Robert Creeley Award. Currently, Sonia Sanchez is one of 20 African American women featured in "Freedom Sisters," an interactive exhibition created by the Cincinnati Museum Center and Smithsonian Institution traveling exhibition. In December of 2011, Philadelphia Mayor Michael Nutter selected Sonia Sanchez as Philadelphia's first Poet Laureate. *BaddDDD Sonia Sanchez*, a documentary about Sanchez's life as an artist and activist by Barbara Attie, Janet Goldwater, Sabrina Schmidt Gordon, was nominated for a 2017 Emmy®. Additional awards include the 2016 Shelley Memorial Award of the Poetry Society of America, the Wallace Stevens Award (2018), the Anisfield-Wolf Lifetime Achievement Award (2019) and the Dorothy, the Lillian Gish Prize (2021) and the MacDowell Medal (2022).

These contributors appear in *Black Fire This Time, Vol. 1* (2022), an anthology on the history and legacy of the Black Arts Movement, published by Aquarius Press. ISBN 978-1-7379876-7-3.

THULANI DAVIS

backstage drama

for Miami

They all like to hang out.
Thinking is all rather grim to them.
Snake and Minnie,
who love each other dearly,
drink in different bars,
ride home in separate cars.
They like to kiss good night
with unexplored lips.
They go out of town
to see each other open.
This they do for no one else.
Minnie does it all for God.
Snake does it all for fame.
Backstage is where they play their games;
that's why i know their business.

I was gonna talk about a race riot.
They say they've never played that town.
Fleece tells me he's seen an old movie
about a black town attacking a white one.
Sidney Poitier was the young doctor,
accused, abused and enraged.
There were Ossie Davis and Woody Strode,
Ruby Dee and a hundred unknowns.
Also Sapphire's mama as a maid.
"What was Sapphire's mama's name?" says Inez.
I was going to talk about a race riot
but we were stuck on Kingfish's mother-in-law.
Minnie kisses Snake so he'll forget about that
and I say, "They're mad, they're on the bottom
going down, stung by white justice in a white town,
and then there's other colored people,
who don't necessarily think they're colored people,

leaving them the ground."

"That's just like the dreads, the Coptics,
and the Man-ley-ites," one drunk says too loud,
"I and I know," say he.
Snake yells, "Are you crazy? No, it ain't,
and no, we don't."
"That's just like Angola," Terri chimes,
"Sometimes it's not who but what,
sometimes not what but who."

I'm trying to talk to these people
about this race riot,
someone is walking on the bar,
and every one of us belongs even now to Miami,
to people we have never seen.

Pookie and Omar want to know what's goin' on.
They always do,
'cause they're always in the bathroom
when it's goin' on.
They do everything together and not for God,
and not for fame, but for love.
At least that's what their records say.
They are a singing group that's had 13 Pookies.

Omar asks me, "What do you want to say?"
Inez interupts, "She don't know what to say,
she just wants to say something,
I understand that."
The 13th Pookie chirps, "This race riot sounds like
all the other race riots."
Fleece says, "And you sound like
12 other Pookies, Pookie."

I am still trying to talk about this race riot.
Minnie looks up and says, "We don't have anywhere
to put any more dead."
Snake puts on his coat to leave alone,
"We never did, we never did."

ALDON L. NIELSEN

Aldon Lynn Nielsen, poet and scholar, is the George and Barbara Kelly Professor of American Literature at the Pennsylvania State University. He was the first recipient of the Larry Neal Award for Poetry, and has since received the SAMLA Studies Prize, the Josephine Miles Award, the Darwin Turner Award, The Kayden Prize, the Gustavus Myers Citation, The Gertrude Stein Award and a Sigma Tau Delta Outstanding Professor Award. His edition of Lorenzo Thomas's *Don't Deny My Name* received the American Book Award. In the past he has taught at The George Washington University, Howard University, San Jose State University, UCLA, Loyola Marymount University and Central China Normal University.

All The Places We've Been
—A Prayer for Gil Scott-Heron

Take Me to the Pilot
Played on the radio
But we didn't know
You in our first class

Gloves out at fingertips
Braids beneath leather cap
Busied yourself then
Busied us

Busy as you were
The Fender Rhodes Scholar
Of Bluesology was to be
Our pilot who the cap fit

That first minute
Of that winter day
When nobody knew
What to say

We were to be
Writers on the storm
Time was right
Up on us

Time was tight
The now that was more than
Ever was what brought us
Together

Federal City's ungranted
Land housed our
Unmitigated band
We were the unruled unruly

We thought we'd call it morning
That storm music
No small talk
At Second and E

Did you hear what they said
Back home
A toast to the people
Ain't no new thing

From South Africa to South
Carolina we wrote
And writing rose
Within our souls

We couldn't know
Watching
Your hands spider across the keys
How you were to end

How drift away was to be
The closing number

Precious Lord
Take his hand

JIMMY GARRETT

Jimmy Garrett is a former SNCC worker and student at San Francisco State College. He was a pioneer of the Black Campus Movement. Garrett arrived at San Francisco State in the spring of 1966 with the intention of relocating the Black Student Movement he had participated in the last six years (as a member of SNCC and CORE) from the community to the campus. In the next two years, more than 90 percent of the sit-in demonstrations by Black students occurred on college campuses in 1967 and 1968.

Garrett also conjured up the idea for the discipline of Black Studies—an idea that soon circulated throughout the nation. After leaving San Francisco State in 1968, Garrett co-founded and served as the director of the Center for Black Education in Washington D.C. and he was one of the principal organizers of the 6th Pan-African Congress in Tanzania in 1974. Over the last several decades Garrett has stayed active in the struggle for human rights, earning a law degree and doctorate in political philosophy and sociology of education along the way. His play, *And We Own the Night*, first was performed as a part of the 1967 Black Communications Project at the Fillmore Auditorium in San Francisco, where writer LeRoi Jones directed the production.

And We Own the Night: A Play of Blackness

We are unfair
And unfair
We are black magicians
Black arts we make
In black labs of the heart

The fair are fair
And deathly white

The day will not save them
And we own the night.
—LeRoi Jones

Characters

JOHNNY
LIL'T
MOTHER
BILLY JOE
DOCTOR
TWO BLACK YOUTHS
TWO BODIES

The scene is an alleyway, dark, dirty, dingy. A large trashcan sits stage right next to a red brick building. The entire rear of stage right is a line of buildings shaded and faded, red or brown brick or graying white wooden frames. A dim yellow light sits above the building closest to the front of the stage. To the left of the stage is a tall white picket fence, also graying. To the right of stage front, around the trashcan, is a broom, leaning against the building. At the very rear of stage left lies a dead BODY: a black youth. In the center rear of the stage is another BODY, a white man dressed in a policeman's uniform.

The lighting should give an effect of dimness, not darkness though it is night, of muted light, of soft shadows, of a kind of grey dinginess. The time is that of the present and that of death and dying.

From off stage there is the sound of gunfire, in short bursts, then in a long sustained burst, followed by high shrilling sirens. Then more gunfire.

VOICE, *offstage.* Johnny's been shot! Help me!

SECOND VOICE. Is he hurt bad?

FIRST VOICE. Yeah, get a doctor, Billy Joe.

SECOND VOICE. Okay. I'll try to find his mother too.

FIRST VOICE. To hell with his mother. Get a doctor, dammit. We'll be in the alley behind Central Street.

Two young black men enter from stage left as if from behind the fence. Johnny, tall and thin with fine black features, is being crutched by LIL'T who is small-statured and has a high brown face. They move toward the building at stage right.

LIL'T. Come on, Johnny, sit here. *He props Johnny up against the building in front of the trashcan. JOHNNY is clutching his left side where his shirt is covered with blood. He is holding a pistol in his right hand.*

JOHNNY, *breathing heavily.* Lil'T . . . Lil'T . . . Bad . . . Mother . . . fuckin' cops . . . *Clutches* LIL'T . . . caught us from behind . . .

LIL'T. They won't fuck with nobody else. I blew 'em away.

JOHNNY. Good . . . Good . . . *Grimaces, then clutches LIL'T.* Lil'T, find mama.

LIL'T. Cool it, Johnny. Don't talk, brother. *He touches the wound.* You're bleedin' like hell. The doctor'll be here in a little while.

JOHNNY. No . . . find Mama . . . Tell her . . . Stay away. Tell her stay home. Ain't no . . . women here . . . Tell her . . . Lil'T.

LIL'T. Don't worry Johnny. We'll keep your mother away. She knows we got a war to fight in this alley. She knows we're kickin' the white man's ass.

JOHNNY. Naw man . . . She ain't . . . She ain't . . . no good . . . that way . . . keep her away . . . til we win . . . then she'll understand. Not now . . . not yet . . . *He nods his head from side to side.*

LIL'T. She can't stop us Johnny. Nobody can. The white man can't. Your Mama can't. Nobody. We're destroying the white man. There's wars like this in every big city . . . Harlem, Detroit, Chicago . . . all over California. Everywhere. We've held off these white motherfuckers for three days.

JOHNNY. Yeah . . . If we can keep pushin' . . . we'll win . . . we'll win. Keep Mama away . . . Keep her away . . . til we win. I'm scared. I can't fight her and the white man too. *He clutches his side and grimaces.*

LIL'T. Cool it brother . . . You the leader Johnny. You ain't scared of nothing, everybody knows that. You're smart. You know how to fuck to whitey. You fight too hard to be scared of a woman.

JOHNNY. You don't know. Lil'T. You don't know . . .

LIL'T. What you mean, I don't know. I've known you for three days . . . three days of fire. I know how you fight . . .

JOHNNY. No. You don't know. On the street, in the alley, I'm a fighter. But in my mama's house I ain't nothin.

LIL'T. What you mean?

JOHNNY. She's too strong. She about killed my Daddy. Made a nigger out of him. She loves the white man . . . She'll take me home.

LIL'T. Home. This is home. This alley and those bodies. That's home. I'm your brother and you're my brother and we live and fight in alleys. This is home. And we'll win against the white man.

JOHNNY. We're brothers.'T but mama believes the white man's God. *He lapses into silence nodding his head from side to side.*

LIL'T. Cool it Johnny. Don't be so uptight. Where's the fucking doctor?

VOICE, offstage. Go for soul! LIL'T turns his head toward stage left and rises. A short, stocky, black faced young man enters. A rifle bangs loosely at his shoulder.

LIL'T. Where's that doctor, Billy Joe?

BILLY JOE. I got him. I found him hiding at his home. Come on in the alley, Doc. A little dirt won't hurt you.

DOCTOR *enters, crouching low moving slowly, passes* BILLY JOE *toward* LIL'T, *who is standing. He looks around as if expecting to be shot. He is a light-complexioned Negro in his late forties, dressed in an expensive-looking gray suit.* LIL'T *goes over and jerks him forward.* BILLY JOE *leaves.*

LIL'T. Come on, Doc. We ain't got no time to be jiving. Johnny's bleeding bad.

DOCTOR, *standing above Johnny.* I don't . . . I don't know what I can do.

LIL'T, *raises his gun.* Man, you'd better do something quick. DOCTOR *leans over* JOHNNY *and kneels.*

DOCTOR. That boy rushed me so quick I didn't get a chance to get my tools. I just stuffed what I could in my pockets. *The* DOCTOR *presses the area where* JOHNNY *is bleeding.* That's a bad wound.

JOHNNY. Aw. *He slides away from the* DOCTOR. Be cool, man.

DOCTOR. Be still, boy, or you'll bleed to death. *Two* BLACK BOYS *rush on stage from the right, one carrying a pistol, the other a rifle.*

FIRST BOY. Lil'T. He stops to catch his breath. The cops've broken through the barricade on Vernon.

LIL'T. Which barricade? What happened?

SECOND BOY. The one on Vernon . . . The cops come in buses, five of 'em.

FIRST BOY. Yeah, looked like fifty cops a bus. The cats saw all them cops, an' ran.

LIL'T. Where'd the cats go? Up to the park?

FIRST BOY. Yeah, they set up another barricade.

SECOND BOY. We got to think of something or them cops'll break that 'un too. We came to get Johnny. He'll know what to do.

LIL'T. He can't move. He got shot lil' while ago. The TWO BOYS *turn to go over to* JOHNNY, *but are held up by LIL'T.* Naw, man, don't bother him

... He's been hurt bad. Wait til the Doc's finished.

FIRST BOY. Man, we can't wait. *They rush over to* JOHNNY. *The* FIRST BOY *kneels in front of the* DOCTOR, *the other stands behind him.* JOHNNY *rolls his head around.* Johnny, Johnny. Wake up brother Hey, what's wrong?

DOCTOR. I gave him something to kill the pain.

SECOND BOY, *kneeling, grabs* JOHNNY *by the arm.* Aw, fuck. Wake up Johnny.

LIL'T. Whyn't you cats leave him alone. *Moving over to the group.*

JOHNNY. Oh. Oh. Waking. What Wha ... Lil'T. Lil'T.

LIL'T, *kneeling.* It's all right, Johnny. These cats ...

FIRST BOY. Look, Johnny. We know you hurt but we need your help, man. Them cops're rushing the barricades in buses. Hundreds of cops.

SECOND BOY. Man. We got to stop them buses or they'll wipe us out. Cats ran from Vernon. They're all the way down the park now. Got another barricade goin'. But it won't hold long!

DOCTOR, *as* JOHNNY *sits up listening.* Wait a second. I'll be through with this bandage in a minute.

JOHNNY *to* DOCTOR. Yeah, yeah. Look here. Throw broken glass in the streets. Then pour gasoline up and down the street for a block or so. If the glass don't stop 'em, plant cars in places so they can hide with fire bombs. An' when the buses get in the middle of that gasoline, chunk them bombs under 'em.

FIRST BOY. Roasted cops!

SECOND BOY. Wow! Oh, man ... outta sight. Outta sight! Come on. Let's go. We'll get 'em. Go for soul Thanks Johnny. You're a heavy cat. *They exit.* Go for soul!

DOCTOR. Boy, if you don't be still, you'll bleed to death.

LIL'T. He's right, Man. Ain't no use in you cuttin' out on a humbug. You blowin' too much soul. BILLY JOE *enters.*

BILLY JOE, *to* LIL'T. I saw Johnny's mother down at the barricade.

LIL'T *takes* BILLY JOE *to the side of the stage left.* She's not coming here

And We Own the Night 143

is she?

BILLY JOE. Yeah, man. I told her to come. I thought Johnny might die. I thought his mother should . . .

JOHNNY. Lil'T . . . Get this dude off me.

DOCTOR, *turning to face* LIL'T. I'm just patching him. He's restless.

LIL'T. It's okay, Johnny. Take it easy Doc. *Back to* BILLY JOE. Look man . . . We got to keep his old lady away . . . She's a bitch. Johnny don't want her around. Go keep her away.

BILL JOE. But. She's his mother . . .

LIL'T. I don't give a shit. Keep her out of here. Go on. *Pushes* BILLY JOE.

BILLY JOE. Oka man. *He rushes out.*

LIL'T *turns toward* JOHNNY *and the* DOCTOR.

VOICE, *offstage*. Look out son. You nearly knocked me down. Where's my son at? Where's Johnny at?

BILLY JOE, *backing on to stage*. You can't come in. Lil'T says you got to stay out . . .

JOHNNY'S MOTHER *enters, backing* BILLY JOE *into the alley. She is an imposing black woman, wearing a simple dress of floral design and flat shoes. She never smiles.*

MOTHER. Boy, don't you mess with me. Where is my son at? *As she speaks,* LIL'T *turns. He is blocking* JOHNNY *from his mother's view.*

BILLY JOE. I don't know where the dude is. *Realizes he is in the alley and stops.*

LIL'T, *walking toward them*. I told you to keep her out.

BILLY JOE. I . . .

MOTHER. Johnny! *She rushes over to* JOHNNY *and kneels, pushing the* DOCTOR *out of the way.* BILLY JOE *shrugs his shoulders and leaves.*

JOHNNY. Mama. Mama. Go back home.

DOCTOR. Don't shake him woman! He's been shot. He's bleeding inside.

MOTHER. My son. He's my son. *She speaks loudly but does not sob.* You the doctor? Will he be all right?

LIL'T, *clutching the woman by the shoulders and trying to lift her*. He's all right. Come on now. Billy Joe'll take you home.

MOTHER, *jerking loose*. Naw. Let me go. Who are you? Why'd my son get hurt like this? You're the cause of it.

LIL'T. He got shot by a white cop.

JOHNNY. Go way Mama. T get her out of here.

MOTHER. Don't you talk to me like that. You bad boys. Sinning. And this is what you get. *Points at* JOHNNY'S *wound*.

LIL'T. Ain't nobody sinning but the white man. Now he's payin' for it.

MOTHER. Johnny layin' there bleedin' and the white man's payin'. Help me doctor. Help me take him to the hospital.

JOHNNY. Mama leave me alone.

LIL'T. Johnny ain't goin' to no white man's hospital. Them motherfuckers would just let him die.

MOTHER. Don't you curse white people like that. Doctor help me.

DOCTOR looks up at LIL'T who has lifted the gun. No we shouldn't move him. I've slowed the flow but he's still bleeding internally. He'll die if he moves around too much.

MOTHER. But he can't stay here in this alley. Oh lord help me, what can I do?

DOCTOR. I've got to get that bullet out quick. I'll go back to the office and get my case.

LIL'T. Okay Doc. Billy Joe can take you and make sure you get back. Billy Joe? *DOCTOR rises.* BILLY JOE enters. Take the doctor back to get his stuff.

BILLY JOE. Okay, come on, Doc. *They leave.*

MOTHER. Is it bad son? Is it bad? Oh Lord. What can I do? I need strength.

JOHNNY. Mama, don't pray. It don't do no good.

MOTHER. I told you to stay home. Out here fightin' the Police. Burnin' down white folks' businesses. I'm ashamed of you. God knows why you're doin' this.

JOHNNY. I'm bein' a man. A black man. And I don't need a white man's God to help me.

MOTHER. What you say? What you say 'bout God?

JOHNNY. Forget it.

MOTHER. Where'd you learn all that stuff. *She rises and turns to* LIL'T. Did you teach him this sacrilege?

JOHNNY. Nobody taught me.

LIL'T. He's leader. He knows how to fuck with whitey.

MOTHER, *to* LIL'T. Boy, can't you talk without cursin'? Don't know child like you need to talk that way. To JOHNNY. Your daddy's a man, and he don't curse.

JOHNNY. Where is he, Mama?

MOTHER. He's at home where you should be 'stead of out here in this alley.

JOHNNY. Is he hidin', Mama?

MOTHER. Naw he ain't hidin'. He's just stayin' close to his home.

LIL'T. While his woman's out on the street. Bullshit. A man don't need to hide. Can't. He'd be out here fightin' like us.

MOTHER. You're wrong boy. God knows you're wrong. You out here breakin' laws. Killin'. Look at what you've done. *She points at the bodies lying on the stage.*

LIL'T. People die when they face the white man. Better to die like a man, bringing the white man to his knees than hidin' at home under a woman's skirt.

MOTHER. My husband ain't no sinner. He don't break laws. He works hard . . . He don't bother nobody. He . . .

JOHNNY. He's still a nigger.

LIL'T. He believes what the white man says.

MOTHER. You don't know him. You don't know what he believes.

LIL'T. Be a good nigger, work hard, pray, kiss ass, and you'll make it.

MOTHER. How do you know? How do you know?

JOHNNY. I know, Mama.

MOTHER. I'm gonna take you home. Away from this sin.

JOHNNY. Don't bother me, Mama.

MOTHER. I brought you into this world. I clothed and fed you. And now you don't want me to touch you? I'm taking you home. *She tries to lift* JOHNNY. LIL'T *rushes over and grabs her by the shoulder, pulling her away.*

MOTHER. Let me go. *Breaks away from his grip.* Don't put your hands on me again.

LIL'T. Well you leave Johnny alone. Can't you understand? He's a man. He's a leader. He's my brother. We're gonna stay here in this alley and fight the white man together. Right Johnny?

JOHNNY. Yeah, brother.

MOTHER. You ain't no leader, boy. You ain't even got no mind. *Turns to* LIL'T. He's got the mind. A dirty mind. Why don't you leave him alone? He's just a boy. He didn't know about hatin' and killin' til he started running with you.

LIL'T. Killin' ain't no dirty thing to do to a white man.

MOTHER, *rising.* Murder ain't never been clean.

LIL'T. Except when the white man did it, right?

MOTHER. Who are you, the devil? I ain't speakin' of the white man as you call it. He ain't done me no harm.

LIL'T. He beat you and raped you. He made a whore out of you and a punk out of your man.

MOTHER. Naw. The white man ain't done nothing to me. But I don't know you. Where are your folks?

LIL'T. My mother and father are dead. They died the first day fightin' the cops. My brother's in jail. My sister's somewhere fightin' or dyin'! My home is this alley and Johnny is my brother. This where I live or die.

MOTHER. You don't have nothin' left. You don't feel nothin'. You ain't found God. You don't have love.

LIL'T. That God you pray to is a lie. A punk. The last dick the white man't got to put in you.

MOTHER. You see, Johnny. He's got no heart. He's got no love.

LIL'T. Love! Love! Everybody knows that love ain't enough for the white man. He don't understand love. You got to kill him. Love! Ass suckin' love. Askin' him for forgiveness when he'd done wrong. Lettin' him shoot you in the back while you're on your knees prayin' to his God.

MOTHER. Jesus said . . .

LIL'T. Another punk . . .

MOTHER. Jesus said love those who are spiteful of . . .

LIL'T. Strokin' his rod, cleanin' his shit . . .

MOTHER. Forgive those who do harm . . .

LIL'T. Blowin' up black children in churches . . . Beatin' pregnant women . . .

MOTHER. We must pray to God for salvat . . .

LIL'T. Kill that motherfucker! Cut out his heart and stuff it down his throat. Bury him in his own shit.

MOTHER, *quietly, slowly*. I will not strike out at white men. They have been good to me. Fed my son. Gave me shelter when there was no work for my husband. Gave me a job so I could care for my family. White men have done me no harm. Only niggers like you trying to take my son away and lead him to sin.

LIL'T. The white man gave you a job and took away your husband's balls. You have the money and your husband's a tramp in his own home. Ain't that right Johnny?

MOTHER, *to* JOHNNY. *She speaks quietly at first, then building to the end*. Johnny. Son. In God's name, you know how I love you and your Daddy. How I've worked and slaved for you all. And you know how white man's folks have always helped us. They're smart. They know what's right and what ain't. We got to trust in them. They're good. They run the whole world don't they? How come you're out here killin' white men. I don't understand. Livin' in this filth. Crawlin' around alleys bleedin' to death. You call yourselves men. Don't no men act like that. The white man don't crawl around, cussin' and stealin'! You ought to be actin' like the white man 'stead of tryin' to kill him.

JOHNNY, *tries to rise*. Mama . . .

LIL'T. Sit still Johnny. You'll start bleedin'.

JOHNNY. I'm already bleedin'. *Tries to rise. He gets to his knees and stops, breathing heavily. LIL'T starts toward him, then stops.*

MOTHER. Don't try to get up son.

JOHNNY. Just stay away . . . I'll make it . . . I should try to be a white man, huh? White as snow. White as death. Don't you wish I was white Mama. Clean and white like toilet paper.

MOTHER. Johnny . . .

JOHNNY starts to rise from his knees. He is holding the pistol with one hand and clutching his side with the other. And Daddy. Don't you wish he was white too? Daddy's smarter than I thought he was. He had to decide between bein' a white man and bein' nothin' and he decided to be nothin'!

MOTHER. Sit down Johnny, you're bleedin'!

JOHNNY. So I'm bleedin'. It's blood comin' from a black body shot by a white cop. Or don't that matter?

MOTHER. You were doing wrong.

JOHNNY. The white man decides what's wrong. The white man's right no matter what he's done. Right Mama. I'm wrong from the time I was born. You love the white man. And I kill the white man.

MOTHER. You made yourself into a criminal.

JOHNNY. My name is criminal. I steal and kill. I am black and that is my greatest crime. And I am proud of that crime.

MOTHER. I didn't raise you to be no criminal.

JOHNNY. You raised me to be white, but it didn't work. The white man is my enemy. I wait in alleys to stab him in the back or cut his throat.

MOTHER. But that is heathen.

JOHNNY. I have been a heathen for three days. He has for three hundred years. But I am not guilty. I feel passion when I kill. Love. He don't give a shit for nobody. He kills efficiently. I kill passionately. He is your God and I have sworn to kill God. Can't you understand, Mama? We're gonna build a whole new thing after this. After we destroy the white men. Black people don't want to kill. We want to live. But we have to kill first. We have to kill in order to win.

MOTHER. But you can't win. They've got guns and bombs. *Loud explosion. They all stop*—startled. God, what is it?

JOHNNY. It's the police buses, they got to the police buses.

LIL'T. Blow them motherfuckers away! I'll go see. *He leaves stage right. As soon as he is out of sight a second explosion roars. He rushes back on stage jumping wildly.* Boom! Man, Johnny, you should have seen that scene.

JOHNNY. Are they gettin' to 'em?

LIL'T. Goin' for soul. Gimme five brother. *He extends his open palm to* JOHNNY *who takes his bloody left had away from his side and slaps* LIL'T's *palm.*

JOHNNY. See. See mama. We're winnin'! *Dabbing his side.*

MOTHER, *quietly.* I don't see nothing boy 'cept you lost your mind. There's nothin' I can do with you. *A third explosion.*

LIL'T *rushes up to* JOHNNY *and spins him around seemingly not remembering that JOHNNY has been shot.* Forget her, Johnny. She's too old. JOHNNY *spins around with* LIL'T, *stumbling but trying to acquiesce to the dance.* This is judgment day, and we're the judges. Motherfuck the police. Motherfuck the white man. JOHNNY *is stumbling, holding the gun and clutching his side.*

JOHNNY. And motherfuck daddy and mama and all them house niggers. Death to the house niggers! *A fourth explosion.* JOHNNY *tries to dance and falls to his knees.* It's all over for the white man, huh T?

LIL'T. You damn right. *He picks up his rifle.* I'm going out to the barricade. I ain't gonna stay and wait for that Doctor no more. We got a war to fight.

JOHNNY. Okay, brother, be cool.

LIL'T. *Walks up to* JOHNNY *who is breathing very heavily while his body falters.* I hope you don't die brother . . . But you know how death is. It's over with. Ain't no more after that. Gimme five. *He extends his hand.* JOHNNY *slaps it with his last expression of strength.* LIL'T wipes the blood onto his shirt and leaves, not looking back.

JOHNNY. Mama . . .

MOTHER. You ain't my son. I don't know you. You rejoice when you kill white people and don't even feel sympathy for each other when you are dying. That boy did more toward killin' you than any white man but you love him.

JOHNNY *falls forward bracing himself by his elbow.*

JOHNNY. Mama . . .

MOTHER. Don't Mama me. I don't care about that no more. You steal and kill and curse God. You call yourselves criminals and feel no remorse. You hide in alleys cuttin' throats. You blow up buses and burn down property. That boy left here knowin' you'd die and he was smilin'. I don't understand. He'll probably be dead himself in a few minutes. I just can't see it. I know you're wrong. The white people would never do those things. You must be wrong. I don't understand. They'll make it right. They'll explain it to me. They'll show me the way. I trust in them. Ain't no nigger never been right. *She turns slowly and walks toward the stage left.* And never will be right.

JOHNNY *points the gun at her back.* We're . . . new men, Mama . . . Not niggers. Black men. He fires at her back. *She stops still, then begins to turn.* JOHNNY *fires again and she stumbles forward and slumps to the stage.* JOHNNY *looks at her for a moment, then falls away. There is a loud explosion followed by gunfire.*

James E Cherry

James E Cherry is a poet, professor, fiction writer, essayist, literary activist and social critic. He lives and creates in Tennessee.

A SURVEY OF AMERICAN HISTORY
IN 7 MINUTES & 46 SECONDS
(after George Floyd)

With guns trained at your temple, they drag you
from your car (make/model will not save you)
handcuff the remaining minutes of your life, slam you
face first into the street. Any street or nigger will do.
They kneel for as long as it takes for blood & urine
to fill a gutter or God and your mother to answer a prayer.
They do not cut off your genitals to formaldehyde
in some museum's collection. Instead, they stand
around and make you watch your own death,
make others unsee a history that daily reinvents itself,
teaches you that you are responsible
for your own noose and gasoline, blames you
for not knowing the difference
between fire and air.

A BLACK BOY WAS HERE
(Gil Scott-Heron Historical Marker Dedication)

Just south of Jackson, a black boy learns love
in his grandmother's arms, her hands a comfort
and refuge through segregated streets.

On Cumberland Street, a black boy grows
precocious at his grandmother's table
from bread, Blackness and words

of a poet who has known rivers, sits him
upon a rickety stool in front of a hand
me down piano for lessons on 88

broken keys until the room blossoms
into handclaps and hallelujahs. A black boy
in his bed past midnight, music from Beale

scratches against his window invites him
outside to walk among the stars. A black boy
enters an all white house of learning

on a cold January morning to teach a nation
what it should have known long before 1954.
A black boy discovers his grandmother

has taken up wings, left her body
in the only home he'd ever known. One day
he too would leave this place for good

and carry this small southern town all over the world.
Today, Jackson, Tennessee genuflects, honors
the years that forged a black boy into a black man

his image now adorns this city's walls,
his spirit rests upon this city's shoulders.

Mwatabu S. Okantah

Mwatabu S. Okantah holds the BA in English and African Studies from Kent
State University (1976) and the MA in Creative Writing from the City College of
New York (1982). A Professor and Chair in the Department of Africana Studies
at Kent State University, his published work includes *Cheikh Anta Diop: Poem
for the Living*—published as a limited trilingual edition in English, French and
Wolof (1997/2017), *Reconnecting Memories: Dreams No Longer Deferred* (2004),
Muntu Kuntu Energy: New and Selected Poems (2013) and *Guerrilla Dread:
Poetry for the Heart and Minds* (2019).

i, too, am a witness
(for James Baldwin)

no,
we are not their "Negro"
or their "Nigger"
or their "Black" or their "Minority"
or their "Person of Color"
or whatever they think to call us next—
always something other than
who we have always been
or who we might be
or who we might become.
in this ever-evolving world
truth is rinsed white
while the dispossessed
are expected to forget what we know
to be true
deep in our bones.
we live with anger.
sleep with it.
wake up with it.
carry it around.
pass it up
from one generation to the next
making a way out of no way.
in this world
being conscious and black
(no matter the shade)
is too black
and to love being black
is still considered
dangerous.

A blue-black on black crime
(for Tyre Nichols)

people don't
have to ask why

we fear
the police
any
more.
five brazen blue-black brothers
beat
down
another black mother's Sun
beyond senseless into another same old American
death.
could have been
one
of them caught
on the wrong side of
their "protect and serve"
blue line.
demented white supremacy in
black
face.
black self-loathing
showing out in brute-badge
blue-black on black crime.

HERINA AYOT

Herina Ayot is Kenyan American, a mental health scholar, and a storyteller crafting compelling narratives that reframe trauma, pain, and redemption. With a background in psychology and psychopathology, she believes in telling stories that reveal nuances of humanity and examine psychological trauma and post traumatic growth. Her personal essays and nonfiction have appeared in Ebony Magazine, The Root, Human Parts, and The Huffington Post. Herina was a 2014 Hurston/Wright Fellow and the 2019 winner of NYUs Threesis Academic Challenge where she discussed her completed manuscript that centers on themes of victim and perpetrator, childhood trauma, and redemption.

Baby Butterflies

Death is one word that comes up. Loss.
An ending. Pupa.

These are the words that come to mind when I attempt to characterize the last twelve months.

This time last Christmas, I bought myself a necklace. A tiny butterfly pendant, that symbolized a metaphorical representation of my favorite creature, life and death, metamorphosis and transformation, and the completion of my manuscript titled *A Kaleidoscope of Butterflies*, a novel that I had been writing for three years. Whatever the cost, I remember telling myself I deserved a fine piece of jewelry, and reckoning the money spent would find it's way back to me in the way of a book deal, a monetary inheritance from a dead family member, or another one of life's surprises. I wore the necklace religiously well into June. Then I lost it. I don't know what happened to it. When I went to feel for it, it simply wasn't around my neck anymore. Those things happen sometimes.

I lost an earring on a night out a few weeks ago.

I lost a pair of $300 sandals and later found them clenched between my dog's teeth, the leather straps shredded like a tattered rag.

I lost my children this year. Because I lose things.

Loss denotes pain that can sometimes be debilitating. But I am learning that pain is just pain. Not good. Not bad. Just part of being a human being. I've always been incredibly fascinated with the art of being human. It's a creative process, no? I liken living to writing a story, or painting a picture, or posing for a series of photographs. The way we wear a life is a fashion statement, pairing garments we find in our closets together ever so boldly, or eccentrically; the makeup of our years is the fabric of our inner and outer lives.

My interests have always been twofold. I studied psychology in undergrad because we become what we think, how we think. We become the stories we tell ourselves about ourselves. But, I studied creative writing in grad school, because at the end of the day, aren't we novels… sagas spanning decades and generations of curses and blessings, blood and tears, foolish decisions and lessons learned? Science is the study of what we are. But literature is the study of who we are. We're layered, nuanced, a complicated equation of will, power, grace, and limitations. Can anyone ever know us? I'm afraid, more often than not, we're all largely misunderstood.

I met a man last month on a cruise ship to the Bahamas. We struck up a conversation over lunch that lasted well into dinner. I love those kind of chance meetings, when you happen to sit down next to someone who tells you a thing or two about yourself. It was an easy conversation, intimate but lighthearted. Sincere, with sprinkles of humor. It started because he asked me what I was reading. It was a book by Viktor Frankl on the meaning of life and how the writer was able to survive the horrors of Auschwitz's with his mind in tact. Then I told him my own story, the fires I've survived, the places in my own life where I've stopped breathing, but determined to walk even breathless through a wilderness dense with trees. I told him the things that I've lost. He listened intently and then told me I wasn't special.

His words were a knife wrapped in gentleness that sliced through my abdomen and chest cavity, splaying me open like a gutted fish. I felt seen, and in a way found out, the story I had been telling myself and the world for years ripped apart and examined for what it really was, a flimsy mask at best that characterized me as a victim in a heartless world, and a blatant lie at worst because none of what I said actually meant anything. Nothing means anything, except the meaning you assign it.

Of course life happens. Things happen. People die. We lose things. But to characterize the loss as something to be endured, a fire to survive, well that is simply the way one is choosing to describe it, bad writing in a novel where the scribe tells the reader what to think and how to feel as opposed to laying out the facts and allowing them to have their own way of sorting through it.

So I'm not special. Because aren't all of our lives a concoction of joy and pain. I write about mine, not as a gritty tell-all seeking a spotlight, but rather as a way to help others feel less alone in the world.

tWitch, a dancer I had become familiar with over a decade ago when I used to watch So You Think You Can Dance with my then, five year old twins in the evenings on the couch shoveling lo mein into our mouths, completed suicide last week. I was shocked, not as if I knew him personally, but because I felt like I did. On screen he was always full of light and positivity, a smile always plastered across his face. He had a wife and three children and I let that fact sit because I've known intimately the desperation of wanting to end an agonizing suffering. It is a physical pain of which anyone who has never experienced will never quite understand. But for me, in my most difficult moments, my saving grace was remembering I had growing children who yet needed me. At this thought, I imagined tWitch, and the immense pain he must have been sitting in rendering his own children not enough to keep him here.

Writing for me has been a tool I've used time and again. It is a rope to which I've fastened myself to climb out of the dark well that circumstances in life threw me into. It is a therapy that has worked wonders in my life, and one I hope to gift others in offering them a way out of their own prisons of grief, shame, or despair. It is a way to make peace with the lost things. The act of creative writing and other art therapies can mimic the effects of experiencing literature, and "traveling" outside of one's immediate surroundings to explore the elastic capabilities of the mind.

In psychotherapy, the common understanding in creative writing is to separate the client's story from their deeper associations, and this separation allows them to put some distance between their identity and what happened to them. It changes their relationship with the events of their life and their thoughts and feelings connected to it. It is a method of Acceptance and Commitment Therapy helping clients move from the stories about their lives to the stories in their lives, that is, to move them from a narrative that skims the top of their experience to one that unearths it. Frankl says, in Man's Search for Meaning,"...everything can be taken from a man but one thing: the last of the human freedoms – to choose one's attitude in any given set of circumstances, to choose one's own way."

Science tells us what we are. Trauma produces something called an iconic image, that is, a mental picture that is stored deep within the brain in the limbic system and is not easily available to the cerebral cortex. But narrative tells us who we are. It is these iconic images that must be accessed if a story about the trauma is to be told. Narrative is the chain that links moments together. It finds closure with the things we've lost. Image is what is seen in dreams, what is remembered when recalling loved ones. It is image that burns itself into the mind, and it is image which can free us from a past that will always have a hold on us until we look straight at it. Image is the lifeblood of the personal essay.

Consider oatmeal for instance. It is simmering in a pot on the stove in my old Maryland apartment that I shared with my then partner and newborn twins. I am recovering from a grueling birth, cesarean section surgery, and in the throes of postpartum depression. I am making breakfast. I turn abruptly, my elbow knocking the pot from the stove, and sending oatmeal splatter all over the white linoleum floor. In this moment, I break. My legs can no longer hold me and I fall with the pot of oatmeal, crumbling into a ball on the floor, my knees pulled into my chest, thick tears welling in my eyes. Somehow my inability to properly make oatmeal meant I was also inadequate as a mother or a respectable member of society. I was, in essence, an overall disgrace of a human being, and maybe I didn't deserve to live.

Months later, my then partner would share with me a time in the thick of those days when during a routine visit, my obgyn pulled him to the side, looked him in the eyes with sincere concern and said, "she needs you." Hormones run amuck after a woman gives birth and for some women, and by some, I mean me, they were especially off kilter creating a severe chemical imbalance. That coupled with financial troubles, and the abandonment I felt from those closest to me sent me spiraling into a space and period that I simply refer to now as the time "when I was sick."

But it got better. I got better. The days turned into months, and the months into years, and I found a rhythm with my twins, a dance that made life pleasant. I enjoyed raising them, joyriding in my drop top convertible that I nicknamed Diana Ross, their car seats perched in the back. When life evolved and the children were starting preschool, we had another car, this one without a removable roof. The older twin, in his childlike innocence implored me once to "take the top off Mommy!" He was thoroughly confused when I explained this one doesn't come off.

We shared movie nights, huddled together on the couch with a bowl of popcorn and a blanket. And long talks in the bathroom, the twins in the tub, soap suds in their hair. Once my baby boy asked me what he was made of.

"Mommy, God made me right?" "Yep."
"But what did he make me out of?"
"Hmm… blood and bones and flesh and skin," I said playfully pinching his arm. He wasn't satisfied. *"But where did he get the stuff to make me?"*

He was inquisitive, and that was my favorite thing about him. As they grew, I remember another apartment, another conversation, when one of the twins asked me about babies. He was learning about reproduction in his fourth grade science class and had read that when sperm meets egg, a baby is conceived. *"But how would it meet the egg?"* he asked. *"Wouldn't it have to travel through the air?"*

Oh how my heart aches with fond memories. Memories that now seem so distant, so…out of reach. Children grow up as they often do and so it is not as if I didn't see the inevitable coming. What I didn't expect was that the children I knew would morph into someone else entirely. They will be 17 soon and this year was riddled with adolescence, rebellion, and bitter arguments that I found no shield or comfort from. I found myself depleted and so I slept. When I awoke, I learned my children were gone. The revelation reminded me of my own adolescent years, and the trouble I had with my mother. It ignited a terrible compassion , and my heart broke for her, seeing at once her humanity and sitting with her in the loss of a child.

Being a young mother, I've raised my children into adulthood before I've reached 40, an age where friends of mine are just beginning their journey into parenthood. The caveat is that I've journeyed alone, feeling feelings that are hard to explain but can only be known. It is losing a person, not to death, but to life. It is coming to terms with the realization that the children I knew so deeply were gone. That is a pain that feels like death. So I mourned. I prayed. And then I let go.

Here is a list of some things I've lost in my journey through time and space.

My first Jersey City apartment
$500 to a tourist scam artist
A ceramic bowl I made in Costa Rica
A collectors Monopoly game at an ex's apartment
A pair of leather flip flop sandals in the Atlantic Ocean off the coast

of Ghana.

Two of my teeth (I had them pulled 3 years ago as part of my orthodontic treatment. The doctor said I wasn't allowed to keep them when I asked. I wasn't allowed to keep my own teeth.)

The last voicemail my dad left me My dad.

I would say I've lost several boyfriends, but in truth, they lost me. I never really wanted them anyway and I don't say that here simply to save face. I've never found a person I've wanted to spend the rest of my life with. Notwithstanding, I love the idea of marriage. A happy marriage. Even more, I love the idea of having a life partner who lights my soul on fire. I'm not interested in mediocrity. So unless and until I find that, I'm comfortable living life on my own terms, meeting people on my journey who inspire me, and love me, and I them, even if not for forever. The time being can be magic.

I'm in awe of my mother The way she has fashioned a life for herself, finding pure love, where the rest of the world may have thought only dead things lay. She is a spectacle. Both supernatural and human. Her and Christ have that in common. The possibilities of my own life excite me, the supposition that my best years are still in front of me, the idea that I haven't yet met all of the people who are going to love me, the anticipation of not knowing how my story will end. Either way it's mine. And its beautiful. And I like to write about beautiful things.

Kincaid explained it best. She said "for me, writing isn't a way of being public or private; it's just a way of being. The process is always full of pain, but I like that. It's a reality, and I just accept it as something not to be avoided. This is the life I have. This is the life I write about."

Caterpillars crawl into pupa to die. They spin themselves into their silk coverlet. They build their own grave and dangle from a twig. Here, they shrink, shed their skin and their insides turn to mush.The grave turns from its fresh green lime color to a rusted brown resembling tree bark. It hardens and dries and hangs like evil, burned at the stake. Caterpillars don't merely sleep. They die in there, and what emerges is another beast entirely. A beautiful beast, with colorful wings that can take them anywhere. They suffer in agony first before they learn to fly. True transformation is like this.

It's not tweaking, rearranging or augmenting. It's a complete overhaul. Deconstruction. In this, the essence of the worm knows a kind of death and yet knows a kind of life. He dies, and behold, he lives. From the violence, the death, the loss, something better emerges…something that would have otherwise never existed.

C. LIEGH MCINNIS

C. Liegh McInnis is a poet, short story writer, Prince scholar, retired English instructor at Jackson State University, former editor/publisher of Black Magnolias Literary Journal, and author of eight books, including four collections of poetry, one collection of short fiction (Scripts: Sketches and Tales of Urban Mississippi), one work of literary criticism (The Lyrics of Prince: A Literary Look), one co-authored work, Brother Hollis: The Sankofa of a Movement Man, which discusses the life of Mississippi Civil Rights icon, and former First Runner-Up of the Amiri Baraka/Sonia Sanchez Poetry Award. Additionally, he has been published in magazines, newspapers, and anthologies.

"Mississippi Like…"

What is it to be Mississippi?
Where Capitol Streets cross cotton fields and
Margaret's *Jubilee* jams with Eudora's Festival
even when there are college cuts, controversy,
and the Klan, with plenty of revolution, religion,
red, ripe tomatoes, and rebel's ruby racist rag;
this is all my Mississippi.
It's little boys puttin' dirt in abandoned tires
then rolling the tires by little girls in their Sunday dresses.
It's hangin' out at Big Sam's Juke Joint on Saturday night
and jukin' to "Sign Me Up" on Sunday Morning.
It's pickin' wild berries and stealin' Mr. Wilson's plumbs.
It's mowin' everybody's yard 'cause yo' mama said so.
It's where time out means…
mama takin' a break from whippin' yo' leathery hide,
and the thought of a swarming strap still causes you to wake up
in the middle of the night in a cold sweat.

It's Ross Barnett damming the doorway of education
and James Meredith bulldozing over his ideology.
It's the Sovereignty Commission playing
hide-n-go-seek with the lives of invisible citizens
while Ebony voices declare "We Shall not Be Moved"
under the salacious sites of riffles and German Shepherds.
What is it to be Mississippi?
It's no matter how highbrow we get
we still have hot sauce on the table when we eat.
It's having a special jaw bone from being double-voiced,
being bi-legally lingual enough to talk with two tongues:
a democrat on tv and a dixiecrat under the hill—
wearing black suits in the day
and white sheets during the night.

It's cinnamon and coffee leaves hangin' from faded olive trees,
a warm Thanksgiving and a cool Christmas,
where rain steals center stage from snow, and a brief frost
can close school like the notion of the ending of segregation,
as Southern Apartheid is kept alive every Sunday morning.
We still don't pray together even though our children
can hopscotch over to Ole Miss and play together.
What is it to be Mississippi?
It's the peanut butter and jelly sandwich
of Archie Manning and Walter Payton
where some like peanut butter more than jelly.
Yet, half a sandwich rarely fills a whole belly.
It's the quiet confusion that becomes
too cantankerous to ignore—like when the doctor says
today is the day to stop eating pork.
Or, when the pork politics of "good ole boy" kick backs
become too fattening to nurture democracy.
What is it to be Mississippi?
It's having one street with two names so that
the white folks can habitat on Hanging Moss
and the Black folks can wither on West Street
until the Black folks march up the street

"Mississippi Like…" 163

'causin' the Confederates to retreat to Rankin County.
What is it to be Mississippi?
It's being the mirror of the world with a
Chrysler chrome reflection too bright to face.

Someone spat that to be Mississippi is to be dumb and stupid.
If that's being Mississippi, then [i] wanna wear the crown of dumb and
stupid:
dumb and stupid like Medgar Evers and Richard Wright
        who used the pen the carve evil into pieces,
dumb and stupid like Margaret Walker Alexander
        who used the paint of the past to illustrate
new school prophets,
dumb and stupid like Etheridge Knight and Robin Roberts
        who weaved words into portraits of dignity,
dumb and stupid like Robert Johnson and B. B. King
        who took tears of bluespeople and made
lemonade for the world,
dumb and stupid like Charlie Pride
        who put on white face with false camouflage
        to melt the plastic illusions of pale listeners,
dumb and stupid like Tennessee Williams and Eudora Welty
two silver knights who believed that souls could be
saved with secular bibles laced with gospels of the South,
dumb and stupid like Elvis Presley
who took the juke joint of the ebony Delta to pallid patrons,
liberating them one hip thrust at a time,
dumb and stupid like Bennie Thompson and Aaron Henry
        who sculpted voter registration cards
into weapons of liberty,
dumb and stupid like Charles Tisdale and Mike Espy
        who wielded language like lumberjacks
decimating a forest of fools,
dumb and stupid like Jake Ayers and Hollis Watkins
        who used the stallion of truth to stampede
centuries of concrete lies,
dumb and stupid like Bob Moses and Alvin Chambliss

who combined the artistry of agitation
with the sword of litigation,
dumb and stupid like Gene "Jughead" Young and my father
who paid my college tuition with jail-time currency,
dumb and stupid like Fannie Lou Hamer and J. R. Lynch
who taught that freedom is the only medicine
for oppression,
dumb and stupid like Henry Kirksy and Roy McCory
who wore intelligence like a finely tailored suit,
dumb and stupid like Dr. John A. Peoples
who with a gardener's love cultivated JSC into JSU,
creating Mighty Magnolias of Mississippi's Modern HBCU.

So, to be Mississippi is knowing that decency, courage, and
forgiveness are not a three-piece suit that can be removed
when they are no longer fashionable.
Like, when you say yes ma'am and no ma'am because
manners are the concrete foundation of civilization,
that's the Mississippi in ya'.
When you open the door for a woman,
not as a prelude to a rendezvous,
but because women are the fertile soil of our futures,
that's the Mississippi in ya'.
When a family reunion is a Sunday dinner,
that's the Mississippi in ya'.
Or, when you send a plate over to Ms. Mary's house 'cause
all of her children took the exodus train North,
and she can't navigate the stairs like she used to,
that's the Mississippi in ya'.
When you go to school because education is the sledge hammer
to knock holes in the walls of injustice and oppression,
that's the Mississippi in ya'.
When you vote, even though there are two flap-jack
politicians on both sides of the ballot, and the concept of
Statesman is nothing more than a mascot for Delta State,
yet you pull the lever anyway because Medgar's blood
is the only registration card you need,

"Mississippi Like…"

that's the Mississippi in ya'.
When being baptized in the blood refers to the plasma of
Jesus and the crimson of the Civil Rights Movement,
that's the Mississippi in ya'.
When you speak to people whom you don't know
as you pass them on the streets, that's the Mississippi in ya'.
And then after speakin' you ask them,
"Who yo' folks baby?" That's the Mississippi in ya'.
Or, when you see a stranger with a familiar face and ask him
if he's Ms. Ruthie Mae Johnson's boy,
who lives over the tracks, under the hill,
that had that daughter who married that Williams boy
whose family owns the stow next to the Saw Mill Inn,
that's the Mississippi in ya'.
Or, when you got a whole lot of cousins,
but yo' mamma and daddy ain't got no brothers or sisters,
that's the Mississippi in ya'.
When you stand 'cause a woman approaches yo' table,
that's the Mississippi in ya'.
When you refuse to call a woman
after ten p.m. or anything but her name,
that's the Mississippi in ya'.
When lovin' your fellow man as you love yo'self
is your political platform, and feedin' little Leroy
is your social welfare program, that's the Mississippi in ya'.
When you pay your bills despite them vampire interest rates,
not because you scared of colorless collectors,
but because yo' granddaddy's word was as solid as the Earth,
and yo' daddy's word is as true as the seasons, and you don't
want to drive down the value of your family's name by being
as unreliable as a politician's promise the day after election,
that's the Mississippi in ya'.
And when you do unto others as you would have them do unto you
because it pleases God and yo' grandmamma,
that's the Mississippi in ya'.

EL-RA RADNEY

An African-American Detroiter, El-Ra Adair Radney's background was solidified in the Pan-African/Afrocentric currents of Detroit's Black community by his middle school years. One of those formative occasions was a 6th-grade trip to see a performance of the Afrofuturist musician Sun Ra. Since he was a kid growing up in Detroit, his family nicknamed him 'Professor'. Hence, a strong sense of Black pride, and positive connections to Africa, had been cultivated in him from the Black performing arts pulse that had resonated from the front porch to the record shop, to the barbershop, and from the influence of several educators.

The Dawn-Song: The Rising of the Astro-Afro Time Traveler

How can we look around
and walk away from these (fallen souls) of Black masks
they have made you wear
we must not be as these lost, once-spirits
for sale again, sold into swollen tight jaws of paradox
they never find their way back
Imani, they want our bodies
But Afro-woman, I will not leave you here
you must tell the long heartbreak to find its defiant songs
because you begin… the life of this world begins
you beckon the turned-on bright-light
the stay woke eyes
from alone-nights, we found it
unbreakable solace
in the stamina, it takes for courage
to not be burnt out dreams
you brought the first sign
I heard your sensible telepathy
in the parts not corroded
through all the wandering of this time
though the Broken promise-verse
left its scarred marks inside
did you try too hard to find another way, love
tell me why did they hide you from me

The Dawn-Song

break our bonds we once laid
seek me gently again 1st-woman
give me back our power
do not send the machine
send your human touch of joy to warm me
to touch the bond that matters
the one that has lasted
from the ways before
from the before time
I had held the wise people up
sought out my forgotten tales
many roses were still growing in the cracks left
told me this was not the end of our days
not the last - piece of our people's love
and the love between you and I
this was the long unresolved pain breaking in on itself
what the Sage dust must burn away
what it knew as keys to color madness
its stains you can't unsee
suffering on the rocks who cry out now
you knew the magic the Black Stone once possessed
tried to tell me
(I did not listen)
tried to tell me... must chase away... attack of dream-killers
truth of what BrownOracleWoman-told
they be dream-eaters, carnivorous thins
not the thick of soul or thick of love they have
"they eat we dreams"
Black dream-killers same as Brown dream-eaters
imposed on sacred ground
where they took our bodies
necromancers worshipping things that
make the Black and Brown dead
they want our bodies, beloved
push their way inside your inside places
find nothing wrong in trying to un-make you
in trying to fake you
amazing grace—they have unsweetened its sound
the hidden ones

came that night made their unmistakable choice
the one sent back it was me
I was supposed to love you
markings on my forehead trace waterlog souls
when the sea vomited stolen memories
other Astro-Afro travelers
fought-weary on passage of motherships
when the Zong crypt tied their fate
what cleansing spell do these hurt lockers require
ghosts of slave captains
unsacred blanched things
fill their hymns of what is relevant
with the cutting off of your Black and Brown bodies
keep trying to steal even the great mercy
of love public and private, few have ever had for us
who must change the dark nights
of their white unvanquished soul
but you see they are the real threat that takes over
makes the sweet lose its right mind
I feel why the caged bird must sing mother of words
Imani, tell her
we will not rise from a confused tribe of sleeping enemies
tell them Corrine Gaines will not
be the last of our angry daughters!
these captors think of themselves as giants
to black oak trees, they falsely make small
I know many men are the blame for
the confirmation of this anger you seek
still why not together
can we conjure the whole Afro-human to be
bitter seeds must grow into the Sage dust
to burn away the giants' failed myth
teach The Rising how to be human again
are we not masters of human science
I have seen much of your good ways-forgotten
in hidden figures
in limitation
in broken sight
it was the wrong him and his false prospects of words

The Dawn-Song

this thing we call your magic
has seen many un-magic days from all the wrongs of him
passed and left their disruptive fades in you
cosmic knives to a place that punctures
divine honey parts do survive
what they cannot hide
the places where you defined your strength of peace
I have seen the contribution of your mind
felt the touch of justice
more than twice in your African arms
we made our freedom into love
that could not be broken thru the night
held its song in the mighty-strung fire of our voices
I remember all nine of your aromas, 1st mitochondria woman
it fills me enough
what original cool did they kidnap too
do not believe their twisted mathematics of crime
they try to make only our stories
all that we made has given us The Rising
and what do they want to take us back to
the days of Rosa's pain
that time shall never be again
a time of your love is greater than
any white delusions they call great!
these captors only want to make sunken places
their great nostalgias
or what they did to us left out of plastic pages
beloved, I can't even astral-travel close to this pavement
without tripping over African bodies
cargo sprawled in the angry long of afternoons
suffering in their own blood from sirens
that cast dark shadows
on altars of normal terror
the strange meaning of these Anglo fruits
classified cultures of unlawful law-stealers
shields that stink with unwashed odors
they may wash them, but they do not own their stains
let them know you will remember these-41 shots
who made their job our job to patch

the holes in the peoples' broken walls
we will see them for what they are
not for what they told us to believe in
let them know we do not forget or forgive
this easy back oven of false faces
they say we should---take the high grounds and wear
what high grounds have they ever taken beloved?
Dunbar's lying grin still wants its revenge
Mantan Moreland's lying grin wants its revenge
Hattie McDaniel & Butterfly McQueen's lying grin still wants it
revenge!
and no this pain will not be my only shape
I am six hundred thousand unsung Afro-man stories
rolled up and blown out in smoke trees
tell them they created their own white fear
tell them this is their monster
their Negro beast
their primitive
their super-predator
their n-word
their b-word
their h-word
their D. W. Griffith brute
their Bigger Thomas or unbound Prometheus
their civilizing mission
behind the white kryptonite bullet
their numbers masquerading as fake science about
crimes and deficit
how do you reclaim Toby-language not even yours
tell them we will not fall in honor to any of this filth
they will not make us this conquered
this is not our mess alone!
Imani let me use my power on them
Am I not a traveler for the hidden ones
Who gave me this to not be scared
to shake the earth no more
Who gave me this to not be scared to strut and dance in our African
ways with you beloved no more
Not that man-blind as you think of me

The Dawn-Song

I see things and I see into smoke walls
like Old Time told me he once did
do not think we build out of thin-Black and Brown air
there is much of us
laid out in this screaming underground
in the grand lies about who brought 'the light'
you have been made not to see your African self
they take our bodies!
they take our bodies!
it takes a special kind of blindness
they make in these laboratories
what's leftover has
the permission to abuse
I know your backs tell tree stories
a map to why we got lost
they take our bodies
invasions of Black and Brown body snatchers
down the street, where the sirens come
how do you make the Black mold think it's only second
Imani this bleached boy myth of science
is the intellectual terror we should tell our children about
in The Talk
and the color madness Toni Morrison
be-loved us into seeing
lurks the familiar evil of a thousand things stolen
from you in the machine
pays Stacy Dash to spit bullshit for the rent
more dope… pushing lethal opiates of white lies
this is revolution of the real-thinking people
even great hearts are not responsible
to fix these people of denial, not the Blue Nile beloved, Denial
paid them well to say the same crooked things
Black milk who never wanted to be Flint water
Done contaminated even her divine nipple
this self-made touch, he boasts ain't Midas
but poison-baby
he tell you – you must drink it
poison
anti-Black and Brown Kool-Aid to die

and then sit like Zombie
faking you alive on the Supreme Court
and yes I am thirsty for you 1st woman!
you keep wearing rejuvenation
you sustained the old dances in your sway
two can be one
the Book of Curtis said it was the righteous way to go
little will they know
or believe when you told them so
how you are second to none
the loud bass of Nile Valley blues heard you before
Cleopatra stealers painted glyphs in bad-faith bedrooms
Don't let them fool you, Mississippi continuum is just the Nile
the nappy soul of the force
bequeathed me a red, Black & green lightsaber
colors of proud heritage for the poetic son of Mahoganies
& he is still too loud
All the answers will be made visible when you love
the African in you America
where are the Refuge places
I need to access your love
my strength will flow there
like flow a tree, or trees flow
a Sankofa of a thousand warm flames
coming back to its life in conjure-woman hands
lands in the restoration of unbroken voices
Imani—we can make the dawn find its songs
Remember something different than this lost way
in the before time
the hidden ones chose me
the one sent back
I came back to love you
And no matter how many times I travel
I will not forsake you

MEGHA SOOD

Megha Sood is an Award-winning Asian-American Poet, Editor, and Literary
Activist. Literary Partner with "Life in Quarantine", at Stanford University.
Member of National League of American Pen Women (NLAPW), and United

Nations Association-US Chapter. Author of two chapbooks and one full collection including Chapbook ("My Body is Not an Apology", Finishing Line Press, 2021) and Full Length ("My Body Lives Like a Threat", FlowerSongPress,2022).Previous contributor and event organizer for BFTT Vol1. Her co-edited anthology "The Medusa Project" has been selected to be sent to the moon as part of LunarCodex Project in collaboration with NASA/SpaceX.

Topography of a Wound

What is the topography of a wound?
The origin and provenance of its existence
its presence defined by its gaping mouth
by the broken semantics of love, hunger, and acceptance
An old haggard face trying to find its identity
in shattered mirror trying to salvage the possibility
of finding its crochet voices in haunting
broken cold corridors of life
What is a vernacular of pain?
When it screams, haunts, and rattles
us in the night
trying to find flesh lodged
between its saw-edged teeth
A ghostly presence—
This scar, this wound, has deeply etched in our souls
its haunting melody, like a protracted fog in winter
bouncing off thickened concrete.
like a bullet ricocheting in the dark,
like a faint voice in the shroud of the night,
An elegy is an acceptance of the truth—
A black body in the middle of a protest
bare naked with arms splayed
pinned like a monarch—
ready for the dumb menageries
Another news making the headline
for its mindless span of a news cycle
prey ready to be devoured
trying to find that sliver of empathy
in the white of your eyes
Pinning knees on the harsh concrete
as it makes deep impressions

into the hollowed past of this country
asking with a bowlful of questions
in its bleary eyes
A question laced with a deep hunger and empathy
a hunger that rises in my throat
panic throbbing like a taut wire
devoid of its symphony
Fear courses in my deep black veins
as the thick blue knees are pressed
a little harder than the last time.

JACQUESE ARMSTRONG

A 2022 Black Fire—This Time Anthology Summer Fellow with Aquarius Press and, author of birthing yourself naturally: motivational reflections on a mental health journey (2022) and blues legacy (Broadside Lotus Press, 2019), Jacquese Armstrong was the recipient of the 2019 Naomi Long Madgett Poetry Award and a 2015 Ambassador Award from the State of New Jersey Governor's Council on Mental Health Stigma for promoting wellness and recovery and reducing stigma through the arts. Jacquese is a writer/speaker/poet who educates, motivates and inspires from her lived mental health experiences and interprets the pain etched on her mothers' wombs.

sister sonia (she tends to the Light)

lions lay awake in your thunder sister
sonia you
keep check on greed and its
acid rain effect on burgeoning flowers
blooming in young minds…

say our lives are political

start humming
ask how can you be a citizen

you are
medicine woman
make words chant healing powers
you say

resist
be human
what does it mean to be…
take minds to a place above
regularly scheduled programming
designed to pry our spirits loose
from integrity and
castigate technicolor imagination
expand and share
that spirit called
human dignity

lean in
say resist
become Life
teach Love
follow Light
let a Dream be a walking stick on rough terrain
                    …tend to the Light

CONNIE OWENS PATTON

Connie Owens Patton is an African American poet and spoken word artist. In September of 2023, she received the California Arts Council Individual Artist Fellowship in the category of Emerging Artist for the Central Valley. Her work has been published in B*lack Fire this Time, Volume 1*, *African Voices, COVID, Isolation and Hope: Artists Respond to the Pandemic, The Fire Inside, Volume II* and *The Fresno City College Review*. In 2020, her poem "Lie to Me" was featured on Heard/Word Galleyway, an online audio series. To hear her work in spoken word listen on Soundcloud at Kaanee.

TROUBLE

They say trouble don't last always.
But this, this trouble
been long and hard
centennials and centennials.

Generations
been birthmarked
by this here trouble.
This trouble been
cruel and bloody
bent backs
cracked bones
stripped flesh.
Looted bodies.
This trouble lays claim
to what is already owned
spoken for, passed down.
It colonizes, gentrifies, covets.
It appropriates, swallows,
then sells you back to you.

This trouble shoves your face
into pavement, puts a knee on
your neck.

It snatches your life in pieces
inside concrete walls.

It hides in language

This trouble fictionalized history.
Built ghettos on legislative foundations
then fenced them with redlines.

This trouble is fake news, indoctrination,
A manifesto with a gun, murdering
in grocery stores and God's house.

Overcome?
Then what?
Here comes something else.
Another mountain needs climbing,
another race to run.

But you are weary.
Because this race you keep running
don't have no finish line.

Historical Rewind

Same old story
Insert black man's name
Perpetrating the same ol' game
He was aggressive
I was afraid
He fit the description of _____
I thought he had a _____

Insert name
Result the same
Once he's dead
Smear his name

Go hunting for a black man
With your dad, shotgun in hand
Block his path

Black, terrified, alone
White faces, guns, country road

Georgia, on that historical deja vu
Slave catchers, wagons,
Bloodhounds, guns,
Black man runs.

Insert name _____
Result the same
Once he's dead
Smear his name

REGINA YC GARCIA

Regina YC Garcia is an award-winning African American poet who resides in Greenville, NC. Her written and video poetry has been published widely in a variety of journals, reviews, compositions, and anthologies such as South Florida Poetry Journal, Main Street Rag, The AutoEthnographer, Amistad, The Elevation Review and others. Her poetic work for The Black Light Project, a documentary focused on real and often untold narratives of African American males in the United States, was featured on a Mid-South Emmy-Award winning episode of PBS Muse. Garcia's debut book, The Firetalker's Daughter, was released by Finishing Line Press in March 2023.

Afro-futures Unnamed Nonce: Black is a well

Black is a well

Deep
That is
what must be
said, deep and dark
dark, deep like a well
Like a well, stretched bottom unending

Unending
That is
what must be
said, unending and full
full, unending like invisible tears
Like invisible tears, bitter and sweet

Sweet
That is
what must be
said, sweet like knowing
knowing, sweet like whispered promise
Like whispered promise, like oracles, prophecy

Prophecy
That is

what must be
said, prophecy like hope
hope, quietly prophesying, being sentient
Like sentient histories, dead and living

Living
That is
what must be
said, living and creating
Creating living from no way
Like sending way -buckets into blackness

Blackness
That is
what must be
said, Blackness and lifting
Lifting eyes towards dark skies
Like skyways, folkways, Diaspora, *Sankofa*

Sankofa
That is
what must be
said, *Sankofa*, remembering, gathering
Gathering for today and tomorrow
Like tomorrow is well, beautiful, *Black*

Black
is a
well, welling in
my soul...

Speculation
A consideration of the before life and death of Tyre Nichols
(June 5, 1993- Jan 10, 2023)

If our forebears could've
'died their torture' (just once)
& buried the institution of depravity

(just once)
& burned the *humiliation* of that which
happened
& spread the ashes deeply in dark soil
& placed a guard over it
& sealed it in silence
& reverence
& put the pain to bed (just once)

Perhaps this collective trauma, this *remembrance of shame,* would not have
awakened in the generations showering

  the wounding whispers that madly
  echo the lie (over & over again)
  the captors' lie (over & over again)

    uncivilized (over & over)
    uncultured (over & over)
    inhuman (over & over)

      you children of nowhere-no language, no land, no history (over
& over)

If we could have just kept these
murderous words
from seeping into our bones
& passing through our life seed
& filtering into muddled minds
& settling into ulcerated places
& casting them onto others

Perhaps, *if we could've killed it…*
      (just once)

five midnight men clothed in
      protectors' blue
      badge-pinned shimmering

Speculation 181

> brown skin gleaming in the glare of
> street lights/headlights/sky cams
would've chosen peace over pummeling

& perhaps

Suspected recklessness would have been verified or put to rest with no
notions of
> bashing batons
> a taser's shock
> furious flights of fists
> cruel, compounding kicks

& perhaps

those wrapped in enforcement
authority
could have understood
the true toll of the terror
of disappearing flesh
> of stifled breath

inflicted in the then
> in the now

…when humanizing peace does not abide

& perhaps…

if they had known it

> *if we had known it/killed it*

Tyre Nichols
could have gotten up
three days later…

> *with all power in his hands*

instead of being one more
black boy
gushing blood red
100 yards from his house
piteously wailing for his mama

Over and over again

TAMARA MADISON

Poet, writer, editor, Tamara J. Madison, is the author of Threed, This Road Not Damascus (Trio House Press – print and EAT Poems audio). Her writing is inspired by her ancestral research. She is the creator of BREAKDOWN: The Poet & The Poems, a YouTube series promoting poets and their poetry as inspiration for everyday life. Tamara has also shared her poetry on the TEDx platform. She is a MFA graduate of New England College and an Anaphora Arts Fellow (2021). She currently teaches English and Creative Writing in central Florida and is working on a new full-length poetry collection.

Afrotica

Eyes pried open, we
transcend their fears,
how desperately they,
always in need of a jesus,
seek to crucify us.

Conjuring, we
turn away, turn
inward, us wrap
one another:
backs braced,
titanium-laced,
tightly sealed,
force-fielded, so
uni-breathed, we
time/lie/knife/knee/bomb/badge/bullet-

proofed...

Wake

a social gathering associated with death, usually before a funeral, and traditionally held in the home of the deceased with the body present

After the claustrophobia and paranoia of the global pandemic, police brutality and white supremacy on relentless rampage, protests after protest, death upon death, stress after stress,
on August 28, 2020,

Chadwick Boseman passes,

leaves us, and I am struggling. So much rampant, goddamned brokenness on every billboard, screen, page, and platform, just blasted brokenness everywhere on viral repeat, my soul bared to the blistering fever of Earth where every melanated birth is threatened with extinction upon its first breath.

Chadwick Boseman is dead at 43,

seemingly another win for those who eat sin for supper, regurgitate, and serve it on a plate to the emaciated as repass.

Chadwick Boseman is gone,

and the world is just too god-damned broken, so I gather what breaths I have left, the itch on my fingers, and my soul-folk wit to fix something, anything. I spy the defunct CD player poised on the entertainment center, no longer the center of entertainment in a grieving world anaesthetized with entertainment, in my grieving world with Chadwick and so many others leaving broken and brokenness behind them.

I must take the pieces of something, anything into my hands and sculpt some semblance of solace. I gather the tools, loose screws spill them onto the living room floor. I pick, pull, pry, punch the jammed switch and tray that refuses to open. These speakers haves not sung for years, but I need a juke joint jam session and a choir and Congo Square, my living room, so fix something, anything I must. I summon my soul-folk through my heart chambers, pray for direction. My awkward fingers pick, pull, pry until the switch clicks. The Parliament CD finally drops.

The once-stuck tray sweeps it away. The digital display twinkles before my eyes.

Under the direction of Supreme Commander George Clinton, the royal funk begins to rise from the singing speakers, parts the sea of grief rushing at my feet. Snatched by the G-spot of conjure, somewhere between resurrection and victory, I stand, dust my hands and begin to dance. As Boss Bishop Bootsy's base, tuned to ancestors anchoring the MotherShip, ricochets in every corner of the room, my 16-year-old son with the aged bourbon soul catches the holy funk-ghost. His body bursts aurora borealis as if he were birthed in the manger of a psychedelic 70's scene. Transcending tragedy, my heart stops bleeding, my soul no longer mourns as angels fall in formation, take their place in the Soul Train line.

Before they ascend, Chadwick-T'Challa performs the rites of the cake walk, and a host of the breathing-while-black, gone-too-soon, melanated martyrs remove the shackles of their brokenness and rise, commence a boogaloo of praise and bless the ballroom of my jubilee.

BILL MARABLE

Bill Marable is an African American poet and member of the Griot Collective of West Tennessee, a poetry workshop in his home town of Jackson, Tennessee. His poetry has appeared in the Skinny, Spilled Ink, and the Detroit Writer's Guild, among others.

I have seen dreams come true, nightmares— two in particular stopped my searching for the light in night sleep, and yet I daydream about things I have seen in my life

I have seen the shuck and the jive
of games and hustles live

I have seen George Clinton and Parliament on stage,
in the 70's when they were the rage

I have seen the 'Godfather of Soul' sing the National hymn,
at a Hawks NBA game, stood right next to him

I have seen sorrow at times too
I have seen it a-plenty spread like the flu

I have seen blood spurting from the chest
of a nigger taking his last breath

I have seen a nigger proclaim his own demise,
then close his eyes

I have seen a killer too,
eye to eye- these streets ain't for you

I have seen yellow brains on the street,
brown ones on a plate—nigger eat

I have seen rainbows in the sky
and wondered why
I have seen people die
in their search for pots of gold- a lie

I have seen a fool and his money part way
scratching off hundreds a winless day

I have seen a nigger hobo the love train,
no ticket, bitch rattled his brain,
flipped the game,
broken; Nigger never was the same

I have seen a woman handled like a man,
I have seen a woman with ten kids -
struggling the best she can,
raising them with a stern hand

I have seen a brother
kissing another
in the middle of the street
broad daylight, two bulls in heat

I have seen a bastard grow
to produce more bastards you know;
seen bastard twins go blow for blow
and the referee was they mama you know
and they fought til they couldn't no mo,
then the ref intervened, said "get up let's go"

I have seen the Law out of order,
issuing blue light specials
from the hood to the boarder

I have seen a homeless man
with a dog begging at the red light,
and a van pick them up at night

I have seen four leaf clovers and would pluck them up,
place them in the Bible for good luck

I have seen rain on a sunny day;
"Devil beating his wife," the elders say

I've seen many-a-thing on this road called life,
roadblocks- potholes of toil and strife

I have seen those things and a hella lot more,
traipsing through life has not been a bore;
pray for days abound
as I strive to remain above ground

JOAN CARTWRIGHT

Dr. Joan Cartwright has toured with her swinging brand of jazz and blues in 20 countries, including the U.S., 8 European countries, Brazil, Mexico, Ghana, Gambia, South Africa, Jamaica, China and Japan. She performed with jazz legends Philly Joe Jones, Shirley Scott, Sonny Stitt, Freddie Hubbard, Dr. Lonnie Smith, Lou Donaldson, Dorothy Donegan, and hundreds of others, during her career. A Doctor of Business Administration/Marketing from Northcentral University (2017), Joan holds a B.A. in Music and Communications from LaSalle University, and a M.A. in Communications from Florida Atlantic University. She founded http://wijsf.org

Blues Women
The First Civil Rights Workers

Blues women were the first civil rights workers because their songs symbolized liberty in its rawest form by tapping into the human spirit. Blues women spoke to and for black people, providing them an open door to emotional escape. Blues lyrics referenced unrequited love and provided a means of articulating pain, suffering, endurance, and overcoming. These women were permitted to sing in public forums and Africans in America realized they had something to say about their treatment by slave owners, traders, rapists, and punishing spouses, whether they were white men with whips or black men betraying them. From generation to generation, the replacement of one Blues singer by another created a hierarchy of rhetorical agents clothed in the beaded dresses of entertainers. Each woman understood that she provided an emotional outlet for her people.

Since the beginning of the 20th century, Blues was performed in the South, but none were recorded due to racism and the assumption that African Americans couldn't, or wouldn't buy record players or 78s. **Mamie Smith's** *Crazy Blues* "changed all that, sparking a mad scramble among record execs to record blues divas" (Obrecht, 2013, p. 1). Smith's *Crazy Blues* sold 80,000 copies in one month, revolutionizing pop music. "The song could be heard coming from the open windows of virtually any black neighborhood in America" (Ibid.). Noted New Orleans jazz musician, Danny Barker said, "That record turned around the recording industry [and] every family had a phonograph in their house, behind Mamie Smith's first record" (Ibid.).

Following in Ma Rainey's footsteps, **Bessie Smith** became the voice of Blacks migrating to the North and West. In <u>Blues Empress in Black Chattanooga: Bessie Smith and the Emerging Urban South</u> (2008), Michelle R. Scott outlined black life in Chattanooga, in "Ninth Street's saloons . . . the few veiled environments in which they could be truly human, a humanity that was powerfully expressed in the blues music that Smith perfected as a stage performer and recording artist" (Goodson, 2010, p. 179). Bessie's song *Poor Man Blues* beckoned the rich man to open up his heart and mind and give the poor man that fought WW I a chance.

For Kari Winter (1998), **Alberta Hunter's** lyrics "empower the singer toward feminist self-affirmation, agency, movement, and change" (Kuribayashi and Tharp, 1998, p. 204). Hunter's childhood, filled with abandonment, abuse, molestation, and communal disdain, gave her the self- determination to rise to the top and stay away from trifling men, which resulted in her feminist lifestyle. Her most noted song, *Down-Hearted Blues*, declared that anyone who wanted her company must succumb to her command. This song put Hunter and Bessie Smith "on the road to international fame in the 1920s" (Kuribayashi and Tharp, 1998, p. 202).

Throughout her 77-year career, Hunter understood the power that writing wielded for African Americans but also took precautions because the mere act connoted the connection between freedom and "the decolonizing of identity—processes undertaken at tremendous risk [because] literacy was outlawed [and] African Americans authors endangered their lives with the same strokes whereby they claimed ownership of their lives" (Kuribayashi and Tharp, 1998, p. 203). As

James Baldwin put it, "the blues artist risks 'ruin, destruction, madness, and death to find new ways to make us listen, [encouraging listeners] to leave the shoreline and strike out for the deep water" (Ibid.). Having composed into her eighties, Hunter "participated in the blues philosophy that resisting Master Narratives inspires energies that undermine, bypass, subvert, and exceed patriarchal logic" (Ibid., p. 204).

Ethel Waters, a "pioneering Broadway, film, recording, and television star" (Frank, 2011, p. 98), "was the first African American to be billed above the title in a Broadway show" (Ibid.). Waters was the first black woman to have a radio show and the first to sing *Am I Blue*, *Stormy Weather*, *Heat Wave*, and *The St. Louis Blues* by W. C. Handy. In Heat Wave: The Life and Career of Ethel Waters, Donald Bogle (2011) recounted "the adulation, money, critical acclaim, and long runs [going] into great detail on how Waters rendered a song to make one feel transported" (Gill, 2012, p. 256).

While touring Vaudeville as "Sweet Mama Stringbean", Waters encountered continuous, life-threatening experiences. She sang *Little Black Boy* at the funeral of a "lynched black youth deposited on the floor of the lobby of a theater where she was booked in Macon, Georgia" (Saltz, 2009), and "she had to plot a fast escape from the menacing theater manager and the police" (Ibid.). Waters' dramatic performances on stage and screen included the Broadway musical, *As Thousand's Cheer*, and the films *Mama's Daughters*, *Cabin in the Sky*, *The Member of the Wedding*, and *Pinky* (Gill, 2012) for which she was nominated for an Oscar.

Offstage, Waters was mean due to a "lifetime of slights, [due to] economic, aesthetic, and racial politics of 1920s-60s popular culture" (Frank, 2011, p. 98). She was bisexual and her voice could not be quieted. His Eye Is On The Sparrow (1951) is a raw and memorable account of the injustices Waters suffered from childhood in Chester and the ghettoes of South Philadelphia, Pennsylvania, three failed marriages, since the age of 12, and through her turbulent journey from stardom to eventual poverty, before her death in 1977. As a postscript, Ethel Waters should have spent her last years treated with the reverence and respect due a person of her accomplishments. Unfortunately, she distanced herself from militant black colleagues by starring as a maid on the TV series *Beulah*, aligning herself with Billy Graham and Richard M. Nixon, and proclaiming, "I'm not concerned with civil rights. I'm concerned with God-given rights, and they are available to everyone!" (Erickson, 2014).

The performances of singer and dancer **Josephine Baker** were "a popular form of entertainment [and] tools that she used to display and communicate her resistance to 'white imagination' [Baker] used nudity to display her own opposition against being placed under the same gaze" (Bennerson, 2011, p. 9) as Sarah Bartmann, the South African woman put on display in European side shows because of the size of her buttocks. At 11, Baker witnessed one of the worst post-WW I race riots, in 1917, in St. Louis, Missouri, which left thousands homeless and 39 people dead. A victim of domestic abuse from an early age, Baker "rebelled from her teachers because she wanted to be seen; . . . rebelled from her mother because she saw how unhappy her mother was, and . . . rebelled from her husband because she saw herself falling into the same trap of poverty as her mother" (Bennerson, 2011, p. 45). Her performance career began in a troupe, The Jones Family. She moved from them to the tutelage of Blues singer Clara Smith.

After two failed marriages, Baker joined the casts of *Shuffle Along* and *Chocolate Dandies*, solidifying her career as a comedienne in New York. In 1925, Baker moved to Paris, where her career as The Banana Dancer skyrocketed. "Acceptance of her sexuality suggested that Baker believed Black women were more attractive than white women, French or American, and throughout her career she used herself to prove it" (Bennerson, 2011, p. 50).

Although many Black artists ceded to Paris, where the French marveled at *the Black experience*, the presence of racism loomed large, influenced by *class ranking in Parisian society* (Bennerson, 2011, p. 52), constantly reminding Baker that she was still a second-class citizen.

Ironically, this icon's "original dancing style [and] nudity gave Baker the ability to 'talk back' to her audience. By refusing to wear clothes, she challenged her audience to face their curiosity and fear about the Black female body" (Bennerson, 2011, p. 61). She to used exaggerated eye movements to force the audience to reflect on their own sexuality, placing Baker in control of the total experience. Baker "chose to go against what people expected of her . . ., creating a platform for the future voice of resistance for those who have not yet spoken" (Bennerson, 2011, p. 62).

Baker's implicit control spilt over into her radical activism around racism in Europe and the U.S., where she toured in 1950. Baker "demanded that she perform only for integrated audiences at every venue. If curfew and segregation ordinances were still in place, she requested that they be lifted for the duration of her performance in the hope that they would change permanently" (Leigh, 2012, p. 165). As an agent of change for American Black people, Baker "championed Willie McGee, a man accused of and convicted of raping a white woman in Mississippi [and] . . . called attention to integrated housing in Cicero, Illinois, while promoting integrated hiring of bus drivers in Oakland, California" (Ibid.).

Baker's activism attracted the attention of the FBI and the NAACP named May 20, 1951, Baker Day for her civil rights efforts. Baker spoke about the devastation of racism, worldwide. On August 28, 1963, she was the only female speaker at the March on Washington (Leigh, 2012, p. 166). Her efforts resulted in the desegregation of night clubs in Northern cities. But the ultimate reality of Baker's insistence on diversity was her adoption of 12 children from varying nationalities and her insistence to educate them within their respective cultures.

In 1939, **Billie Holiday** sang *Strange Fruit* by Abel Meeropol under the pen name Lewis Allan. This was "the first significant song of the civil rights movement and the first direct musical assault upon racial lynchings in the South" (Margolick, 2001). Holiday sang it at Cafe Society in New York, revolutionizing the struggle it personified. Holiday's rendition was "poignant and raw and saturated with pain, evoking another time and place and yet is still utterly relevant to race relations in the United States" (Casper, 2012). The song, a testament to "the civil rights movement . . . examines the lives of . . . Holiday and Meeropol, the Jewish schoolteacher and communist sympathizer who wrote the song that impact[ed] generations of fans, black and white" (Margolick, 2001).

The bastard child of a raped, 14-year-old cotton field worker in South Carolina, **Eartha Kitt** debuted in the film *Casbah* in 1948, at 16. She was a student of Katherine Dunham. In 1960, she was blacklisted in the United States for speaking out at a Women Doer's Luncheon at the White House with Lady Bird Johnson. Kitt explained to this elite group that crime in the streets could be attributed to "American youth . . . rebelling because of the Vietnam War" (Mezzack, 1990, p. 745).

Since 1953, Kitt taught dance to black children, who could not afford lessons. In 1966, she founded the Kittsville Youth Foundation, a non-profit that served children in the depressed neighborhoods of Watts in Los Angeles (Ibid., p. 747). Youngsters in Anacostia, a neighborhood in Washington, D.C., asked Kitt to help them fundraise for Rebels with a Cause. She contacted Congressman Roman Pucinski, and they went before the House General Subcommittee on Education of the Committee on Education and Labor regarding the Juvenile Delinquency Prevention Act of 1967, and won a grant for Rebels with a Cause.

In June 1967, Kitt was appointed to the Citizen's Advisory Board on Youth Opportunity by President Lyndon Johnson, however, she was not cleared to be on the board due to the remarks she made at the Women Doer's Luncheon in 1960. In January 1968, Kitt was cleared to attend another luncheon at the White House, where a panel of speakers discussed crime in America and the Vietnam War. Once more, Kitt admonished the Johnsons that crime was connected to youths having to go fight an unjust war. Although many in the room disagreed with Kitt's statements, while hailing Mrs. Johnson for her retort to Kitt, several citizens sent correspondence to the White House, stating that Kitt spoke the words that millions of Americans, especially, mothers of sons who had lost their lives. One woman wrote, "So Lady Bird cried – well, doesn't she know that the mothers of 15,000 boys murdered in Vietnam by her husband's foreign policy cry every night" (Mezzack, 1990, p. 752)? Others felt that Kitt's remarks were "a release of frustrations built up over decades in blacks humiliated and discriminated against" (Ibid.).

Dr. Martin Luther King, Jr. said, "Kitt's remarks were a very proper gesture [that] described the feelings of many persons" (Ibid., p. 753). The leader of the Welfare Rights Movement, Etta Horn described Kitt's claims as *beautiful*, while Dick Gregory said, "Someone in Mrs. Johnson's position ought to be informed" (Ibid.). Baseball pioneer Jackie Robinson was quoted in an editorial in *The New York Times*, stating "because whites have not experienced the pain and humiliations blacks have suffered, they could not understand the anger" (Ibid.).

Despite disparate comments from many supporters of The Johnsons, Kitt's remarks resounded throughout the nation, bringing awareness to the problem of crime and enlisting the support of many organizations on the issue, including 15,000 chapters of the General Federation of Women's Clubs, B'Nai B'rith, the District of Columbia Anti-Crime Crusade, National Federation of Business and Professional Women's Clubs (250,000 members), National Association of Colored Women's Clubs, Association of Junior Leagues of America, and 7 Keys to Freedom, a rehabilitation center for ex-inmates. (Mezzack, 1990, p. 754).

Kitt's career suffered because of reports from the FBI, Secret Service, National Security Agency, and the CIA sent to the White House a week after the luncheon. Kitt lost several contracts and a radio station KHEN in Oklahoma stopped playing her records. Nevertheless, with all the

Blues Women 193

bad publicity generated about her regarding her outspoken stance on "the luncheon was symbolic of what many who were opposed to the war believed was insensitivity on the part of the White House to their views" (Mezzack, 1990, p. 745). Kitt was the voice in the wilderness for minorities to whom it appeared the Johnsons had turned a deaf ear.

Contemporary Voices

A study of young feminists and leadership found that, when asked to identify outspoken feminists, most young feminists point to music icons, exemplary of *emotional mobilization* empowering women (Reger, 2007). In recent years, the song *Wild Women Don't Have The Blues* penned by **Ida Cox** in 1924, became a feminist anthem because she wrote and sang about sexual freedom, a subject rarely broached by African American women (Harrison, 1988). This song was the theme song for the W.C. Handy multi-award-winning feminist/black power group Uppity Blues Women, or Saffire, led by singer/songwriter **Gaye Adegbalola**, who said the group's music was about empowerment, following in the tracks of those divas in the 1920s.

Adegbalola's group sang "about sex, its joy and its pain [and] . . . topical things like *School Teacher Blues*, *Nothing's Changed*, and *1-800-799-7233*, the national domestic violence hotline number" (Harrington, 2005, p. 6). She said, "the whole point of the blues is just to get the pain out."

Nina Simone "located American race relations in an international context in ways that drew attention to gender as well as race" (Feldstein, 2005, p. 1373).

She was a "black women who evoked international [and] American issues in discussions of race" (Ibid.). Simone's fight for gender equity induced her to use "her body, her music, and her words to forge links between Africa and African Americans and disseminated ideas about black freedom that were not specifically about the U.S." (Ibid.). Simone said, "I started to think about myself as a black person in a country run by white people and a woman in a world run by men" (Feldstein, 2005, p. 1373). In *Go Limp* (Appendix I), "Simone played with an older tradition of African American female singers who [sang] about sex . . . [like] second-wave feminists who would write about sex" (Feldstein, 2005, p. 1376). Their "protest and politics converged in Simone's music [and] gender and sexuality informed her denunciation of racial discrimination" (Ibid.).

Nina Simone befriended vocalist **Miriam Makeba**, a staunch activist against South African apartheid to the point of exile. She joined her protests to "American calls for black power when she married Stokely Carmichael in 1968" (Ibid.).

Conclusion

The Blues are neither mournful nor the cries of victims. According to Baldwin, they "articulate a hard-won affirmation of life and self. Blues artists 'fill the air with life,' with their own lives that [they] understand contain the lives of many other people" (Kuribayashi and Tharp, 1998, p. 204). Most Blues singers shine light on the darkest scenarios of existence, bringing laughter to center stage as a form of relief for themselves, the audience, and accompanying musicians. Blues women instituted the primary healing of the human spirit with their musical dalliance that we can forever be delighted with and grateful for.

Blues is a breath of fresh air in the stagnant world of discrimination, racism, physical and psychological abuse, and over all inhumanity towards children, women, men, and whole groups of people. It is no wonder that Blues permeate the planet, wherein, people from all nations and all levels of society enjoy the sound of the flatted third, as the foundation of lyrics that light up the face of the most sardonic human beings.

References

Bennerson, A. J. (2011). You must not know 'bout me: Reviewed   resistance of Sarah Bartmann, Josephine Baker, and Beyoncé Knowles. State University of New York at Buffalo. 103 p. http://search.proquest.com.proxy1.ncu.edu/docview/879554866

Bogle, D. (2011). Heat wave: The life and career of Ethel Waters. Harper Collins. 624 p. ISBN: 9780061241734

Casper, M.J. (2012, April 7). On race, trauma, and "Strange Fruit". *The Feminist Wire*. http://thefeministwire.com/2012/04/on-race-trauma-and- strange-fruit

Cartwright, J. (2009). A history of African American jazz and blues. FYI Communications, Inc. 156 p. ISBN: 9780557060108

Cartwright, J. (2008). Amazing musicwomen. FYI Communications, Inc. 112 p. ISBN: 97805570373229780557037322

Davis, A.Y. (1999). Blues legacies and black feminism: Gertrude "Ma" Rainey, Bessie Smith, and Billie Holiday. 464 p. New York: Random House.

Davis, A.Y. (1983). Women, race, and class. Random House, NY. 271 p. Erickson, H. (2014, September 21). Ethel Waters: Biography. *The New York Times*. http://www.nytimes.com/movies/person/74929/Ethel- Waters/biography

Feldstein, R. (2005). "I don't trust you anymore": Nina Simone, culture, and black activism in the 1960s. *The Journal of American History, 91*(4), 1349- 1379. http://search.proquest.com.proxy1.ncu.edu/docview/224896917

Frank, J. (2011). Heat wave: The life and career of Ethel Waters. *Library Journal*, 136(1), 98.

Frymer, P. (2008). Black and blue: African Americans, the labor movement, and the decline of the Democratic Party / Paul Frymer. Princeton: Princeton University Press, c2008.

Gill, G. (2012). Heat wave: The life and career of Ethel Waters. African American Review, 45(1/2), pp. 255-256.

Goodson, S. (2010). Blues empress in black Chattanooga: Bessie Smith and the emerging urban south. *The Journal of Southern History, 76*(1), 178-179. http://search.proquest.com.proxy1.ncu.edu/docview/215777983

Harrington, R. (2005, Sep 02). Saffire lightens up the blues. *The Washington Post* http://search.proquest.com.proxy1.ncu.edu/docview/409881577

Harrison, D.D. (1988). Black pearls: Blues queens of the 1920s. New Brunswick, N.J.: Rutgers University Press.

Hayes, E.M. (2007). Songs in black and lavender: Race, sexual politics, and women's music. African American Music in Global Perspective.

Hayes, E. & Williams, L.F. (eds.) (2007). Black women and music: More than the blues. University of Chicago Press. 261 p.

Kuribayashi, T. & Tharp, J.A. (1998). Creating safe space: Violence and women's writing. 239 p. ISBN: 9780791435649

Leigh, J. L. (2012). Who shall let this world be beautiful? Seeds of black female creativity in Josephine Baker and Octavia E. Butler. Morgan State University. 229 p. http://search.proquest.com.proxy1.ncu.edu/docview/103044450 0

Margolick, D. (2001). Strange fruit: Billie Holiday, Café Society, and an early cry for civil rights. 168 p. Harper Perennial. ISBN: 978-0060959562

Mezzack, J. (1990, Fall). 'Without manners you are nothing': Lady Bird Johnson, Eartha Kitt, and the Women Doers' Luncheon. *Presidential Studies Quarterly*; 20(4): p. 745.

Obrecht, J. (2013). Mamie Smith: The first lady of the blues. Jas Obrecht Music Archive. http://jasobrecht.com/mamie-smith-the-first-lady-of-the-blues

Reger, J. (2007). Where are the leaders? Music, culture, and contemporary feminism. The American Behavioral Scientist, 50(10), pp. 1350-1369. http://search.proquest.com. proxy1.ncu.edu/docview/214762259

Saltz, S. (2009, September 18). Review: Ethel Waters: His eye is on the sparrow (U.S. 1). http://www.passagetheatre.org/index.php/about/press- archives/107- review-ethel-waters-his-eye-is-on-the-sparrow-us- 1

CYNTHIA MANICK

Cynthia Manick is the author of No Sweet Without Brine (Amistad-HarperCollins, 2023), which received 5 stars from Roxane Gay and was selected as a New York Public Library Best Book of 2023; editor of The Future of Black: Afrofuturism, Black Comics, and Superhero Poetry; winner of the Lascaux Prize in Collected Poetry; and author of Blue Hallelujahs. She has received fellowships from Cave Canem, Hedgebrook, and MacDowell among other foundations. Manick's work has appeared in the Academy of American Poets Poem-A-Day Series, Brooklyn Rail, The Rumpus and other outlets. She lives in New York but travels widely for poetry.

Eintou for the Matriarchs

I come
from a long line
of bad nanas. Some top-
heavy, others light with the spoon.
Each pair of eyes – hips taught
me something old,
yet new

Dear "Is the Rainbow Enuf?"
for Ntozake and Anastacia

I wish you

the last slice of cheesecake

a scalp that knows tenderness in the chair and out

a short line to the ladies restroom after a concert or game

dreams about Prince serenading you on stage

an air conditioned and clean subway car on the way to a job you hate

a job that creates ventricles that makes you happy and whole

a mother who sees you as wildness blooming and doesn't taper it

the last slice of pizza after the late shift

a smile that feels like purple glory

lemonade tart as the sun in a frosted polka dot glass

sorcery needed to start the heart of any man or woman

light when the electricity bill is due

a father who teaches you how to stay for love

a father who teaches you to put out any fire that burns too bright by leaving

knowledge that the Blues don't mean tragedy

an expensive pair of shoes where only your size is on clearance

the burnt corner of baked mac and cheese

a shoulder when you are tired and you've lost an hour due to Daylight Saving

knowledge that a body built big boned or small deserves all the things

a sashay walk down the street where the only catcalls you hear are the ones
you give yourself

a partner who washes your hair bonnet and places it in the drawer
without being asked

the kindness of muscles that always heal

window succulents that respond to your voice

knowledge that you are full of okra, carrot seeds, and tales

the power to name what you need or want

words from this poem to tether you here

I.C.Y.

I.c.y., a writer and award-winning library administrator, has a B.A. in journalism (creative writing minor), a M.L.S. in Library and Information Science, and a certificate from the Institute of Children's Literature. Her articles and stories are published in a variety of magazines ranging from "Highlights for Children" to "XXL (Hip Hop) Magazine". She grew up outside Chicago, proudly African American, and remains closely connected to her deep south roots. She currently reside in New England, where her first play was produced after being read at the Schomburg Center for Black Culture, a research division of The New York Public Library.

daughters of the lost tribe

they breathe
through spirits
of inherited helpers

having mastered
Mantic piano
Ancient domino
Missioned hopscotch
Affricative voice
mirrors of gold coast beauty
jump double-dutch
in lynch ropes
rain godesses
dousing KKK fires
with rhythmic arms they emancipate
with holistic hands they heal
generations
alienated from their native
noblesse oblige
they remain
survivors
in new worlds
land they raise

CURTIS L. CRISLER

Curtis L. Crisler, Indiana Poet Laureate, was born and raised in Gary, Indiana. Crisler, an award-winning poet/author, has six poetry books, two YA books, and five poetry chapbooks. He's been published in a variety of magazines, journals, and anthologies. He's an editor and has been a contributing poetry editor. He created the Indiana Chitlin Circuit and the poetry form called the sonastic. He is the Indiana Poet Laureate and Professor of English at Purdue University Fort Wayne (PFW). He can be contacted at www.poetcrisler.com.

LAST STOP TO DINE
a ten-minute play

CHARACTERS

SADIE aka NANA MAMA   She's an elderly lady that
                                    works as a waitress and
                                    cook at *Gabe's Heaven*. Late 50's.

GABE aka LIL' GABE   Owns *Gabe's Heaven,* a diner he got f
                                    Big Gabe. 40 something.

AFRICAN-AMERICAN MAN   Customer, 30's.

AFRICAN-AMERICAN WOMAN   Customer, 30's.

AFRICAN-AMERICAN BOY   Customer, teenager.

SETTING

Gabe and Sadie are inside *Gabe's Heaven*. The diner is on the outskirts
the city. It is the last stop to dine before hitting a long stretch of highwa

TIME

Afternoon.

(Inside Gabe's Heaven we see N
MAMA *and* GABE. NANA MAM
behind the counter wiping it down. Sh
on her cat-glasses, a hair net, and an a
over her loud muumuu. GABE is dress
jeans and an ordinary colored shirt. G.
is going back and forth all over the p
while moving boxes.)

LAST STOP TO DINE

NANA MAMA

Gabe?

GABE

What you want Nana Mama, you know I gotta get this
inventory done?

> (*He keeps going back and forth, moving boxes.*)

NANA MAMA

Gabe, why you gotta be such a mean ass donkey? Oops, that's
redundant.

> (*She laughs.*)

You know you're nothing like Big Gabe was.

> (GABE *stops in front of the
> counter looking at* NANA
> MAMA *with his fists on his
> hips.*)

GABE

You're not like Big Gabe. No, I'm not like Big Gabe. I have to work
and put every ounce of sweat into this place. Some heaven. No,
I'm *not* like Big Gabe and *you're* no Halle Berry yo'self, humph.

> (*He continues moving the
> boxes.*)

NANA MAMA

> (*She walks from in back of the
> counter out to where the tables
> are located.*)

Lil' Gabe, I ain't gone let you worry me. As the young folks say,
don't hate the player, hate the game. Ooo, my feet hurt. They're
starting to swell up again.

> (*She grabs a chair and sits down at one of the tables. She kicks her shoes off.*)

I just get so tired, now. I would help you but my back hurts and my rheumatism is acting up. I...I'm gonna take me...

> (*She says yawning.*)

a little nap until we open up. Is that o...

GABE

> (*Exasperated.*)

Nana Mama...huh... just do what you have to do. I'm gonna get the milk, butter, and cream done and then I'll take care of the pies.

NANA MAMA

> (*Bobbling her head.*)

Okay, baby. I'll be here. I'm just going to put my head down for a few minutes, just a few minutes...

> (*She fades off into sleep.*)

GABE

Nana, oh, forget it.

> (*In a huff he leaves through the kitchen door behind the counter.*)

NANA MAMA

> (*She wakes up.*)

Oh, that man. I love him but he sho'nuff work my nerves. Whoo, these dogs are barking like bacon in a skillet.

> (*She rubs her feet, takes off her glasses, and then lays her head down on the counter and starts snoring. Long pause.*)

LAST STOP TO DINE

GABE

> (*Comes from kitchen with a broom in his hand.*)

Nana Mama! Nana Mama!

NANA MAMA

> (*She wakes up.*)

Aaaahhhhh! (*She grabs at her heart.*) What the hell, Lil' Gabe?

GABE

Did you see it? Did you see it? (*Swinging the broom like a baseball bat.*)

NANA MAMA

See what, Gabe? And stop swinging that broom fo' you break something.

GABE

The rat. The doggone rat. It was about this big.

> (*Still holding the broom he places hands apart about a foot.*)

NANA MAMA

Oh my Lord, I thought you were talking about something. Boy, you damn near gave me a heart attack. Could you please leave that little old mouse alone? *This* big.

> (*She gestures with her forefinger and thumb.*)

That little old thing? I can see why Big Gabe bought the farm. (Pause.) Cause his son is a legitimate fool that drove him crazy as hell.

GABE

> (*Upset. Stomping around the restaurant.*)

You mean to tell me you know about it?

NANA MAMA

(She smiles.)

Boy, been feeding that thang since Big Gabe was here.

GABE

NANA! If the Health Inspector finds out about that rat I'll be shut down. Why don't you use your head for once? Just like him. You are just like him. Stubborn, bullheaded, and careless...just like him. It's a wonder he kept the diner as long as he did.

NANA MAMA

> *(She puts her shoes and glasses back on and goes back behind the counter.)*

Gabe, get on out of here. The way you acting you'd think it was up your butt. Anyway, here comes a customer, I heard somebody pull up.

> (GABE *looks towards the door then mumbles walking back through the kitchen door behind the counter. Music starts.* BLACK MAN *enters and comes to counter. The music fades. The Light comes on, which is a spotlight, not too far from the counter.)*

NANA MAMA

Hey, baby, would you like to try one of our specials today? Our motto is if you can withstand it we can dish it out.

MAN

> *(He looks up at the menu behind her and points to it. The menu is flashing* **Today's Special: Faith.***)*

LAST STOP TO DINE

Yes, I'm knee deep in a journey

from downtown to movin-on-up…

NANA MAMA

(*Confused.*)

Say, again? I mean, excuse me, sir? What did you say?

MAN

It's a down beat with high

frequencies/ trepidations & trap-doors

'cause I'm affirmative action in progress

NANA MAMA

(*She breaks in.*)

Down beat? Affirmative action? I don't understand a darn fool thing you are saying.

(*She scratches her head.*)

MAN

(*Unmoved by her astonishment.*)

I'd like America on the side, with cheese,

maybe supersize it fo' twenty mo' cents

right/ left, sound off, a-quota

right/ left, sound off, a profile

left/ right, sound off, one, two, a thug since I sometimes

enjoy a baseball cap on my peanut head

(*Pause.*)

I tried to be a father to that

child for her but couldn't deal/still

had latefees on my dreams

> (*He looks at her. Her mouth is agape. He turns to walk away.*)

NANA MAMA

Sir, are you okay? Am I crazy? I'm trying to put it together baby but I just don't get what you are saying. Are you on Prozac? Are you slow in the head, son?

> (BLACK MAN *turns back around and comes back to the counter.*)

MAN

> (*Hurriedly.*)

I tried to be a husband to my wife but we

never married/in the reel of sensation

do you still have 3/5ths or 3/8ths of black

man on your menu? It's from the ghetto

> (NANA MAMA *puts her hands over her ears and shakes her head.*)

to the suburbs/ want some of that green

    grass / blades

for new shaver in/ stead of concrete

realities   I need   handfuls

    of happiness   and a cool

crisp breeze off the lake, please

NANA MAMA

Honey…honey…I can't…

(*She peers deeply into his eyes.*)

MAN

(*Dejected.*)

I would like to accentuate this grub in the comforts of my own destiny, but…

(*Music plays.* NANA MAMA *and* BLACK MAN *look at the customer that enters the diner. It is a* BLACK WOMAN. *She stops just after she enters the door. The* BLACK WOMAN *fumbles through her purse. The* BLACK MAN *looks back at* NANA MAMA.)

NANA MAMA

(*Gesturing in irritation.*)

Thank you, honey. Can you step over there? It looks like there is another customer coming.

(*He looks at her perturbed. Then, he steps aside into The Light where he squirms as if the heat of The Light burns him.* GABE *comes from out of the back. The music stops.*)

NANA MAMA

Lil' Gabe, I think, I think I'm more tired than I thought.

GABE

You didn't see the rat again, did you?

(*She shakes her head.*)

Nana Mama, I know I'm hard to get along with but I do need you here. Ain't nobody else for this job that I can trust. (*Pause.*) You do look a little peaked. Are you sure you are okay?

NANA MAMA

(*Nervous.*)

Uh, I think I can manage. (*Pause.*) Could you...could you... Oh, forget it.

GABE

Well, let me get ready to cook up some stuff.

(GABE *walks back through the kitchen door.*)

NANA MAMA

But he ordered...he ordered...ah forget it.

(The WOMAN walks to the counter and looks at the menu. The menu is flashing **Today's Special: Forgiveness**. NANA MAMA looks at the MAN and he looks back at her with his arms folded.)

NANA MAMA

Okay, okay. Maybe that dude was just a little crazy. I'll get it together.

(*The* WOMAN *looks at her puzzled.*)

LAST STOP TO DINE

Oh, please forgive me, I'm just talking to myself, child. Can I interest you in our special for today, sugah?

WOMAN

> (*She looks up at menu, again,
> then back at* NANA MAMA.)

No, thank you, Sister-in-a-bind

NANA MAMA

Sister who?

WOMAN

> (*She points to the menu.*)

Girlfriend, I would like to spend time with those

dreams I put under my mattress, I would like that

world full-of-love my man promised me,

> (*In the spotlight the* MAN
> *looks at them with contempt.*)

NANA MAMA

Love? Love your man *promised*? Oh no, no child. This isn't...

WOMAN

that trunk full of child-support and

man-to-son one-on-one he owes me

that swing set in the back yard and those

Friday night hot oil foot massages

but arrears is his haven and

> (*She looks at* MAN *to the right and turns her nose up at him. He looks away from* WOM- AN *as if he is just blistering in the hot light. She looks back at* NANA MAMA. NANA MAMA *smiles uncomfortably.*)

WOMAN

I suffer like a cockroach on the tip of scientist's pin

Sister-in-a-bind, I changed my mind

NANA MAMA

I am not in a bind, *sista.*

WOMAN

> (*Looks at* NANA MAMA *indifferently.*)

give me an application to

wonderful so I can plant

my feet in the ass of all those players kickin' game

git that lemon-lime love out my mouth

> (WOMAN *wipes mouth with hand.* NANA MAMA *gets her an application while she shakes her head.*)

NANA MAMA

Lord, lord, lord. Have I forsaken thee?

> (*She looks up to the ceiling with both hands in the air and shakes her head. She puts her head down on the counter.*

LAST STOP TO DINE

211

> GABE *comes back in to the diner. He has on a white chef's hat and white chef's shirt. He is carrying a wooden spoon in his hand as if it were scepter. His demeanor is serene. He stands behind* NANA MAMA.)

WOMAN

the aftertaste is attorney's fees

and I can't write off the taxes

> (*She puts the application into her purse.* GABE *points the wooden spoon towards the* MAN. *The* WOMAN *goes reluctantly over to where the* MAN *is standing, in The Light. They turn their backs to each other. A* BLACK MALE TEENAGER *walks into the diner. He looks over into The Light and sees the* MAN *and the* WOMAN.)

NANA MAMA

> (*Raises her head off the counter.*)

Ma'am, could you take two steps that way?

> (*She points to her left and notices the* WOMAN *is not there. She sees* GABE.)

GABE

> (*Authoritatively.*)

She's already there.

NANA MAMA

What's happening Gabe? I don't understand it. Why is everyone talking so…

> (*She is frazzled. Rap music starts.*
> GABE *touches her shoulder with*
> *his hand.* NANA MAMA *looks at*
> *him.* TEENAGER *approaches the*
> *counter. The menu flashes* **Today's**
> **Special: Honor**. *The rap music*
> *stops.*)

NANA MAMA

All right. I'm not crazy. I'm not crazy.

GABE

Take his order Nana Mama.

NANA MAMA

Okay. Hey, little man. Would you like something? Something to *eat*?

TEENAGER

Uh, nawh? My Mama told me 'bout taking

sweet-no-things from strangers and how

people can corrupt a child if a child

don't watch out for corruption   but since I am

NANA MAMA

Corrupt *you*? Corrupt you, *child*? What in the hell is going on!

> (*She slams her hands on the count-*
> *er. The* TEENAGER *looks at her*
> *perplexed. The* MAN *and* WOMAN
> *are startled and look to where the*
> *sound comes from.*)

NANA MAMA

I'm sicker than I thought, Gabe. What is it that you are trying to say
to me, son?

LAST STOP TO DINE

GABE

Just take his order Nana Mama. *Listen* to him, Nana. Listen at what he is saying.

> (*She looks at* GABE *perplexed then back to the* TEENAGER.)

TEENAGER

being the man of the house, now,

I'd like to take a big stake in my future/

the man of the house, then,

> (NANA *looks at him. The* WOMAN *looks at the* MAN *and the* MAN *turns from her in shame. The* TEENAGER *looks over at the* MAN.)

TEENAGER

that one called *sperm donor*

didn't come through so me

a latch-key-kid waiting for

opportunity's rattle on door/

Mama's boyfriend or a not there Poppie / hungry

for compassion in deep Barry White voice/ I want a sister

> (*He looks back at* NANA MAMA.)

NANA MAMA

Son...

GABE

No Nana. Don't say a thing. Listen to him.

> (*All eyes are on the*
> TEENAGER.)

TEENAGER

I want another sibling to romp around with

to eat cake with   and dream tomorrows with

do you have education on the half-shell?

can I purchase stocks and bonds in knowledge?

I want to know what it's like to be a full-course family

wanna know how to plant turnip greens/ mustard

greens/ tomatoes   like Grandma

want to sing to sadness, a happy Sunday morning tune,

like Mama, I want a Daddy I can call Daddy

for a Daddy reason/ want Daddy

to rub my head, show his concern

Uh, and I'd like some type of cherrypie jubilee, that's all/ that[s] all in my head

> (*Looking at the* TEENAGER,
> GABE *points the spoon in the
> direction of the* MAN *and*
> WOMAN. *The* TEENAGER
> *walks over to them with his
> head down. They are aston-
> ished to all be next to each
> other. The Light fades down
> on them and we only see their*

LAST STOP TO DINE

215

> *shadows. The menu flashes*
> **Love** *three times and then goes*
> *out.)*

NANA MAMA

> (NANA MAMA *and* GABE
> *look at them.)*

Lil' Gabe I'm sicker than I thought. I don't know what kind of virus or bug it is. Either they sound like crazy people or I'm out of my mind. Who are they? What are they doing here? They never ordered a thing, Lil' Gabe. They just babbled on incoherently like grown babies.

GABE

That's because they are Earth Walkers, Sadie.

NANA MAMA

Earth Walkers? What? Lil' Gabe, you called me Sadie.

GABE

I know. Sadie, those three are Earth Walkers, still. They are not ready to order from here, that's why you can't understand them. They haven't broken the belt. They are not ready for the diner, yet.

NANA MAMA

Gabe, what are you talking about? I'm sick, okay, just too sick. I…

GABE

You aren't sick, Sadie, and you'll never be sick anymore.

> (*She looks at* GABE *in*
> *surprise. The Light comes back*
> *up on the* MAN, WOMAN,

and TEENAGER. GABE *points to i
with the spoon and* NANA MAMA
and him look at them. The WOMAN
*places both of her hands on the sides
of the* TEENAGER'S *face. She looks
right into his eyes. The* MAN *looks
at both of them. The* MAN *gets on
one knee and the* TEENAGER *hugs
him as the* WOMAN *looks down
on the two. The* MAN *then hugs
the* WOMAN *around her waist
as he still holds the* TEENAGER.
*They are in a group embrace. The
Light changes to red on them. They
look over to* GABE *and* NANA
MAMA. *The* MAN, WOMAN, *and*
TEENAGER *smile and then their
faces quickly become expressionless,
blank—eyes shut. The Light flickers
a few times, like a strobe light, then
it blacks out.* NANA MAMA *covers
her mouth. The Light comes back on
and the* MAN, *the* WOMAN, *and
the* TEENAGER *have disappeared.*
GABE *looks on without batting an
eye.* NANA MAMA *looks at* GABE.)

NANA MAMA

What was *that*?

GABE

They always do *that*. It's good. They don't have to come here.

NANA MAMA

Why is that good, Lil' Gabe? Don't we need customers?

(GABE *looks at her and smiles. He*

puts his hand on her shoulder.)

GABE

Believe me, Sadie, it's good that we don't see them now...but time is a funny monster—just when you think all is well, it isn't.

NANA MAMA

Hunh?

GABE

(Smiling.)

We'll see them again, believe me, no one gets passed us. We are the thresholds. We are the greeters. We are infinity and beyond.

NANA MAMA

(Dejected.)

We're dead aren't we, Gabe? I mean, am I dead?

GABE

(Smiles.)

Sadie, for the first time *you* are alive—alive forever more.

> (GABE *kisses her on the forehead. The lights go out. Music starts. The menu lights up in a fluorescent color. When the lights come back on* NANA MAMA *has on a white chef's shirt and a white headscarf. She is not wearing glasses and looks fresh—younger. She is wiping down the counter. The music fades down.)*

NANA MAMA

Gabe, we got a customer!

(*The Light comes on. The music swells up, again.* SADIE *looks toward The Light then to the door. She smiles. The lights over* SADIE'S head *fade down illuminating her fluorescent headband and shirt. A few seconds pass and the music fades, simultaneously, with the lights over* NANA MAMA *and the m board. The only thing that remains on The Light.*)

Looking for Hurston in a Triptych

I. Zora (letter one)

You were your name before you were
named. I went old school, dropping things
in the mail. That is why I'm coming to you—
to know your failures as much as your goldens.
You have become the *it* & the *they* & the *we*.
Hell, I'm feeling all kinds of broken—the hour
that includes the minutes & its seconds—
the forest that includes its animals & its trees.
The computer, its motherboards & its chips.
The screams of us—our terrors & our heart-
aches. But, still, there is no name for how we
lose. Hell, we lost you before we found you.

I am burnt raw—in machinations where you smile under the brim of your hat.

I wanted God to rearrange the matrix.
Thought he'd do that Superman thing—
go backwards, around the world, &

put words back into their proper lexicon,
make time cooperate? But God ain't down
with human commands. You would have
conquered the world, & we'd have it all:
the Eiffel Tower, consciousness & blue
note, the Euphrates, a harvest from seedlings
to how black life gave its birth dazzle—
the language of babies still learning to jazz.

*There were no women with your tongue & your color kicking
anthropology & ethnography.*

I'm writing to you because I'm a boy with
a flat line, in a man's body. I'm searching for
that *Mule Bone* glow—before it all went
south—for a phrase from another black
woman because it's always black women
who save me. If you were dead, I wouldn't ask.
How are you with this new migration, *this*
blackness? Today, again, I play in your name—
in the tepid water puddles, letting the sun
dry me naturally because this poem's all natural.
More sunflower than bougainvillea blooms
about the earth surrounding me. More dandelion
than juniper. It seems you know something
about dying, about living, about resurrection.

*So, I'm calling out to you: Harlem Renaissance, Niggerati, Janie, Tea
Cake, Barracoon.*

II. Before You (letter two)

I am looking at you while
I'm looking for you. I may not
have stated it correctly in my last
missive. It's hard writing to someone

who's too busy to reply. I'll keep doing so
until you say stop. I know you are

getting them. I know you are reading
them. I know it bothers you too—
all this world. You know, it's like you
created Florida, with all that Eatonville

patois—a sound that reverberates through
the womb, like coming out of a tunneled
slide, a child with bubbles in her stomach—
that echo of release. That's where I'm at,

succumbing to your trickster smile & what's
                        behind your eyes. I see there's a convoluted

aura mixed with the mud and thickets of
resilience—then, some. Now, what am I
to understand about a black woman discarded
like the unwanted touch a child's never to

talk about? I mean, they couldn't find you,
your gravesite, the life you owned—until
they did. You weren't even on the record.
You were lost. Then, you were found. Now,

there's a headstone. Now, there's your books
taking up space in Barnes & Nobles,

in university classes with a swelter of minds
determining you should be constellations, or
some closer connection to our solar system.
I am improvising, in the cut, figuring out

the how, the to, the why of where water enters
& where it breathes before it leaves or
evaporates. All I'm doing is evaporating like
a song fades, then there's nothing but the needle

in the groove keeping time. Somedays all
the beautiful things in my life break my heart.

III. All Up In This (the Zora dreams)

You come to me like the night trying
to hide the moon—halfway out its pocket.
I can see night's hand caressing its rim.
But, maybe the way I'm seeing it doesn't
sound like a perfect sphere. My sights a little
off, correcting from the blare of all day
laptop screens, & I don't have my readers
on. Motion can fool you into believing
you're in a minefield full of poppies,
& you are high & low, simultaneously,
dragging your nightmares into daylight.

You come to me like the day moon—
try to say it isn't bloated on passion—
so heated, it rises like a Chinese
lantern left to float into airspace to show
everyone a soul can rise. This is my soul,
lifting into the blue, stretching my arms
across the sky to hug you forever.
I never knew how to demonstrate love
when it's just us. So, today, I'm trying to
hide the sun in my pocket. It's hot,
for sure. I love yellow—to grab passion,
place it next to my 49¢ & have the coins
burn their imprints into my thigh. Only
this abuse can satisfy the ache from the sun,
the smoke from my bones. In the heap
left stirring, you won't recognize me.
You won't find any lies lifted from my ashes,
before the wind propels me about
the air, singing with your name.

CONRAD PEGUES

Conrad Pegues is an African American Southerner from Memphis, Tennessee who has been writing for over 20 years to himself as an exercise in maintaining sanity. He has taught college English courses and is now a librarian which rounds out his love of books and words. He published a collection of short stories on Amazon entitled The Sweet's Price for Edenville and Other Stories of Black Gay Males in 2015. He is currently a librarian at the University of Tennessee at Martin. He has two sons and one granddaughter.

waiting

h. r. trainers keep saying
Boss
the person over you
at work
like it has no history on the ear
every time
antebellum scenes erupt in my mind's eye
like over ripe boils
black backs bent low
in a still sea of white
under the yellow blaze of a high noon sun
and I want to burn something down
in protest of bosses
who capitalized on unpaid labor
for centuries
passing the payday on to country and children

NAOMI WILSON

Naomi Wilson is a poet and photographer from Holyoke, Massachusetts with a background in journalism and an MFA in Creative Writing from Texas State University. Naomi Wilson is a poet and photographer from Holyoke, Massachusetts with a background in journalism and an MFA in Creative Writing from Texas State University.

As Mardou

We see ourselves   however we can.
We act crazy, act dutiful, wear velvet slacks,
        perm, press, strut.

Drink amber beer, get dug, get dug on.
Writhe, bloom, on the barroom floor.
                Play pool,   pretend.

Never apprise,
never acquaint,
always allow.

Our mothers can't talk us out, our fathers
                        don't try.

We try everything once. Magic bullets, talk therapy,
tea, romance.

                Certain things we try
                again.

White man,
making it,
we try again.

In the movies, they make us Leslie Caron.
Transatlantic talking, the Wild One.

The bodies behind the brass are

        well-dressed,
                pink-skinned,
while we're going naked in the world.

LAKIBA PITTMAN

Lakiba Pittman, poet/artist, and educator, teaches diversity, media, race, and social justice at Menlo College and mindfulness and compassion with the Compassion Institute and at Stanford University. While crafting the second edition of *Bread Crumbs from The Soul,* melding art, poetry, and autobiography, she also pursues a doctoral degree in Psychology focusing on Consciousness, Spirituality, and Integrated Health. Her art has graced MOAD, SomARTS, and the African-American Art & Cultural Complex. She was featured at the 50th-year celebration of the Black Arts Movement and in *Black Fire This Time, Volume I.* Lakiba's poetry sparks self-healing, spiritual consciousness, and awareness.

The Dreamers

Yesterday, I experienced myself anew
Awakened as if in a dream, but not a dream
A reality lived centuries ago that is now intertwined in time.
I see myself in the passerby's and hear some of my story
In herstory and history and in their story and in yours
and just a bit of a tear wells up as I listen to the journeys of others
and hear of your dreams and early beginnings.

In our families, some hide the rhymes and the reasons
Some sharing their dreams and a vision and hope
Even when they have given up much of it
Still, they believe in us.
We are the ones who will live a better life, and in that realization
They rest some but work more to ensure a safer journey for us
Dreaming of our education and our growth.
That we will have a better life and so…

May I embody the dreams of my ancestors
Igniting a spark in my mother's eyes, illuminating her soul.
May my father's smile embody a thousand dreams
Inspiring future generations under the warmest sun
That the strength of his hug remains with me throughout the years
Especially on those days when the world seems resistant
In places where my light may not always penetrate or be known

Where my joy is suppressed in those places where I am not welcomed
In the face of adversity, I rise, undeterred

May my father's dream for me be realized as I conquer each new
challenge
May my mother's dream for me broaden my heart's horizons,
and show me the power of self-love, self-care
compassion for others and for myself
May I remain strong. May I show up.
Yes. I am because they believed in a dream that will never die
Now and forever, within their dreams, I take flight.

KARLA BRUNDAGE

Karla Brundage is the founder of West Oakland to West Africa Poetry Exchange
(WO2WA) and board member of the Before Columbus Foundation. She is co-
editor of Colossus:Home which features poets from the Bay Area in solidarity
with Moms4housing and advocating for housing justice. A Pushcart prize
nominee, her poetry, short stories and essays have been widely anthologized and
can be found in Hip Mama, Literary Kitchen, sPARKLE & bLINK, A Gathering
of the Tribes: Black Lives Matter Issue, *Black Fire This Time Volume 1*. Her
forthcoming book *Blood Lies/Race Traitor* will be published by Finishing Line
Press in 2024.

Katrina: A pantoum written on August 29, 2005

Katrina came to New Orleans in catastrophic force,
a merry party girl, wreaked havoc on old structures,
tossing over old lovers like worn out shoes
a collective heartbeat would be no more.
A tempestuous party girl wreaking havoc on old
she wore a luminescent redlined petticoat
a collective heartbeat would be no more
from our televisions we witnessed levees break.
She wore a luminescent blood red petticoat
flooding to rooflines, poles snapped and scattered
from our televisions we could see levees break

stranded families climbed to the roof.
Floods rose to rooflines, poles snapped and scattered
Waves at crushing force moved the whole block
Surging families climbed to the roof
Chaos came bringing the blue and white.
Waves at crushing force moved the whole block
TV news reported, hands were tied.
Chaos came with the blue and white
dazed onlookers frothed with rage.
TV news reported, hands were tied
The Lower 9th Ward was soon under siege
Her fury knocked out the floors
dazzling onlookers who looked on with rage.
What did we do to cause this raging?
Trombones drums and second lines silent
A wailing emitted from front line
Looting was reported, hands were tied.
Trombones drums and second lines silent
Soldiers, tanks guns had turned against them
Looting was reported, hands were tied
As we waited witnessing a collective cry.
Katrina came to New Orleans in catastrophic force
a merry party girl, dogs sensed her arrival
she wore a luminescent redlined petticoat
a collective heartbeat would be no more.

She Roars

The line that one crosses to speak the truth
                    the line that is simultaneously not visible, not true.

Silenced in shadows, lurking in corners, is an affliction I have of
wanting to be heard.
                    I don't speak for anyone.

Could I be the person who suddenly dives in the pool to keep you from
drowning
        a butterfly with one wing fighting until death?

My mother, an Alabama river girl
Myself a Ka'a'awa rock wall girl

Are there women hanging clothes on the line? Hauling water
from wells?
Black eyed wandering from accident to accident? That. Could
be me—me. Then, not
now—you must be questioning my veracity.

I must speak for myself

and children not born of cotton pillows, but borne on their
mother's backs
hard to speak because my mind wraps in doubts of double-c
onsciousness doubly woman, doubly half black and not black.

If I had a voice I would tell it to be quiet and
then probably not listen…

Last night I spoke on the phone, roaring with laughter.
I don't like to think of speaking for anyone.
I like to think of speaking out
    Out of turn
    Out of necessity
    Out of darkness

Doug Curry

Residing in upstate NY, Douglas Curry is a black radio host, actor, writer, and poet, born and raised in Harlem and the Bronx. He is a 1974 graduate of Carnegie-Mellon University, in Pittsburgh, Pa. Mr. Curry's writings deal with the universality of human joys and foibles, and the march of history as witnessed by divergent cultures. He is an especially keen observer of those of African descent whose story is embedded in the soil of the United States.

MICKEY

Love comes in all forms and truly does last forever. Children grow into adulthood and still remember and love their schoolmates. Mickey was one of mine.

We were tenth graders when we met. Both shy, we found comfort and friendship in words. They were our playthings, and our playmates. We could always read and write magnificent ideas, daring feats, and saucy, swaggering, sexiness, the very stuff we were short of - except in our friends, our words. These words, hers and mine, fed upon each other and grew and grew more adventurous, eventually drawing us together, her words and mine. We were friends, schoolmates in 1966.

Mickey told me with all seriousness that she was going to be a journalist. With some embarrassment, I pretended to know just what that meant until I had a chance to go and look it up. Then I encouraged my friend in her dream. For my part, I could only say that I was enthralled with every utterance from the wordsmiths of the day; Malcolm, Martin, Muhammad Ali …. Even the unlettered exuberance of Willie Mays and Yogi Berra held me in its sway.

Square as a pool table, and just as green. My friend Michelle and me.

Mickey was a light skinned young woman of medium height and quiet demeanor. She was not overly pretty but was still very attractive in the way her near high-yellow skin tones contrasted with her straight, jet-black hair. In 1967, that kind of thing was still very 'in.'

Life happens …

Life happened to Mickey, and to me. Mickey got mad when I missed English class, and the next time she saw me I was glassy-eyed and high. *Reefer madness...* She was disappointed when I suggested that we cut school one day and go hang at a friend's house whose parents were at work. Mickey was not *that kind of girl.*

But now, it was 1968. In the nation, the struggle for civil rights was giving way to a demand for Black Power. War raged in Indochina, and directly threatened life and limb of all whose legal draft age approached. The kind of person you were was changing every day before your very eyes. With the explosion of information from all sides, most of it incendiary, every day you morphed in ways that surprised even yourself. And while I was busy marveling at my own changes, I didn't even notice those that were going on with my friend. I never paid much attention to the ghetto-rich, baby-faced drug dealers and hustlers who suddenly were everywhere. Decked out in alpaca sweaters, silk pants, leathers with Persian lamb collars, and 'gators, they swarmed over and preyed upon my friend Mickey, and all the unsuspecting, shy but vain girls like her. I never noticed Mickey beginning her descent. Before I knew anything, she went spiraling down, down, down ... Mickey went from snorting skag, to skin-popping, to mainlining. Heroin was her first pimp. After a time, she walked around glassy-eyed and too cool, purring a Billie Holiday-ish moaning slur when she talked. She gave me a Janis Joplin album and proclaimed her a genius.

There went one of my very best friends, ever.

One day I walked into the wrong classroom at school and as I chanced to look over in a corner of the room, I noticed my friend Mickey. She was deep in a junkie's nod, her head never quite touching the desk as she nodded down, but never quite reaching an upright position when it recoiled upward again.

My friend Mickey was a stoned junkie. It was now 1969.

I went away, off to college, where if Mickey could only have landed, she no doubt could have become that journalist in her dreams. Times were changing for women, but things had already changed too much for Mickey.

The last time I saw my friend Mickey was in the summer of 1970. I was within hours of leaving New York City to avoid some street trouble that sometimes comes some people's way. The last time I touched her hand, kissed her sunken cheek, looked into that now vacant abyss where her sparkling eyes once were, was on the corner of Southern Boulevard and Elsmere Place in the Bronx in June of 1970.

I held her hand. I kissed her. I turned and, without ever looking back, walked away into the '70s. I didn't know I would never see her again.

While at college, I got a few cards, even some letters with loose ten-dollar bills, wrapped in Mickey's love and her admonition to never let what had happened to her ever happen to me. And then, the war, Jimi Hendrix, Huey P. Newton, Nixon, Kent State, and the youthful, illicit pleasures of the 1970's all conspired to nudge Mickey into the far reaches of my consciousness. For me, then, she became but another Bronx tale.

Even though the last time I saw Mickey she was fully a woman, I will always remember her as a troubled child of a turbulent time and place. I often wonder what became of her. It is my suspicion that she died long ago, a slow pain-filled death, unavoidable to so many, and narrowly escaped by far too few ghetto children. I think of how close we were, similar in so many important ways, and I realize that Providence and good fortune surely have smiled upon me.

The kind endurance of my years is not without the bittersweet moments when I pause and contemplate Mickey's memory. I know now that we were only children when we met, feeling what was both a child's platonic empathy for each other and an adult romantic love -- for us, forever unrealized.

We had walked together away from our childhood, into the uncertain realities of being grown. The winds of change were swirling with menace. But we had faced this, encouraged by each other's words of hope.

We were *friends*.

Amoja Sumler

Recognized by Poetry Slam Inc as a "Legend of the South," Amoja Sumler (author of "Fables, Foibles, & Other 'Merican Sins") is a nationally celebrated Black poet, essayist and one of the preeminent emerging voices of leftist intersectional social advocacy. Amoja has headlined poetry festivals such as the Austin International Poetry Festival, the Bridgewater International Poetry Festival, Write NOLA in New Orleans and Rock the Republic in Texas. His poetry appears in the *Pierian Literary Journal, Muddy Ford Press*, the *Antigonish Review* and elsewhere.

Afro Futurist

We done jumped to the eventual
(There was skipping and hopping
like country kids in lilac pastures.)

Here the big bad done been slayed;
the great 'They' ain't been seen in years
not hide nor hair since *that reckoning*.

In the now we just love and fire
our shiny sable canon. We pop
that thang like old time rap tunes

it's a different vibrato each time:--
here even our ghost notes are blue. We fire
and fire and fire and can't seem to miss.

Jet iron roars till reddening
& I hear Rita
& I hear Patricia

This be that new new N word.

& I hear Natasha
& I hear Nikki
& I hear Nikky

& hear at one time long
long long ago it was just
gonna be Langston

cause there could only be one:--
like we was still up in Scottish
Highlands taking heads for immortality.

Charlois Lumpkin

Charlois Lumpkin, aka Mali Newman, is a native of St. Louis, Missouri and a member of the Eugene B. Redmond Writers Club and its performance troupe, the Soular Systems Ensemble. Her work has appeared in *Drumvoices Revue, Valley Voices—A Literary Review, Merge Literary Magazine, Crossing the Divide from the Poets of St. Louis*, and *The Hoot and Holler of the Owls*, an anthology published by the Zora Neale Hurston/Richard Wright Foundation. Most recently she appeared in *Black Fire This Time, Vol. I* and appeared in the 2022 documentary *Poetry in Motion: St. Louis Poets Take the Mic.*

Going Cotton
a 10-minute play

"…it is the melancholy distinction of cotton
to be the very stuff of high drama and tragedy …"
—David L. Cohn

An elderly ex-sharecropper leaves the South at the end of the Great Migration to join his family now settled in the Ville neighborhood of St. Louis, MO. Upon arrival he attempts to forge a relationship with his grandson by sharing a history of emotional truths.

Characters

GRAND DAD
ISAAC (GRAND SON)

AT RISE: A wooden makeshift porch (two chairs can be used for substitution) a metal pail containing ice and two small bottles of soda pop. On stage are four wood planks forming a garden bed holding four plants with white bolls of cotton. It is autumn and GRAND DAD is teaching ISAAC the proper way to weed and check the plants for weevils and aphids. ISAAC has a hoe and is beating the ground, as his GRAND DAD looks on.

GRAND DAD
No. No ISAAC, not so hard. You have to beat the earth like you would a woman-real genteel-like.

Going Cotton 233

(HE gives ISAAC a quick demonstration, then gives him back the hoe.)

ISAAC
Like this Grand Dad?

GRAND DAD
Yeah son, like that, tender and easy. Now you're choppin' cotton. Get rid of the weeds so the plants can breathe.

(They give each other a quick smile and continue working.)

ISAAC
I heard Mama and Daddy talking. They say you've lost your mind planting a cotton patch in the Ville. They wish you would plant something that made sense . . . like tomatoes.

GRAND DAD
You don't go repeating everything you hear in this house. It's not respectful, besides they don't know everything.

ISAAC
Mama and Daddy won't talk about Mississippi. Whenever I ask, they say they can't remember anything. (Short pause) What was it like down South when you were my age?

(GRAND DAD gives a sigh, then smiles.)

GRAND DAD
Doesn't matter how long you're away from the South, the South never leaves you.
I can still hear my Daddy 'Get to that field fo' I dust yo' breeches, and I'd high tail it out the door, shirt tail flying in the breeze.

(GRAND DAD moves his arms like HE'S running. The image tickles ISAAC'S funny bone and they both share a laugh.)
In the fields your eyes squinted from the sun, and as far as you could see a blanket of white seemed to soften everything around it.

(GRAND DAD stares off like HE has it stored in some corner of his memory.)

Mama didn't look so old, Daddy didn't look so tired, the earth didn't look so hard and the clouds didn't seem so far away. Back then the stalks stood tall and white. Whole families worked side by side, row by row. Men, women and chill'n all heads bowed from sun up to sun down.

ISAAC
You mean bowed like in church?

GRAND DAD
Yeah… only not so holy, and we sang to keep the rhythm going so as nobody would fall behind.

(Voices off stage sing with GRAND DAD.)

One day I'll pack up
and fly away
Won't see you no mo'
till judgement day
Bend down
Bow to cotton
Bend down
Bow to cotton
Uncle Joe dropped dead
Right where HE stood
Not gone fo' cotton
HE'S gone fo' good
Bend down
Bow to cotton
Bend down
Bow to cotton

GRAND DAD
In the summer time when the fields were in full bloom, the owner would come round and tell us "Pink in the fields mean green in the pocket." His pocket.
(Pause) Seems like I've spent most of my life plantin' or pickin' somebody else's cotton.

(Female voice off stage.)

Going Cotton

GRAND DAD, ISAAC – dinner in an hour.

ISAAC
GRAND DAD did Uncle Joe really drop dead?

GRAND DAD
Yeah…in nineteen and thirty-eight on one of the hottest days of the year, I was working along- side Josiah when he dropped to his knees and fell flat on his face. The land giveth and the land taketh away. That's why you must be careful how you treat it. (GRAND DAD plucks a cotton boll from one of the stalks and spreads it open.)
Look ISAAC. Now I'd say this here cotton is of fair middlin 'grade. That means it's pretty good.

ISAAC
I guess that makes US pretty good city farmers.

GRAND DAD
I'd say we were pretty good quarter hands, and not bad at all considering city soil. (Still holding the cotton, boll HE takes a seat on the porch. ISAAC sits on the step beside him. GRAND DAD pulls two bottles of soda pop from the bucket, opens them with a church key and hands a bottle to ISAAC. They take a sip.)

ISAAC
Aren't we going to finish picking the cotton?

GRAND DAD
No son. You and I are going to sit here, drink our sodies and watch it.

ISAAC
Watch it? (Short pause) For how long?

GRAND DAD
Till it rots.

(HE takes another sip of soda as the house lights slowly fade.)

THE END

TUREEDA MIKELL

Tureeda Mikell, Poet Author Story Medicine Woman, called activist for holism, hell bent on asserting life named word magician, by author/professor, Ngugi wa Thiongo, is hell-bent on asserting life. D'Jele Musa, aka woman of truths, is a Qigong energy consultant of 36 years; has published 73 CA Poets in the School anthologies for at risk students. Her full length collection, *Synchronicity, The Oracle of Sun Medicine*, was released on 2/2020 and was nominated for the California Book Award. Her full length collection, *The Body: Oracle of Memory* released, 2/2024, published by Black Lawrence Press, NY, faces many awards.

LIFE LIGHT REMEMBERED

We are soldiers on the battlefield
With life light in our eyes, said Sister Sonja.
1994, 23 years after volunteering
At the George Jackson free health clinic,
The Tribune calls, asks,
How many guns did you have at the
Black Panther Clinic?
How many guns?
Not how many services were provided?
Not how many programs were implemented?
Not how many doctors or healthcare workers volunteered?
Not even why we'd care to put
Into practice such a program
With so many hospitals in our community.
No, didn't ask any of that!
Wanted to know how many guns we had.
Not what illnesses or diseases
Most affected our communities
Or how often we screened for diabetes, sickle cell,
Or checked for high blood pressure, if at all,
Or
What may have been my specialty
At that time.
I would have told them about
Certain grains to regain genetic memory.
But they were more interested in

How many guns we had.
Not who ran the clinic
Or what hours or days
Of the week we were open
Or
Who was our hero or she-roe
To set about such a task that sustain
Our health needs today.
No, the reporter didn't ask any of that.
They wanted to know
How many guns we had.
The revolution is coming whether we want it or not!
It is coming whether we want it or not!
We must be politically prepared for what is coming.
The revolution will not be televised
Not be televised
Not be televised.
The revolution will be live!
How many guns did we have?
We were soldiers on the battlefield with
Life light in our eyes.
We are soldiers on the battlefield with life light in our eyes.

Thurman Watts

Thurman Watts was born in San Francisco and is an alumnus of Willamette University. In the '70s he formed the Nairobi Poets with David Rages and Joseph McNair. His work has been seen in The Pan Africanist, Black Creation Magazine, Holloway House Publications, The San Franciso Examiner, The San Francisco Chronicle, Cadence Magazine, and Blues Blast Magazine, among others. In 2022, his short story "Mbombe's Glass" was featured in the anthology *Black Fire This Time, Vol. 1*. His collaboration with Lester Chambers, *Time Has Come—Revelations of a Mississippi Hippie* was also released in 2022.

30 African Triplets

i was born in hunters point authentically
a joint in itself
on the outskirts of toxicity

my middle name is a Langston Hughes character
that once got his mental pocket picked
as a sad young man sitting at a bar

at sixteen, a reading of Giovanni's Room by Baldwin
prepped me for my first bad acid trip
that happened befo twenty

took that orange sunshine at college, in a blessed twist of fate
my name mighta been Tim Peebles
had i gone to sf state

what the world needs now is a black sonic boom
I wrote to N. Giovanni
she wrote me Black

my potna stole her letter
fame is fleeting like a motherfucker
the Butler of East Palo Alto did it

as fully fledged & pledged Nairobi poets
Stanley Crouch sent us a gin bottle that had no pig feet
when we blew Black Art psalms for alms on his turf

our feats on the throttle for what
we had birthed we met Eugene Redmond in Sac
Quincy Troupe in berkeley north, on earth

troped Troupe, seek ye the Reed of Ishmael?
come back after the nazis try to claim the boogaloo
the coast might be clear then

30 African Triplets

Black Arts other Sarah Fabio whose counsel we did covet
showered us with grace and purpose
the storm cometh hinted she, and we's smack dab in the eye of it

caught in a cointelpro spell and shenanigan
they killed a girl i had for a bit
went to the nut ward at least thrice, to wit:

the poets broke up
crack came for my head
i gave up my pen for a season instead

Rasta threw me a lifeline as I roused rabble
I spoke with Joe Higgs, Marley, Peter, and Andrew Tosh
still, i continued to dabble, not to mention the babble

David Henderson brought ghetto follies to town
i took his picture instamatically
he gave me a beer for it

knew nuthin' bout my roomie coked out
middlemanning a Pryor deal
at the start of the "is it something I said" tour, at the circle star, no doubt

undercovers everywhere
outside the crib, on the road, in the highway light
when they came for my roomie, I was on that nut ward flight

when old man death came for Marvin
i contemplated rehab
and said, yes, yes, yes

saw Big Mama Thornton's last gig
in berkeley at the Julia Morgan
she looked like my Grandpa's voice from beyond

Black Community News Service fall '91
We did the 25th Panther anniversary issue
i wrote in quotes of Garvey for the people's sum

on the bay bridge one day i saw Ed Bullins
handed him a one-act
that i never saw again

burst into radio with musica
interviewed Smokey, Mavis, and both B.B.'s on air
T. Watts, i thought you wuz a white man said Mavis takin' me there

ghostwrote a tome for Sly's sister Vet
they went on the road
y'all know the rest

went to a record party
met Suga Pie DeSanto and Senior Jimmy Mo
De Thang Johnny Talbot too, at a club called down low

went on the road with the Suga
Chitown Bluesfest, Norway, Italy, the price of fame; the game of wages
nonetheless, the Suga burned stages

spoke with Masekela's biographer, professor Cheers
took me 11 years to finish Hugh he said
Hugh said, bra, i don't think it took 11 years, i'd be dead

sojourned with Lester Chambers telling his story from life's files
mingled with the retrospective vapor
of Owlsey, Hendrix, Betty & Miles

so now you're convinced that pandora is a music portal
and most everything is square
but my children, be not still, beware

all prophecy is not real
protect spirit, soul, and la familia
be on alert for all attempts to kill ya

you might miss me dough
in this super flow
of the world crashin' and cashin' in on me

on me, on you
it matters not who
handles this business fo we's thuu

MARK ALLAN DAVIS

Mark Allan Davis, MFA, is a native New Yorker and an Assistant Professor of Africana Studies in Black Performance Studies/Dramatic Literature and Music/Theatre History at San Francisco State University's College of Ethnic Studies. His explorations and research focus on the politics of the black body on stage and in dramatic literature, Black Lives Matter, the Politics of African-American Performance on Racial & Social Movements. Minstrelsy and Vaudeville on Broadway Song & Dance, as well as the reemergence and rediscovery of the impact and evolution of the Black Arts Movement on contemporary theatre & dance creation. Mr. Davis is an Original Cast Member of 'The Lion King' on Broadway and is an accomplished director/choreographer, & dramaturg, and playwright, both domestically and internationally.

Why is Monumental Reckoning, "Monumental?"

Friday, January 12, 2024
Farewell Ceremony for Monumental Reckoning
Esho funi-(Buddhist concept) the oneness of life (as art)
and the environment.

I was fortunate to meet this incredible manifestation of fortitude and power embodied in one, Dana King, four years ago. There was an immediate connection. I too am an artist. People like Dana, me, any person who has journeyed from one location of transformation to another, have a stake in that great dividend of profundity knowing that something in their lives has moved. James Baldwin wrote in 1962 in the essay The Creative Process,

"There are, forever, swamps to be drained, cities to be created, mines to be exploited, children to be fed. None of these things can be done alone. But the conquest of the physical world is not man's only duty. They are also enjoined to conquer the great wilderness of themselves. The precise role of the artist, then, is to illuminate that darkness, blaze roads through that vast forest, so that we will not, in all our doing, lose sight of its purpose, which is, after all, to make the world a more human dwelling place."

Regarding the empress, Dana King, she, together with Illuminate, have created a work that makes this city a more human dwelling place. Why is it monumental? I'll be getting to that.

Her work in sculpture, in statuary art, captivates because our lives intersect on that great highway of contemplation where we reconcile the dislocations of the Black body, not only in the public sphere, but also in our collective consciousness.

To 'reckon' or 'reconcile?'

I was on a working visit in the former Soviet Union in 1990 during Perestroika. Moscow is a HUGE city, vast. It is over 50 miles in radius. Being driven around and witnessing their monuments was overwhelming. Not only were the roads very wide, the buildings were set very far back from the roads. The monument to cosmonaut Yuri Gargarin is jettisoning upwards to a height of almost 43 meters (145 ft.)! One must crane their neck to look up at it. It dwarfs. Moscow's immensity and it's large buildings, and the scale of its monuments, are telling the citizens something. They are telling the citizens that they are puny and insignificant and the Party is foremost. Hearing the Right Wing name calling the other side "Communists, Marxists, and the Radical Left," is comical to me. Moscow's infrastructure was emblematic of the influence of the state to control, and disempower the spirit. In this instance the state, the Soviet government, is not illuminating darkness but exacerbating it. Some things never change.

I am the 3rd generation on my paternal side born free. My great grandfather Zachariah Davis, was born in 1847 in Lowndes County, Mississippi. My great-grandfather was the progeny of rape. I've never found it fair nor equitable that I must undergo the reckoning of this

Why is Monumental Reckoning, "Monumental?" 243

ancestral trauma 'alone,' or, that my European brothers don't have to, or won't. What a great privilege. Many can't, but my father's memory, and his family's, told me about Zachariah. They breathed him into life for me as well as the burden of having to learn of him.

I had come to a crossroads in my personal life that forced me to address trauma, abuse, and not just in my life but in my father's and mother's lives. They are no longer here, and I feel it's my duty to become happy. In order to do that, I have to reconcile, deeply, actively and daily, that I am the son of America's greatest sin. I'm not the only one. I know this. But I am responsible for my life. The causal acts were in place long before this nation was a nation. But I do this act of reconciling my existence. I must. It's my American legacy, my American obligation. I'm proud to do it as I know Dana King is proud to realize such a vision as we gather here to say farewell.

Fundamentally, this is my existential crisis. One recent morning I saw a video clip of an interview with a MAGA person. An elderly, white woman-who hemmed-and-hawed, with darting eyes showing she couldn't answer the question, "what was the Civil War about?" Unbeknownst to her she was trampling all over my history, on my very existence. The privilege of her arrogant ignorance was disturbing and monumental. Many of us are like Marty McFly in the film Back to the Future with this sense of us simply fading away from a Polaroid, as if we were never here, and never had been. While our compatriots have the privilege of the unconscious, the Un-woke, the walking dead, our ancestors are here embodied in these soon to be departed figures, alive, alight, to enlighten and yes, illuminate.

This is another reason why this artistic work we're celebrating is monumental.

I've had to deeply reflect on the fact my skin color, as a high-yella brother, affords me privilege. It also mplaces me in a caste within a caste. This caste can be resented by some of my Black brothers and sisters. It's also afforded me a proximity to racism which I most emphatically wish it didn't. I have to reckon With that every day.

If we forget a moment about race and acknowledge caste-Black folks participate and codify each other along with the rest of the world, and in some cases, we can do it better and brutally, as well.

Billy Paul's 1972 hit *Am I Black Enough For Ya?* often rings in my ears. Here I am. I'm not biracial but my paternal great-great-grand dad wasn't Black, and he raped my African great-great-grand mother. I then have to hear Florida's Governor tell people, who don't know what the Civil War was about, that slavery was beneficial. Well, yes, I'm here, so that is beneficial. That is why these figures standing here in Golden Gate Park are monumental.

Kehinde Wiley said it best recently, "I'm an artist and a thinker." So is Dana King. So am I. There are many of us out there. The hated 'woke.' As far as Monumental Reckoning is concerned, Dana King achieved something that I brought to her attention when I told her she had decolonized Golden Gate Park she said, incredulous, "I did?"

Words like 'de-funding' or 'de-colonizing,' or God forbid you mention, 'reparations,' this means, somehow, white people must lose something so Black and Brown people might gain something. No, no, no.

Monumental Reckoning represents several things for many people. For me, it symbolizes the difficulty of existing as the progeny of a global system of oppression like that of chattel slavery. People willfully wish to make tepid this history of slavery, from whence I come, as insignificant. No, once a slave your children were and their children. The greater world order and the very society that raised you, conditions you, and still oppresses you, perpetually, ignores and denies it's impact, or even its existence, and this, in turn, damages you.

Monumental Reckoning illustrates where once stood a hundred-and-thirty year old monument to a man most contemptible now stands three hundred and fifty ancestors smiling upwards where he who hated no longer is welcome and was disappeared like so many of the Black bodies he owned and brutalized. That is monumental.

De-colonizing doesn't mean 'replace' it means to reorder. It means to 'recalibrate.' It means to console the restless furies that force salted moisture from our eyes.

Why must I furrow my brow attempting to comprehend the fact my father HAD to risk his own Black life to fight for this nation, in a segregated military in World War II, against tyranny, genocide and hate, in Europe, only to return to it in his homeland? When I asked him he had no answers except he did what he had to do and that's all he said about it. When you hear about the book banning's and the 'don't say Gay' laws, and the expelling of duly elected Black young Democrats from Tennessee's State Legislature for standing up against guns, or a statewide University system denying a living wage to its faculty, you know that it is monumentally difficult to do what Dana King has done here. But she did… do it.

The fact that the words Lift E'vry Voice, the first words of our Black National Anthem, are emblazoned above a temple to music in Golden Gate Park is monumental.

Looking at our world with the gaze of seeing what I need to see instead of seeing what has simply been put there… that is a monumental reckoning. I'd like to close with a quote from the late Buddhist leader, Daisaku Ikeda:

> "The institutions of human society treat us as parts of a machine. They assign us ranks and place considerable pressure upon us to fulfill defined roles. We need something to help us restore our lost and distorted humanity. Each of us has feelings that have been suppressed and have built up inside. There is a voiceless cry resting in the depths of our souls, waiting for expression. Art gives the soul's feelings voice and form."

Thank you so much for your kind attention!

KEISHA-GAYE ANDERSON

Keisha-Gaye Anderson is a Jamaican-born poet, writer, visual artist, and media strategist based in Brooklyn, NY. She is the author of Gathering the Waters, Everything Is Necessary, and A Spell for Living, which received the Editors' Choice recognition for Agape's Numinous Orisons, Luminous Origin Literary Award. Keisha's poetry, fiction, and essays have been widely published in national literary journals, magazines, and anthologies. In 2018, Keisha was selected as a Brooklyn Public Library Artist in Residence. Keisha holds an M.F.A. in creative writing from The City College, CUNY. Learn more about her at www.keishagaye.ink.

Cuckoo

Cuckoos sneak their eggs into the nests of other bird species.
Mother thought she could hide us inside
whiteness, that forgetting the past we
would be safe from the beast that devours
the best of what we are, its long mouth
stretching across oceans and generations
to confine bodies as house girl   helper
nanny   day's worker   laborer
She thought we could start fresh
in Americanness, but we were really cuckoo eggs,
big, and so, so blue. Smuggled into a nest
not made for us. Two of these things
are not like the others.
Girls, you are now other, stretching up into life, solitary,
in search of a story about where you started, depending
on the hospitality of strangers to name all the feelings
you were told to forget.
She said it was good here. She said, "In this country, Ah never
guh to bed hungry yet." But we hungered for a floodlight
to burn off the fog of constant confusion overcast our lives.
Her body braced for danger on every corner as she looped stories
about all di wickid people, lawd have mercy . . .
Then changed the subject, hid inside sleep, a signal for us to forget
about a too-small concrete cube, lashings that let blood for every
misstep, a boy with an ice pick prying through the roof, and scandal
upon scandal. "What won't a big, dirty man do?"
But the story of us is alive, won't be smothered, won't allow us
to forget. Us new-world birds still looking for our own nest.
We fly in our dreams to worlds mapped in our bones, pulled by the need
to know who all make we, truly. Truth trickles up through the skin,
the throat, the aching back. We must act.
Them that is we will not let us forget, want us to know they are the doorway
through which we see, want us to look at the whole thing, find the names
that turn a key to the place where we are not alone, the path
to find our way home, whole.

Mama Lovie

born in 1898
This one will be bright, she say,
swaying with di fat red baby on her jagged hip
under cool Kingston verandah
Mama Lovie, a tall and lean bamboo
Fulani face lost at sea,
skin all midnight and sinew by then
hair, a silver halo parted and pulled back neat
keep the great-grandbaby close
This little one not gon be like dem wild leggobeast
deh bout di yard
who nuh have no ambition
She nuh go be fool fool pickney
This one will win the scholarship
won't wear no red dirt covered shoes
or answer to first name or
come here or
stupid fool or
no! no! no! or
useless black gyal
She won't pick up after English children
who are always Master and Missus
when they call her Iris
Won't bring home the bread ends they don't want
so there can be S.O.S.— "Save Our Souls"—
dinner for the 10 here now
who always want/need
and sleep head-to-foot in two rooms
No, dis little baby won't push and squeeze onto dutty Kingston bus
in frayed, sun-bleached dress
just to go scrub floors into senility,
collect a pittance and then
be cast out one day like a racehorse
ready to become glue
No, dis girl gon leave di tenement yard,
for good

MALIK ABDUH

I am a poet, essayist, and short story writer. I earned an MFA in Creative Writing from Rutgers University-Camden in 2009. Currently, I teach English at Rowan College at Burlington County in Southern New Jersey. My work appears in several journals and magazines, including *Southern Indiana Review, Four Way Review, Exit 7, Some Call it Ballin' Magazine*, and *Platform Review*. My debut collection, *All the Stars Aflame*, was published by Get Fresh Books Publishing (2022).

Two Strikes

The outfielders took their positions, while the infielders fired the ball around the bases. Redds adjusted his cap and looked out from the dugout. The clouds beyond center field had turned black as furnace smoke. "Gon' come down, look like," he said. "They might call it."

"That your excuse for droppin' fly balls," Jimmer said.

Redds spit a brown glob near his catcher's foot. "Catch that, Jimmer, hear?"

This was Redds's third season with the Mobile Black Roosters, but he and Jimmer had barnstormed together for years. A well-known journeyman, Redds had played for six or seven different teams throughout his career. He moved wherever the biggest payday took him. But since Branch Rickey and the Dodgers integrated major league baseball, it became the only real payday, and Redds had tried out for almost every team there was. He knew—everyone did—the Negro leagues were all but done. The legendary players, the top draws, all went with the money and prestige of the Yankees, Giants, White Sox. Redds wasn't complaining much about guys leaving for the majors, just about not being one of them.

Jimmer pulled off his catcher's mask and wiped the sweat from the folds of fat on the back of his neck. "Can't get an angle on Blackburn to save my life. He don't talk about much other than baseball."

Redds pulled his cap over his eyes and shrugged his shoulders. "Why it matter to you? Long as he say what needs sayin' come payday."

Next to Josh Gibson, or maybe Pete Hill, Redds Green was once considered one of the best hitters in the Negro leagues, early on averaging a home run every 13 at-bats. But between getting on in years, and an incident with a white woman outside of St. Louis, most teams wouldn't sign him.

Redds stood up and picked up two bats with each hand and swung them around. "Big man can hit with either hand," Jimmer said.

"What they call double-barrels," Redds replied.

"You up, Redds," Blackburn said.

Shorty Blackburn was the Rooster's owner and manager. No one knew exactly how long he'd been around, but the joke was that he was old enough to have played with white players before Cap Anson helped segregate the game.

"How old you suppose Blackburn really is?" Jimmer said.

"Older than Satch, I guess."

"Shiit, ain't nobody that old. Who tossin'?" Jimmer called out to Blackburn.

Blackburn turned his head slowly and looked at him, squinting. "You'll find out when you stop talkin' and start catchin'."

Blackburn put his fingers in his mouth and let out a sharp whistle that carried across the field. A coach near the rear fence looked up. Blackburn nodded and spat out a mouth full of sunflower seed shells. "Tinsy!" The coach nodded back and turned to the bullpen. A woman, wearing the Rooster's white uniform and black insignia, with the number 20 next to it, sprinted across the field. She couldn't have been more than five foot-two, and no more than a hundred pounds carrying a bag of bats and balls. When she reached the mound, she jabbed her glove a few times then twisted her fist into its leather.

"That Tinsy Smith…from the Stars?" Jimmer said.

"That'd be her," Blackburn said.

"When she get here?"

"Night 'fore last."

"Aw, man, you better hope she ain't hear all that talk of yours, Redds. She liable to put a mud ball right between your eyes," Jimmer said.

Redds bent over and snatched up a few blades of grass. "Man, she ain't stirrin' no grits out on that mound. She preparin' to throw at Redds Green."

"Just be careful she don't stir your grits. You know she put Gibson on his ass once or twice."

"Old wives' tales. But I tell you what, put that church 'cross the road on notice. May need some new stained glass after this."

Redds stepped on the field swinging the bats. He dropped one by the baseline and tapped his cleats with the other. He stood for a moment and watched Tinsy warm up. He'd seen her barnstorming a season or two and knew that a batter had as good a chance of hitting Pluto as he did of hitting one of her pitches. "The bride of Satchel Paige," they called her. Satchel called her "Ms. Duncan," because she could make a ball drop over the plate like a yo-yo. She tossed a few warm-up pitches to Jimmer. Each time the ball cracked in his glove and echoed through the park.

"Don't know about no stained glass, Redds, but I may need a new glove 'fore it's over," Jimmer said laughing.

"You up," Blackburn barked.

Redds stepped to the plate, kicked the dirt around, and dug into position. He looked up at Tinsy. She had her back to him rolling a rosin bag through her fingers. She was looking off into the dark clouds past centerfield. She rolled her right shoulder and turned around with a wide grin on her face.

"You settled in, mister?" she said.

"Good to see someone learnt you some manners," Redds said.

"Taught some, too," Tinsy said.

"This ain't charm school, I'm afraid."

"No sir, this here is finishing school."

Jimmer pulled his mask over his face and struck his glove with his fist. "Strike out, and drinks on you tonight, Redds," he said.

Redds crouched down, tapped his bat on the plate a few times and then brought it up by his ear, choking up on the bat like he was breaking a chicken's neck. Out on the mound, Tinsy leaned forward slightly. Her glove lay on the side of her left leg, the ball cupped in the other hand behind her back. She brought the ball into her glove, kicked up her left leg and released the ball like a slingshot. Redds watched it hurl towards the plate. A seasoned hitter like him knew not to hit where it was, but where it would be. He shifted his weight and swung at it. In his eyes it looked big as a full moon, but once it got to the plate, it jerked and dropped under the swing and down into Jimmer's glove.

"Comin' at ya!" Jimmer said.

Redds straightened up and shimmied his shoulders as if a chill ran down his back. "That was a warm up, little lady."

"I know. I felt the warm breeze out here," Tinsy said.

She caught the ball and rolled it around in her fingers, went back into her stance and threw again. This time Redds caught a piece of it and hit it foul.

"Next one has my name on it," Redds said.

"You must spell that with a K," Tinsy said.

Redds bent at the knees and straightened his shoulders. There were beads of sweat popping up on his forehead. He shot up from his crouched position, waved his hand and stretched his arm.

"One of them Charlie horses, big man?" Jimmer said.

"Even a canon need greasin' from time to time, junior," Redds said.

He stepped back over the plate and spread his legs and held the bat up in the air behind his head. He bent down again into hitting position. Tinsy lowered her head and smirked. She wound up, kicked up her left leg and threw a hard fastball straight at the plate. Redds turned at the hips and swung like he was trying to chop down a redwood. Jimmer's glove exploded in a cloud of dust. He shot up and fired the ball off to the third baseman. Redds stumbled a bit and caught his balance. Standing up straight, he let out a loud grunt.

"Goddamned Tinsy Smith!"

"I hear drinks on you tonight," she said.

Redds took off his cap and waved it at her. "Yeah, but no bubbly," he said. "Cause we ain't celebratin."

***

THE NIGHTCLUB was packed floor to ceiling: ball players, musicians, local politicians—even clergy—were either on the dance floor, at a table, or by the bar ordering drinks. Redds and Jimmer were sitting at their regular table near the front of the room next to the bar. They had ordered and were waiting for Tinsy to come back from the bathroom.

"Good thing you buyin', Redds. I'm quite parched tonight."

"Aw, hush up, Jimmer. Ain't no different than all them nights you forgot your wallet back at the room."

Jimmer picked up his drink and slowly lifted it to his mouth. "It just taste better when you buyin', Redds."

Tinsy came back and sat down. "We ain't come all the way down here to nurse that one bottle, Mr. Green," she said.

"Yeah, yeah, yeah."

He poured the last of the bottle into Tinsy's glass.

"I hear you from Virginia?" Jimmer said.

"Born in Norfolk. But we moved north not long after. My momma found work teaching in Philly."

"That's where you come across baseball?" Jimmer said.

"Yeah, sandlot games. Walked on and asked 'em just two questions.

Did they accept coloreds on the team? They said they hadn't, but wasn't opposed to it. Then I asked could a girl join the team, and since they couldn't find no regulation preventing it, they let me sign up."

"Why baseball?" Redds said.

"What kind of—"

"Now don't get all in a fuss. Ain't like it's been any other womenfolk in the game."

"Have you ever looked up in the stands? Whole lot of us at the park. Just y'all like it better when we clapping for you instead of throwing at you."

"I bet Redds sure wish you had been in the stands clappin' today," Jimmer said.

"Do you ever quit yappin', Jimmer?" Redds said.

"Hard to yap with a glass to my lips."

"Another round then."

Jimmer got up from his seat, picked up the bottle and headed towards the bar. He grabbed a waitress by both hands and began to lead her in a tango. Redds took a drink from his glass and slammed it back on the table. Taking a long pull on a cigarette, he gestured to Tinsy.

"You played in the All-Women's League before this, didn't you?"

"Tried out. Me and two other friends. But they let us know with no hesitation that them teams wasn't for colored girls. Ain't that something? White men don't want them, and they don't want us. I asked them straight. Ain't I a woman? But I may be asking the wrong person. I heard all about your...*indiscretions.*"

"Old wives' tales. I swear before the good Lord. You see me with anything but a colored girl, I'm just givin' her directions. My momma would turn in her grave if I mixed like that."

"You ought to be more worried about turning in your own grave, you keep it up." She sipped her drink. "So why you not playing in the big leagues?"

Redds leaned back in his chair lifting the front legs off the ground. He thought she meant he was too old, or worse, not good enough to make it in the major leagues.

"Shoot, I ain't studyin' them white folks like that. I hit the ball, and fans cheer. What make the sound of white hands clappin' more satisfyin'?"

"I guess someone tell you that you should want something long enough, you start believing it. For me, it wasn't about wanting to play with white folks, just wanted to play. Where else was I gon' go?" Tinsy said.

Two Strikes   253

"Well, you here."

"Wasn't no red carpets rolled out in the colored leagues neither. I had to throw like I was David with Goliath at the plate to make it on the Stars.

"Well, least you made it."

Redds watched Tinsy's face as she sipped her drink. She had a cocoa complexion, with tiny freckle-like moles on her cheeks. Wearing a black felt hat with peacock feathers, he thought she looked more like a jazz singer than the woman who almost made him throw out his hip earlier that day.

"I'm done worryin' bout them white leagues," he said.

"Then why you still addressing it?"

"Say what now?"

"I believe that a person who says he's not worried about something, but always mentioning that something, ain't worried about much else." She sighed.

"Listen, since I was small, I wanted to play baseball. Wasn't bout colored or white, majors or otherwise, cause my kind wasn't to be found in either place. And just so you know, I am worried about it. An awful lot."

"You thought much on the fact that ol' Satch—best there ever was— was passed over almost a year 'fore they decided to let him in?" Redds said. "Gibson died 'fore he even had a chance to dent car hoods in the parkin' lot up Yankees Stadium. You think you got a chance in hell to play with them? I reckon they'd let Mamie Eisenhower play 'fore you."

"Did you ever reckon I would be on the mound in front of you? Odds ain't never been even for me. But like you said, 'Here I am.'"

Redds looked up and saw Jimmer bumping through the crowd rushing back over to the table. On his heels was the Black Roosters' shortstop Eldridge Beale. Everyone called him Sleep Dog on account of his lazy eye. Jimmer's face was bunched up.

"Tell 'em what you just told me, Sleep," Jimmer said.

"I just come from over Rose Marie Manor and—"

"Blackburn dropped dead over at Rose Marie Manor," Jimmer said. Redds sat up and put his glass on the table and loosened his tie. "Say what now? How's that?"

"Looks like a heart attack, Doc saying," Sleep Dog said.

Tinsy put her hand over mouth and shook her head. Redds knew the news would hit her especially hard. It was Blackburn who'd found her and fought for her around the league.

"You all right?" Reds said. She nodded, but said nothing.

***

BIGHT MORNING STAR was one of the oldest Baptist churches in Mobile. It was a stone building that stood on an incline right off Main St. Inside, there were two rows of long wood pews on opposite sides of the church, not one of them empty for Blackburn's home going. The church was hot as a BBQ pit, and the basement kitchen had it smelling like one. Reverend Walcott was slumped down in his huge oak chair beside the pulpit leafing through his Bible. He sometimes worked the games as an umpire in Mobile, and Blackburn had despised him. Redds thought about how Blackburn used to cuss at Walcott's calls, so during the sermon, he was sure Blackburn would roll out of his casket. Redds sat in the third row between Jimmer and Tinsy. Like the other women in the pews, she sat waving hot air in her face with a church fan. Lying in an open casket at the head of the church, Blackburn was dressed in a gray pinstriped suit with a burgundy tie. Everyone mentioned how good he looked. Redds had rarely seen him without his uniform and wondered why they didn't just bury him in it.

"What Walcott mean we may not all make it to home plate, but we all goin' home?" Jimmer said.

"He sayin' every soul gon' taste death, Jimmer. We all got an appointed time."

"So why not just say that? That's why I don't come to church. Can't stand a whole lot of double talk. Don't know nothin' bout no River Jordan. He never heard of the Mississippi?"

"Mind yourself, Jimmer," Tinsy said. She stood up and shuffled her way out of the pew and hastened down the aisle and out the doors. Redds gave Jimmer a hard look. "Watch out," he said. "This probably Blackburn first time in a church anyway," Jimmer mumbled. Redds got up and followed after Tinsy. He found her sitting on one of the benches in the church's yard, scraping at the wood with her thumbnail.

"Jimmer, or Walcott's sermon run you out of there?"

"You know, Mr. Blackburn, he was the first to see me as a ball player, not some daughter. A ball player. Met him when he was in Philly with the All-Stars for a couple weeks, and somehow, he got word about me. Came down to our little sandlot for almost a whole week. I knew he was somebody, cause no one came to that raggedy field that clean. I threw so hard every game till I couldn't lift my arm to brush my teeth by the end of the week. He came up and asked if I was interested in trying out for the Black Roosters' All-Stars. I said, what you think I been doing here all this time? He wasn't a jovial man by no stretch. But he laughed hard at that. Well, I went down a few days later to try out, and them players stared at me like a squirrel had run out to the mound. Shorty just nodded, and I struck out every batter they put in front of me. They was probably expecting some underhand softball pitches, but I was giving them Sunday sermon fire and brimstone right across the plate. And Shorty, he would just give that curled up smirk of his." She sighed and looked over towards the church doors.

"Hell. With all due respect, Blackburn got out at the right time," Redds said.

"Leagues is all but gone. Nothin' left but a few traveling teams. Some days it's more players on the field than folks in the stands. White leagues got all the money, and from what I hear it's greener." Redds smiled and fingered the knot of his tie. Looking up in the sky, he laughed. "Saddest part, the good ole' days wasn't so good neither. Don't know how many times I had to collect my pay with a straight razor. 'Cept from Blackburn. Man kept his word…when he could. Widow already talkin' bout shuttin' it down and countin' her losses, I hear. Can't blame her."

"So, what you gon' do for yourself now?" Tinsy said.

"Damned if I got a clue. I'll let you know after I drink on it a while. You?"

Tinsy shrugged her shoulders. "You know, when they let Jackie Robinson in, I was so proud, so happy. Then in the same moment, this other feeling come over me. They might have integrated the majors, but that was only for half of us. If the man invisible, what that make the woman standing
behind him?"

The organ groaned, and the voices of the choir rose:

The big bell's tolling in Galilee.
Ain't going to tarry here.

Jimmer came out the church. He lit a cigarette and walked toward Redds and Tinsy, gesturing with his hand in a drinking motion.

"I'm going back in and finish paying my respects," Tinsy said. "I'll talk to you at the repass."

"Well, Ms. Smith," Redds said standing up, "one good thing come from of all this. I won't have to buy no more drinks on account of them yo-yos of yours." Half-smiling, he wiped beads of sweat from his forehead with a handkerchief.

Ain't going to tarry here...

PAULETTE PENNINGTON JONES

Paulette Pennington Jones is Professor Emerita of City Colleges of Chicago. She is a graduate of the University of Illinois Champaign-Urbana with a MA. in the Teaching of English. During the Chicago Black Arts Movement Professor Pennington Jones wrote/performed with Dark Meditations Writer's Workshop convened by Useni Eugene Perkins and also authored the *Checklist for Theatre Quarterly: No.18* Amiri Baraka, London 1978.

detail of
 flying african survival song for for baba useni eugene perkin
            dark and bright meditation

this
this is
this is a
this is a flying
this is a flying african
this is a flying african survival
this is a flying african survival song
this is a flying african survival song for our griot useni
in the beginning
was the word
and the word was love
and the word was life
and we became the word
in nommo spirit
we rise
in nommo spirit
we fly
in imani spirit
we fly
away
in imani spirit

detail of
flying african survival song

faith futures us
with our faith
we are lifted
in flight
in our faith
we levitate
in harmony
the energies are coalesced
the manifestation of love, of life
we be

the greening of ourselves
became the raffia grasses
that he dances upon
zooming
transforming ringing winding
zinging
yeah, red
the red lips of sharon
whispering on useni's strong neck
the rose of sharon encouraging
stretching out on faith
big baba useni writing
and reciting poetry
plays, essays,
drama, drafts, documents,
articles, answers, characters, collections,
speeches, skits, scripts, volumes, tomes,
letters, lyrics, lists, journals, jots,
books,
even classroom texts
the guerrilla teacher learning
the guerrilla student teaching
deep in the bush
high on the mountain
all across the continent
close to the delivery of instruction
keep the sacred lip
unbruised yet blushed with

the sunsets of fire
in qunu flaming hope
spear of the nation
at the golden close of day
shouting i am a poet
an african cultural conductor
founder, supporter, poetic producer
wise convener, leader, master teacher
exuding always black love and feeling
advisor, instructor, lesson preparer
superior director who urges, guides, opens,
walking with the ancestors
working with the ancestors
we are our ancestors
multitudes within
shooting star griot
the lover useni
wailing the blues of baraka
in his own kind of way
no misery striding to the boat
body waters in rhythm,
in synch, in the pocket
in king's horseman's style
big bold brave body sway way
yet,
languid lagoon hurricane man useni
his motion moves the tall prairie grasses
heads toward the horizon of open sea
transforms into rushing oceans
being tilted on the axis of the
african world
you represent yourself
your selves
your mother eva, your father marion,
your brothers touissant and robert, your cousins here
andstill on the continent
the artists, the sculptors, the painters,
the musicians, the singers, the wailers,
the carvers, the dancers, the healers,

detail of
flying african survival song

the doctors, the photographers, the illustrators,
the portraitists, the directors, the auteurs,
the engravers, the molders, the potters,
the designers, the planners, the curators,
the surrealists, the romantics, the realists,
the yogis, the writers,
the creatives
making love with materials
casting magic and mojos
that carry us home

your black arts move
your entire gorgeous race
africans all
bringing the good news
good god news
speaking the language
the black arts language
talking loud and saying something
speaking tongues to truth
that people understand
understanding your people
defining racism
speaking good news
of the ancestors
speaking in tongues
talking loud saying something
walking with the ancestors
working with the ancestors
we are our ancestors
multitudes within
big baba useni talking
thank god for building ritual…
for establishing legacy
pharoah useni wraped in cowrie shells
tall spirit warrior man
sing unto the lord
for he has triumphed gloriously

roars soars home
talking about survival
talking about a rainbow
talking about a nommo
a rainbow nommo
a rainbow nommo brother
the colors of our people
as in our brownness
as in our blackness

and in the blackness of our nommo spirit
and in the darkness of our imani meditation
the candle flame flickers
the afro cuban heart beats
the levitation
rushes to the rise
and baba useni eugene perkins has survived
in us all
singing useni's flying
singing useni's flying african
singing useni's flying african survival
singing useni's flying african survival song

circa summer 2023

cynthia sequence
for our sister zubena filled with words

cynthia sequence
              detail from part 1
everywhere i go
i go for her
carrying herself with myself
feeling leaves
four hands
  twenty nails of feeling
and infinitesimal cells
being constantly
recreated in me
me and my sister
2017

cynthia sequence
                day is too small

it was snowing
when she died
as not
the predicted blizzard
sweeps into town
after morning of 24°
warm to black men
who are blanketed by chill
factors of -67° winds
gusts of 50 miles perhour
drifts
on doris's day
of birth and searching
her lines are busy
she hurls herself headlong
toward the blizzard
trailing through snows

walking headlong herself
her way
through thunder and
lightening and
snow
cause alex haley is a 50 year old black man
worth a fantasy
and certainly a social studies lesson
the life of a black man
worth a unit in school til june
alex haley is here and now
'77
our new consumer products
affect the aged antique
even a teapot cannot stay
and burning pots are cyclic
not for us, not the gentle
going home in slow and easy stages

but roots—t.v.ized
comes down too heavy
the white mentality: an addition
not easily stomached
the perversity wallowed-in
76 counts of incest
in preference to feeling,
personal communication, sharing
our tradition, our heritage
buried deep inside
the quasar color
the gloss
at least all the black folks
in hollywood is working
and we are a pretty people
but searching
searching for
something
something more
it is easy to slip
across the lubricated chasm
so readily, inaccurately called death
we are born
we continue our habitual be

we move on
within the cold
snow silence
but what if
anything is possible today,
because it's cynthia's?

28 january 1977

cynthia sequence
                a winning
cynthia and buffy st. marie
singing china blue
the folksinger in all of us

starry, starry night
like strangers that you've met
summer of sould could have had history
if we had played for keeps
sisterly competition
is ugly and feudalism
my mother and my aunts
know
i'm the only on who is
ignorant
the 13 is worse than
playing for money
gamblers never play
on a glass table
the queen of spades
is the antithesis of the
the queen of hearts
put your collar
on with aretha franklin
churching on a monday night
with our heads covered
her death had something to do
with being a woman
singing china blue

going down low
don't get caught
you learn by playing
teaching about the connection
chants/gospel rhythm/blues
on cobblestones and
moist humus soil
i'd have fear
if i had to attack with hostility
"you can have it"
trying to win so hard
didn't know what was happening
it remains to be seen
who has had the grits thrown

on them
.1 montego bay
you gotta have the attitude of a winner
to win
the beautiful brother bartering
light to shadow
shadow to light
we're both taking a beating
in terms of our times
just clean water
to tickle our children
eye and eye
       jnt
it is our fullness
the fullness of the eye
in the creator
      lord of lords
teachment take time
oh lion of judah
       judas didn't have to die
       but he couldn't have the lead role
the black man
stole de show
ashoreing the west indies
of my brothers
sitting up straight
we've got to find a way
be being some loving
if the d.j.'s know this much
are of knowledge

what's going on in duet
for more danger
the glint causer of my eye
high stakes at all costs
with any body
the thrill of the game
the beautiful bartering
hemingway was a child

in the meadow bartering
with the wind
while brother barter
in blood and thunder
lightening
blackness
our beautiful bartering
innocent and naive
street brother
it goes through
you know how it feels
when it goes through
do everything that needs to be done
each sunset will put you
nearer the goal
everywhere i go
i go for her
carrying herself with myself
feeling leaves
four hands
  twenty nails of feeling
and infinitesimal cells
being constantly
recreated in me
me and my sister
as you are accosted
on all sorts
of other levels
moats stocked
with songs of my father
inside i'm locked

this is my first affair
please be kind
intonations of childhood
do you want me tonight
with my veil just below my eyes
or as ellington's sophisticated lady
in satin rehearsal shorts

if they could seeee just
how special you are
they would tree-line
your winning path
what heart can i get under
everyone has their own game
if pennies ain't nothing
take them out of your pocket
momma said
there would be days like this
adding some card scores
on the crisis of
the niggahs and their intellectualism
yawning and yearning for the water
it's not that cold
but the tarantula is in there
rules are created
the scary stuff is past
you cannot quit
do not dare turn back
now
looking out to sea
asking for knowledge
            down the road read
            burma-shave-series-style
what we have absorbed
of the father lands' soils:

going away is a form
of winning
it is; i swear to you
oh lover, abstracted
(my language does not
allow me to
deal with you
any other way)
same time; same space
the muslim sister
in the form of

cynthia as lover of ghalib
circa 1792 and circa 1972
                              circa 2023

Addendum
Sister Zubena/Cynthia McDearmon Conley:

Sister Zubena was a writer and performer in the Chicago Black Arts Renaissance. She was a member of Dark Meditations workshop, meeting at the historic South Side Commuity Arts Center, convened by Useni Perkins in the late 60's.

Sister Zubena authored three poetry chapbooksCalling All Sisters, Om Black, and posthumously self published God's Child her poetic memoir. She is included in several Blacks Arts era anthologies.

Her poems spotlight quotidian african american life that value our experiences with family and community. Rarely recognized Cynthia McDearmon Conley was born in Chicago, the midwest/heartland, 9 October 1945 and at her appointed time joined the ancestors 28 January 1972.

a toast to the people
                    for queen mother sister frankie davis at 101

the sound
it always opens with the sound
of ocean waves lapping
and sisters speaking
creating the narrative
telling our story
a good good story filled with details
in a warm kitchen
a black woman could produce art
prove worth
in action and sound
in a phyllis wheatley moment
she believes
in promises fulfilled
prayers answered
fruit blossoming

thank you expressed
gratitude manifest
praise rising
woman meditation moment
the minister wears
double dark indigo robe
for first sunday
the choir
the members
the guests
all reach want need to touch her hand
as they walk the center aisle
back from the communion alter
silver filligree jewelry
she deserves
rings on many fingers
earrings dangling and waving
greetings of welcome and love
she has dreamed dreams

seen visions
pored out the spirit of our god
as her love flows it grows
in our bronzeville home our
african methodist episcopal zion church
my pew partner prays a no chains legacy
she be our shining example
queen mother sister frankie davis
a toast for mother frankie davis
we now
stand as one
raise our voices
and say
"long years have passed
memories hold fast
essence of a black life
unlost
uncaught in the hour glass
beautiful black mothers

beautiful black sisters
beautiful back daughters"
the essence of black life
voices of children's laughter
this toast ends with freedom

she flies
pageant sister
smooth and smiling
like a feathered wing bird
in a fashionable chapeau of resilience
she makes
dookie chase meals of fried chicken red rice
with green beans love
facing and frying the yes
to all black people
she speaks
gingham wisdom suggestions and statements
she has dreamed dreams
seen visions
pored out the spirit of our god

she lives
disobeying bad law
with defiance and determination
a toast to the people
whose memories hold fast
she lives
the essence of all black people
this toast ends with freedom

SYVILLA WOODS

Syvilla Woods is a Black cultural activist and educator of African-American children for 50 years. A writer of songs, poetry, and plays for children, as well as a mediator for violence prevention. Although she was born in Chicago, her travel includes many destinations throughout the African Diaspora. Syvilla continues thriving through The Blessings of Allah and her Ancestors, particularly, her loving parents. She is most proud of her late Beautiful, African Warrior husband, Arto. She is also proud of her children and grandchildren.

All Praises to African Women Everywhere

Tall Spirit AFRICAN Warrior Women
Walk Among Us Everyday
Gentle Yet Giant Footsteps
Bringing Us Ever Close to Our Rebirth.
Rebirth, The Rebuilding of,
The Rekindling of Red-Hot Embers,
Now Simmering,
Not Remembering.
So, It Takes Another Haile
Gerima This Time To
"Sakofa,"
"Sakofa" Us Back on Wide Birdwings.
To Make Us Remember That Our Fires Always,
Always Burn Bright!!!
That Our Hopes for Our People, Ourselves, Our Children, Are Never
Far
From The Light, The Truth;
The Arms That Carry Us.
The Tall Spirit, Warrior WomenLike My Sista Paula Wright Coleman,
Like Queen Mother Moore,
Like Our Mother Eleanor Tidwell, Like Bernice Hite
And Our Aunt Shera, Like
BeSy Naylor,
Like Willa Bentley and All of Her Daughters.
Like Your Mothers and GrandMothers. Speak Their
Names. Ashe.'
Like Dr BeSy Shabazz, Like Paula Wright Coleman,

All Praises to African Women Everywhere   271

Tireless Worker Warrior Woman, Making A Quilt Out of The African
Diaspora,
Like My Shero Fannie Lou Hamer, Like My Sista Jackie
Like All Our Nanas.
Say Ashe' Somebody!!!
Like Sista Egypt, Sista Doris,
Inshirah and Jean
And My Blood Sistas
Sandra and Jackie,
Say Your Name. Say Yo
Mama's Name, Your
Daughter's Name!!!
Don't Forget Harriet Tubman and Sojourner
Truth, Kamala Harris, and CongressWoman Maxime
Waters Up on The Hill,
And Any and Every Black Activist, Political and Cultural Warrior
Woman
That you have Known.
ALL, ALL, ALL!!!
Praises To AFRICAN WARRIOR WOMEN EVERYWHERE!!!
LIKE MY SISTA Paula Wright Coleman
                    ASHE'

COLE EUBANKS

Cole Eubanks of Mays Landing NJ, an African-American, is retired as an
educator from the Philadelphia (PA) and Atlantic City (NJ) School Districts.
He is Pushcart nominated and a 7x winner of Nick Virgilio's Haiku in Action
Gallery. His work can be found in: *Apiary, F(r)iction, Shamrock, Jalmurra, ,
MiGoZine, Peter Murphy Publishing of Stockton University, Sugar House Review*,
and many other journals and anthologies.

Driving South

> *We used owl calls to signal on the Underground Railroad.*
> -Harriet Tubman

Last night I heard the cello-moan

of that hoot owl again.

Most evenings it sounds like
Pablo Casals, but this time

he was my dead father humming
Italian opera. We rode arias from:

Aida, Tosca, and Pagliacci
straight through to Maryland.

The second he crossed
The Mason Dixon,

the curtain came down.

What Kind of Blue?
after the Blue Note Album Cover of John Coltrane's Blue Train

A blue tinted photograph of John from the shoulders up
The background: dark-blue nothingness.
 Floating out of the bottom right corner
—blue cobra-neck of John's alto sax seeking his mouth.

John's relaxed right fist alights chin—index finger rests on lower lip
—wide-set eyes cast down like he is looking at the river of life.
His left arm reaches behind to grasp his neck—a temporary lid keeping in
all he witnesses in deep exploration of inner-space.

Is this titled *Blue Train* because in April, Miles said, *Motherfucker get
the fuck out of my band with your heroin ways* because he was *Kind of Blue?*
Those words transformed John to a cold turkey with his head in the toilet
—Only to rise in mere weeks—a phoenix from the ashes of his music.

Considered a gifted young lion before he crashed
—his performance here rockets him to the pantheon of jazz.
This was September. How could a spring-time addict fall into godhood?
No, this is not a *blue* of weakness. On the album cover he spells his name T-R-A-I-

EWUARE OSAYANDE

Ewuare X. Osayande is a poet and author of several books including Blood Luxury with an introduction by Amiri Baraka and Whose America? with an introduction by Haki R. Madhubuti. His latest book is entitled Our Breath is the Whisper of Our Ancestors' Defiance: The Poetry Anthology (1993-2023). He is founding editor of The Poetariat, an international social justice poetry journal. He currently resides in D.C. where he is completing a Juris Doctorate.

The Underground Railroad

the ground under our feet
was the tracks that led us to freedom

the ground under our feet
was the tracks that led us to freedom

ground under
ground under
ground railroad.

Moses got her heat on her side
her metal rod to part the waters wide
to steal away
steal away plantation's prisoners
moseying on down to the river
yes
ain't no turning back Black
this here be a one-way ticket
out of the most wicked system ever devised
just keep your eyes on the drinking gourd
and your mind stayed on the Lord

the Underground Railroad carrying a precious load
black gold
our human souls
spirit-combustion
kept this train a-moving

this here Soul Train
was not a Don Cornelius syndicated lip-syncing production
this here train was black-black
black as Coltrane
engine screaming

"bant
baaaaaaaaaa
aaaaaaaaaaaaaaaaaaaaa
aaaaaaaaaaaaaaaaaannn
nnnnnnnnnnnnn"

moving to a rhythm of   "A Love Supreme"
doom doom   doom doom
doom doom   doom doom
doom doom   doom doom
doom doom   doom doom

with a Bessie Smith blues riff
belting out the smokestack
had hell hounds hot on our tracks
looking for familiar marks
on the barks of trees
ancient graffiti
aerosoled on the massa's mansion walls

The Underground
Nat Turner's hideaway
original fugitives
holding counsel with Ogun
machete machinations
creating our own briar patch
where the lash couldn't catch us

we was brer rabbit
outfoxing the fox on his plantation
singing songs and picking cotton
all the while plotting rebellion

The Underground Railroad

is John Henry
born with a hammer in his hand
Black labor resisting them robber barons' laying down the rail
wailing like Fannie Lou
bout being sick and tired of being sick and tired refusing to lose
seeking refuge from water hoses and billy clubs
seeking refuge for New World refugees
refused citizenry
Africa's dispersed and despised
a diaspora of outcasts and aliens
marooned on the island of invisibility
The Bermuda Triangular Slave Trade
paradise lost to pirates
with the skull and cross-bones
of the Arawak and the Carib
buried in their flag

The Underground
where James Brown found
the camelwalk-ing across the Sahara and talked that talk
that only Fela Kuti could stand under
and dig his way out of the quicksand of colonialism
and resurrect the sound of black rage
from Negritude to rude boy attitude
the link between Marcus Garvey and Bob Marley
"there's a natural mystic blowing through the air,
if you listen carefully now you will hear"
Garvey's ghost in the whirlwind and the storm
whistling Africa's redemption is near

and over here
Jimi Hendrix is taking his ax to the flag
reappropriating national sounds and symbols
with guitar picks and tongue licks
the stars for the ones we followed in our midnight flights
the stripes for the whips that marked our backs like branches
the red for our blood shed
the white for our oppressors
and the blues

see the blues be our indigo-stained sorrow
hear him chopping down white cultural dominance
in 68 Olympic proportions
with the learned defiance
in Angela Davis' Black Power fist
that made the hit list
not Billboard's Top Ten
but the FBI's Most Wanted

The Underground as Panthers' lair the Railroad,
how Assata escaped
is now hip hop running for its life
bleeding black feet frost-bitten
breakdancing in a winter wonderland broken
being hounded by vanilla-iced snowmen and frosted eminems
dreaming of a white Christmas
so they can unwrap rap
and go digging in the crates of our story
and sample our very souls
and bite our very being

The Underground is our culture crying out to be free
in double-entendre self-determinations
is the mystery never solved
how we still around
how we
morph
adapt
change
evolve revolve
and revolt

we are the practice that precedes the theory
we are the fact that
we will never be satisfied with not being free
that this train won't stop
til we is free
til we is free
til we is see

getting to the North ain't far enough
til we arrive at that station marked Liberation

doom doom   doom doom
doom doom   doom doom

Next Stop: Reparations

ERIK ANDRADE

Erik Andrade has made impactful contributions to the world as a father, an international organizer, poet, fashion designer, environmental justice educator, leadership development educator, graphic designer, videographer, TED talk presenter, political candidate, disrupter of negative power, thought leader, and founder of La Soul Renaissance. Erik has presented internationally in Standing Rock, Cuba, Canada, Cabo Verde, and all over the United States. Erik featured at Indigenous Peoples Day NYC in 2019 - 2022, the NYC Poetry Festival in 2021 & 2022, and for Jewish Voice for Peace's 2020 Poets For Palestine: Honoring The Nakba & 2021 Boston Hanukkah Event: "Artists Against Apartheid"

Black Magic

Black Boys can
turn to Black Men
who bend
but don't fold
see our magic
we hold in our
inner alchemy
from within the inner
balcony above hate
and love escape
like dove
transcend duality
at peace with
your reality
never cornered
nor blocked

by the corner
or block limits
on your mentality
no more mourning
our immortality
be more moral
paint a mural
where we would
mend our broken
men and then
we can transcend
and end the
tragic trauma
dramatic healing hurt
heart voids
in our mama
Oh Moon
Mother Oshun
please tell
Father Ogun
to let our words
heal old wounds
create spells
that expel all hell
as all hail
wise wisdom
jewels fell
enlightening
even fools
to lead our suns
and daughters
to rebel from
negativity's prison
learning to unlearn
and in turn transform
divisions break free
from social norms
that don't live
and let live

Black Magic

outperform vision of
chaos turn it to order
own our own borders
make magical orders
bound by righteous
laws of Maat
grow smart then
teach smarter
be no martyr
see our suns
and daughters
need fathers
that have seen farther
no need for greed
evil or egos our ethos
is love be and see
equals men bend
but don't falter
solid as a rock
a modern Gibraltar
having the heart
to garden a modern
movement centered
in art of self
improvement imagine
the magic of being
able to change
your mind
incepting a vision
divine like Malcolm
yet manifest a
diferent outcome
dream King, X,
Afeni and Assata
helping Mutulu to
father Tupac who
taught art and unity
to outlaws and
bad boys who grew

to notoriously big
movements of love
peace and community
Black magic is
Black unity plus
the freedom
to dream
you see
you and me
Black boys
and men if
we can feel
deal and heal
we'll realize then
reveal we have
been kings
And a role
For our soul
is to listen
to Respect
and to protect
all children
elders and
QUEENS

Where Do We Go?

where do we go when
we can't afford the "ghetto"?
From New Bedford to Soweto
historically segregated
and hated we are the "blight"
they rewrite outside the margins
marginalized by institutional
racism and real estate bargains
and yet if we speak of the oppression
hoping to reach and to teach lessons
we are seen as "complainers"

that are less important
explaining the pain away
as just some vain "whiners"
who don't take the time
to define solutions well
how about not contributing
to the uprooting of community
and what about solidarity
and unity or listening to the voice
of the "voiceless" or not making
the choice to ignore the impact
on those made poor by the war
on black, brown, moors, and natives
see genocide and gentrification
are so related they are cousins
and "white fragility" has me bugging
seems some more upset about
shame, blame, and guilt
than the pain that is felt
when the only place oppressed
people can claim is the prisons
they built like concentration camps
as "so called" allies stamp
you as irresponsible and negative
for speaking trying to increase awareness
yet "fragility" makes it hard for some
to hear this seems so many asleep
they must have taken a
sedative and deep is the question
so it bears being repetitive...
where do you go when you
can't afford the "ghetto"?

Vanessa Silva

A first-generation Cabo-Verdean American raised in inner-city Boston, Vanessa Silva is a cultural practitioner, artist, poet, story teller, activist, and organizer. She uses her creative expression to transcend spaces, relate across differences, dismantle structures of domination, and co-create worlds that hold a more just future for humanity, the earth, and all beings. As a co-narrator of a film documentary, her work has been exhibited at the Museum of Fine Arts, Boston, Jeu de Paume in Paris, and the Visual Arts Vienna. She has collaborated with Black Artist Movement pioneers and her focus is in Afro-futurism and new possibilities.

Untitled

If I existed outside of hierarchy and white colonial framing, I would be something that
couldn't fit
So vast I would be
Taking up all the space I could In
My Tall Black
Imagination
Everything would be black and in color
outside of lines.
Everything would exist
Everything would mean something
Everything is.

What do we do with everything?
Where did the secret keepers hide the keys
That unwind time
So far back it reaches present,
What do I have to compare
That doesn't belong to everything
I'm too short to reach

Up is one direction
we can stretch meaning
connection
practice
paradigms where value measure vast
grey
like rain sky
Like fabric
Like poverty
like dots
like ceremony.

ELIJAH PRINGLE

elijah b pringle, III is an internationally published American poet from Philadelphia, PA. His works appears in several international anthology: Compagnia de' Colombari's Whitman on Walls, 99 Poets for the 99 Percent, Selfhood, Moonstone Poetry Ink 25th Anniversary Anthology, and Aquarius Press critical acclaimed anthology on the continuation of the Black Arts Movement – Black Fire This Time. Overall, he has appeared in numerous anthologies and journals. Constantly evolving and exploring, he has maintained a voice that consistently reveals his keen insight into the "human experiment", as he would say.

Washing Stockings: Around Midnight

the same fashion Daddy's arms would rest
on the torn edge of his seldom used easy chair
which sat lonely in a corner trying to be unseen
Mom's arms would rest on the lip of the basin
bending over a sink made white with Comex

water would dance 'tween strong sturdy hands
as she scrubed vigorously 'puff of smoke' stockin's
moving the dirt and dust collected from the week
the fixing the kids for school, the pleasing her man
after the day's work* for money to close the gap

between can't afford and thrift shop buying
second handed stuff getting another chance
the ritual of familiar made us all comfortable
we knew it was Saturday soon to be Sunday
Mommy's feet were bunions and corns then

the bottom of her feet black from walking
barefooted because her shoes were too tight
and so was money and I needed new sneakers
just so the white kids wouldn't laugh at me
or we needed something, always something

but Ivory soap lathers up extremely well
when rubbed against used nylon stockings

about to be glory bound in eight hours
after they had dried in front of the heat vent
even in summer the ritual meant everything

Sheila Smith McKoy

Sheila Smith McKoy is award-winning poet, fiction writer, and filmmaker. She is the recipient of the 2020 Muriel Craft Bailey Memorial Prize in poetry. Her full-length poetry collection, *The Bones Beneath* (Black Lawrence Press, 2024) is described as being "haunting." She is also co-author of *One Window's Light: A Haiku Collection*, a collaboration of five Black poets; the collection won the 2017 Haiku Society of America's Merit Book Award for best haiku anthology. A native of Raleigh, NC, she lives in the San Francisco Bay Area.

Far Enough

The birds were singing outside of Lena Scott's window when she first opened her eyes. Two cardinals were playing in the maple tree beyond her window. The female was the usual drab color of Cardinal women. She was nothing spectacular alongside her mate. Her song, though, was dazzling. The cardinals played together, flirting between the tree limbs, close enough to their nest so that they could watch their chicks. Behind the tree, Feltonsville, their small township, was awakening. Workers waiting for the Kings Peach Orchard truck to take them just outside of Raleigh to pick peaches all day were already laughing together in ways that they would be too tired to do when they returned after dark that evening. Highway 55 curved its way beyond their house, leading to the somewhere else she had hoped to one day go. The sun was shining brightly as if all were right in the world. Lena washed and dressed slowly as worked on the lie she would have to tell so she could leave the house.

Her parents sat in their usual silence in the front room, in their usual places. She could hear the Soul Stirrers on their radio. Today, Sam Cooke's unmistakable voice failed to convince her that Heaven would somehow make a way. She was the one who had to do it. She felt lucky that she was not yet showing. She was not going to be like her sister, Agnes, who had to hurry up and leave home when she was just two months along because of her swiftly swelling belly. Their father, Rev. Lewis Scott, Sr., had decreed that no daughter of his would ever bring shame to the family by bringing a bastard into the world. Their mother, Cadie, had often nodded in silent approval when she heard those words, though her eyes showed the tenderness that she would not speak. Cadie knew things. Knew how to work with roots. Knew, often enough, what things were coming their way. Even if she didn't speak, her daughters knew that Cadie understood more than their father's small view of the world.

Lewis meant those words every time he said them, with his finger pointed in one of his four girls' faces while the veins bulged in his neck. He always spoke in the perfect diction that he used from the pulpit when he was preaching. It was a part of correctness that he enforced in his home. He was not ashamed of berating his wife for the smallest offences. He was not ashamed that he had harnessed her to the plow when the mule died. In fact, Lewis was not troubled by that many things. He was not troubled by his habit of fumbling under his female church members' dresses in his church office, inserting only one finger, just enough so that they could pretend it had never happened when they came to his office breathing hard times and desire. He would not, however, bear the humiliation of a bastard in his own home.

That is why Lena's charade had ended the week before when Cadie had dreamt of catching fish for two days running. The dreams were so vivid that Cadie could feel the slippery, wet scales of the fish wriggling as she took them from her line. She knew the sign, and it was clear and present: dreaming of fish meant that a baby was coming. She had questioned each of her daughters, gently and without blame. Lena had not even thought about being pregnant until her mother had asked her the question, but it was as if the very conversation had made her body change. She had awakened the next day with morning sickness forcing her to go to the outhouse in the wee hours of the morning. She needed to tell Hale that they had to get married and everything would be just fine. She loved him. Maybe it was going to be all right.

She dressed carefully and pulled her hair back and tied it with a plain band so that it showed her respectability. The wave of nausea hit just before she was in full view of her parents. If her stomach had started turning just a few seconds sooner, she would not have been able to hide it. She slumped against the wall, waiting for it to end, listening to see if her parents had heard anything. When it passed, she pushed herself from the wall and wiped her mouth. She straightened her skirt to make sure that everything was perfect before she walked to the front room. She would greet her parents and slowly unfold the lie that would get her out of the house so she could go to Hale's place. She failed to notice that the cardinals had suddenly stopped singing.

"Good morning, Daddy," she said in the softest of voices. Like all of Len Scott's children, the "a" in the word stretched towards "eh."

"Good morning, Mama,"

She started past her father's desk towards the kitchen, the floor of which Lewis had never finished in the twenty years that they had lived in the house. Made of smooth red clay, the floor required daily attention. All of the girls took turns wetting it down so that they could smooth it every night. The wetting and the smoothing made it so that no red dust escaped to spread across the house on to the furniture that was dusted every day.

Lena was only two steps away from his desk, when Lennox grabbed her arm. He pulled her closer to him, forcing her down to the floor. Her mother said nothing, but her fingers had stopped shelling the butter beans that she had picked that morning. Her eyes filled with tears that she knew better than to shed for her child.

"Lena, no daughter of mine will bring a bastard into my house. Who have you been laying with, Harlot? What is his name?"
She started to lie, but there was no use. Fear forced her words out short and too fast.

"We . . . we're getting married, Daddy. Hale and me. I mean, Hale and I are getting married as soon as we can." The words tumbled out faster than she could manage them.

"Well, Daughter, we will see about that. Go get your things, and go one out to the car." He let her go so quickly that she fell backwards before she slowly scuffled to her feet.

She already knew how to move like a beaten woman, never moving too fast when her father was angry, never raising her voice, never betraying that she felt anything other than fear. She smoothed her clothes until they were perfect. Cadie lightly squeezed her hand as they got their purses. On the radio, Sam Cooke was still singing like there really was a God. Outside, the stillness of the cardinals hung in the air like a prophecy.

Silence walked with them down the three brick steps out of the house, passed the rut in the driveway that always held water in the summer time. As the sun flung itself higher in the sky, they walked to their 1950 Chevrolet Fleetline, basic black and fitting for a man of his stature. By any measure, Lewis Scott was a small man. He was slightly built and short. He was made even shorter when he walked with his wife who was just shy of six feet tall. All of their children took after her; even his daughters were taller than him just after they reached puberty. Cadie's pale skin also marked his children, only two of them had any undertones of his darkness. They had all betrayed him by taking her waving, thick hair. Lena's was the most beautiful. Her hair, not even dark enough to be light brown, swung when she walked, hitting her in the middle of her back even when it was curled. She was dimpled and meek, just the way the Reverend loved a woman to be.

Lewis walked behind her to the car, watching for signs of the shame. When he saw Lena rubbing her arm where he had held it, he wanted so badly to beat her, to beat her down, but they were in full view of the people of Redsville who were going about their business on a Saturday morning. He had a reputation to uphold. There would be time for beating later. He swallowed hard to temper his anger, but he felt indignation rise in his throat every time he thought about going to the Chavis place to beg their sorry Mama's boy to marry his daughter.

He opened the car door for Cadie and Lena before he slammed it shut. He stood still there, staring at them through the car window, lost in his thoughts. *Lena fucking some no good boy. Cadie letting it happen.* He stood there, clenching and unclenching his fists, the thoughts fueling his anger. He stood there long enough that Lew, Jr., his second son, looked up from where he was hooking his mortar mixer to the family's old truck. When he saw his sister's face pressed against the window and the hollow roundness of her eyes, he dropped the mixer right where he stood and ran to the car, reaching it in a few strides. Already over six feet at only sixteen, Lew, Jr., was strong. He was the only one in the house that Lewis feared.

"Daddy, you need for me to drive you somewhere?" His breathing was easy, his voice calm.

"We are going to Hale Chavis' house to speak with him and his parents. Your sister here is going to get herself married or shamed, one or the other."

Without acknowledging his father's words, Lew, Jr. opened the passenger door for him, then he walked around the car and slid into the driver's seat. He had learned to protect Lena early on, even though she was old enough to have changed his diaper. Lew, Jr. searched for Lena's eyes in the rear-view mirror, but she was staring far away at a maple tree, lost, perhaps, in the troubles of the moment.

He wondered how Lena had gotten to and from Hale's place without him knowing. He knew well enough the kind of man that Hale Chavis was and the only kind he would ever be. Hale was not his friend, but he had a certain respect for him. He had a car, a 1956 Ford Fairlane, and he kept it clean. He worked hard and he played hard. He was not the kind of man that he thought Lena would go for at all. He had always thought that she would choose someone more like her brothers. They could lay brick, plane and build, paint and plaster. The crafts were passed from father to son and to sons-in-law. They could build anything, knew how to make their own bricks if they had to. They had land and they were tethered to it. Leaving was only on their minds when Lewis' fists made them think of different horizons.

The Chavis house was just far enough away to drive. The ride from Old Smithfield Road where they lived to where the Chavis family lived between Highway 55 and West Holly Springs was uneventful. The railroad tracks on the side of the road marked their journey, promising safe passage for anyone quick enough to jump onto the North-bound train. They looked like a family out for a Saturday ride rather than one searching for redemption on the wrong side of the tracks. No one spoke on the ten-minute driver there. Only the radio broke though the car's quiet. A few minutes after they bumped over the railroad tracks, Lew, Jr. turned the car on to the long, dirt road that led to the Chavis place. They rounded the last curve and parked next to Hale where he stood shining his Fairlane.

Hale held his head slightly to the left as he opened the car door for Lena and her mother. Anybody who knew anything about life would have known what the Scott family had come to do. He helped them both out of the car so that he could avoid speaking to Rev. Scott as long as possible.

"We are here to speak with your parents about you and Lena." Lewis held up his hand to stop Hale from trying to explain anything.
Lena would not look at Hale, but she looked at everything else. Her eyes were open wide as if she were seeing everything for the first time. She wished that she had the nerve to speak.

Wished she were like her eldest brother who had struck her father down to the ground before he took off to live his own life. All she could do was to try to make herself small as she was crowded in to the Chavis house.

"Mornin', Rev. Scott," Hale's father said. "Come on in the house and have a seat. So good to see y'all."

"Mornin' Mrs Scott, Lena. How y'all doing?"

Rick Chavis was smiling the smile of man about to find out whether his day was going to hell quick or just damned fast. He was only vaguely black,with freckles sprayed across his entire face. He could feel his face reddening from the moment he greeted the Scotts.

His wife came out of the kitchen and greeted them from the door, cloth in hand. Sharon Chavis had started her supper early, as usual. When the Scotts had come in the door, she had been about to take the corn cobbs and the pea and bean hulls out to the hogs so she wouldn't have so much to do after supper. She had gotten up with the sun to pick some purple hull peas, butter beans, okra and corn, all of which were now done and staying warm on her stove. Her okra were fried just a bit hard. She always added a little corn meal to the flour to make them crunchy. She had wrung the chicken's neck just before she shucked the corn. Like her mother and her mother before her, she used the chicken feet to add flavor to her chicken and dumplings, though she always removed them before serving her meal. The Scotts, though, had stopped dead in the middle of her floor. One look at Lena trying to shrink herself down, her mother's motionless face, and the clench of Rev. Scott's sorry jaw, and she knew what she had to do. She was a lean woman, with the green eyes and tawny skin. She knew how to use her charm and her looks to take control.

"Well, good afternoon; y'all are just in time for super. Before y'all say another word, just wash up your hands and let's eat together. My mama always said that any news was better served up with some food. Come on, now."

Sharon sent her three youngest children out to the porch with plates in hand. She got the Scott family seated. She told her oldest daughter, Sylvie-- Hale's closest confidante – sit next to him to keep him calm.

Sharon already knew that her Hale was dead wrong. She also knew that she didn't want him tied to the family of a jack-leg preacher who used the Bible to make his mean way in the world. There was no need to trouble Lena with her feelings, though. She was a sweet child, too sweet for the life she was about to have. So, she carried the conversation without the men suspecting it. She had everyone agree to a quick wedding the next week. She planned the reception meal down to which of the mothers would make the potato salad, with and without mustard. Rev. Scott agreed that they could live in the duplex on the edge of their property, a place that they sometimes rented to strangers and sometimes made available to their newly married until they could do better.

"Lena, honey, I will teach you how to make red-eye gravy just the way that Hale likes it. We put a little coffee in the grease to make it just right. You will be a real Chavis then."

After dinner, Sharon refused to let Cadie or Lena help clear the table. She hugged each of them in turn as she led them to the door, and out of her house. She waved at their retreating car until it rounded the curve out of sight. She looked her son standing there as if his world had ended. All over a girl naïve enough to open her legs for something as silly as love.

***

Lena rode to the courthouse with her parents and Lew, Jr., who hugged her tightly before they went in to the office of the justice of the peace in Raleigh. Even her sisters came, having borrowed their uncle's car, though the three of them were lost in their separate thoughts about the days they had left their father's house. They helped Lena get ready. Helped her to pin her too-light-to-be-brown hair up on one side. Helped her adjust her dress so that it well. Stopped themselves from telling her to run away before it was too late. Lena was relieved when Hale came, just a bit late, with his parents smiling their apologies. Sharon explained that Sylvie had to work unexpectedly and couldn't come. Then, Lena and Hale said the words that she had dreamed about the night before. They had the reception at the Scott's house where they stayed until dinner time. Lena had never known a happier day.

She and Hale walked to the duplex just before dusk. The sky was darkening and marbled, the night warmer than it should have been. She had wanted to show Hale that she could be a good wife. So, she had gone to their new place early in the morning to cook dinner. All she had to do when she got back was to warm her food and fry her corn bread.
She giggled when Hale carried her across the threshold and kissed her lightly on her forehead. Deep down, she had known that he was a good man.

"Well now, Mrs. Chavis, here we are."

He rubbed his hand across her belly, the first time he had touched her there since she got pregnant. Hale looked at her in a way that he had never done before. It was a long and lingering look that she thought had something to do with their first night as husband and wife. She let herself hope that it would he gentler than the first time when he had forced her. That it would be sweeter than the second time when she had willingly gotten in to the back seat of his car.

Lena almost skipped into the kitchen to get her corn bread going. She heard the screen door in the back of the apartment screech open, then close. She heard Hale's footfalls moving rapidly across the porch. Somewhere in the distance, she heard Sylvie's laugh, heard the Fairlane's engine come to life, its muffler always rattling a bit too loud. By the time she got out to the porch, all she saw were the Fairlane's cat-eyed rear lights speeding down the road.

Later, she could not remember why she set the table for two. She would one day recall waiting unit the crickets took over the night before she realized that Hale might be gone. She would remember eating alone, and that the tears fell into her plate, thinning the gravy of her peas.

**

That night, Cadie's dreams were fierce. She was helping women birth their babies in twos and threes. At one house, the woman bore four babies in a room where bees had made hives in a window. Honey dripped down the pane. She awakened with a purpose. Dreams about birth always meant death, but she had time to do something about it. She called Lew, Jr., and got her bag of herbs ready: raspberry leaf and nettle to hold the baby in; pennyroyal and black cohosh, if Lena so chose.

At Lena's apartment, there was nothing in the place where Hale's car should have been. When they opened the door, it was clear that Lena had taken her first drink.

She looked up at Cadie and Lew, Jr. Lena tried to tell them that the moonshine had a nice fire. That it promised forgetfulness. But her throat was hot and dry, and no words came.

Although the pain had been searing, Lena had used the coat hanger the way her sisters had taught her. Nothing happened beyond the pain, at first. Then, everything had happened all at once. She had already cleaned the floor twice, doing the necessary things to keep from taking the second drink, though it, too, had soon come.

Without speaking, Cadie and Lew, Jr. half-carried and half-dragged Lena to her bed. Cadie slid a quilt under Lena's hips and legs. Then, she went to the stove to make the tea, putting enough herbs into the pot to make it strong. She would need a lot if Lena was going to make it, to do what had to be done. Still warming on the stove was Lena's red-eye gravy, cooked the way Cadie had taught her. A perfect circle of water surrounded the ham drippings, rimming the cast iron skillet just right.

LAMONT LILLY

Lamont Lilly is an independent journalist, Black radical activist, poet, and community organizer based in Durham, North Carolina. His time and experiences in the ongoing Movement for Black Lives spans over a decade. From Occupy Wall Street to the Ferguson Uprising—from Standing Rock to the Baltimore Rebellion, Brother Lamont has been tirelessly engaged on the frontlines. His poetry, journalism, and collective writings echo the struggles for justice and Black Liberation for this generation. Lamont contributed three poems to *Black Fire This Time, Volume One*.

letter to pan africa

you have lifted our wings
and armed them
with resistance
stirring the pot
standing in the face of winter

truth speaker
fire breather
living and brewing the revolution
keeping the seat warm
where Harriet Tubman
once sat

training soldiers
saving souls
daring us to keep up
keeping the seat warm
where Harriet Tubman
once sat
on a move
on a move

bloodline

my bones still remember you
how home loves all of me
the beginning
that still to come
that still to be

the north star may lead me free
but that really ain't home
these bones still remember you
land of Nkrumah, Lumumba,
Madikizela

my bones still remember you
whole bold black
unbroken
mother africa

MALI COLLINS

Mali Collins, Ph.D (she/her) is doula, writer, and Assistant Professor of African American & African Diaspora Studies at American University, where she teaches Black Motherhood Studies. Previously, she was an Assistant Professor of African American Literature in the English department at Howard University. Her creative and peer-reviewed work has appeared in *American Quarterly, Souls: A Critical Journal of Black Politics, Society, and Culture, National Political Science Review*, and *The Black Scholar*. Her first book, *Scrap Theory: Reproductive Injustice in the Contemporary Black Feminist Imagination* will be published in late 2024 by Ohio State University Press.

Young Margaret

So much of what I learned from my grandmother was what my father called nonsense, but what she taught me was the cold, naked truth. To be honest with you, I cared a whole lot about what my Daddy thought of me, of what I did, and what I wrote. But I knew he was dead wrong about this. Not only did I *know* what my Grandmother taught me was the truth, but I had seen real nonsense with my own two eyes that last day of school, May 25, 1918. I learned more of the truth later that day. Daddy said it was always best for an author to surprise their reader and so I'll do that for you too.

The morning was already humid.

When I awoke, I ate my hot bacon straight from the cast iron pan. The sun rays shone through the sole kitchen window and cut through the swirled path of the grease rising to the ceiling. I didn't like the grease mixing with my cornbread and strawberry jam on my small enamel plate, so I ate my bacon standing over the hot stove, much to my mother's distaste—She told me I looked like the help when I did that. She couldn't see me when she and Daddy were out in the parlor drinking coffee and answering letters, so I wasn't worried about her finding me and lecturing me.

Our house was bigger than the classic New Orleans shotgun but was more or less the same size as our house in Birmingham, Alabama. It was neither nicer nor cleaner. The only difference in this city were the people and all the nonsense that happened when I talked to them. The evening before that day of utter nonsense was normal too: I went to bed right before my parents walked in the door from their dinner party. I also listened to my Grandmother, Elvira Dozier Ware's stories after I had washed up from dinner. I tell you her whole name because she started every story with, "I am Elvira Dozier Ware, daughter of Randall Ware and Vyry Ware, and I am about to tell you a story about my mother and her mother before that." She stayed in the room right off the kitchen. If Mother saw me sitting on the scrap rug at the room's entry, she would have had a fit. The room was too small for anyone or anything, except for a small footstool Grandmother used to reach the window when she needed to prop it open with a ruler so to let some air in. In another middle-class New Orleans family, that's where the live-in help would be, but my Grandmother liked her small room close to the kitchen, her twin bed taking up the length of its entirety. This way, the stove was only about 5 feet away. When she sat up in the morning her legs hung off the bed and swung in figure eights for her "exercise" and she stared directly at that cast iron stove with its tall chimney which snaked at one joint and disappeared behind the pale blue wall. The wall to her back had a tiny window that stayed hard to clean because of how much the magnolia flowers fell and mucked up the base of the window. I gently tucked the

Young Margaret

pins that dared to poke out from the bottom of my satin bedtime scarf as I crossed my legs and prepared for her recantation. That night before the nonsense I sat on the floor like I did every night and listened to her stories.

The story she told me that night was about my ancestor's second move across Alabama after being freed from slavery, and how they met a poor white family that had several sickly children. Grandmother told me all of what she could remember without any emotion, never judging the people in her stories or their decisions. She usually told these stories as if she was reading off a scroll in her mind's eye. She did not clip her toenails or brush her long black hair that went down to her back. She simply told the story and let me know that what happened was "pure wrong."

"Tell me about what she used to find her way! How did they know what to do?" I prodded.

"After they found out they were free, they just left," she answered, but not. I knew that my great-grandmother had other tools that helped her homestead. These were the tools that I would beg her to tell me about.

"The North Star is important, but your great-grandmother knew the planets, too." she said.

"Knew them?" I asked.

"Why you asking simple questions. Yes, she knew them. She mapped them. They told her where to move and how to live. And you'd do your best to do the same. If it worked for her, it can work for you. Now start thinking about sleep." I uncrossed my legs and rose to stretch.

She sang her song as I left the room:

"I look up at the stars,
And I look at my scars,
And I look at my children
And I wonder...."

The large glass pane of the oak front door rattled as it opened. Mother and Daddy were home. I ran past the kitchen up the backstairs to my bedroom. The short hallway was lined with a tattered orange rug that muffled my quick steps, but nothing could quiet the thump brought from my door frame to the bed and crawled under the covers, grabbing my tablet and pencil from the shelf from behind my head.

"....every night, woman! Every night when she could be studying, you're telling her your stories!" I heard my father bellow.

Grandmother's voice was too muffled for me to hear much of her response. When it was all said and done, she was his mother-in-law, and we all knew it was Grandmother's say-so that determined the way of the house and especially with the children. I stayed steady on taking notes about the family's migration. I had no dates or times or real sense of chronology—this story was one of many that she would tell. I would have to piece together later. If I took notes while she told the story, I wouldn't listen, so I had to store them up as best I could and spit them out in shorthand from a dull pencil while in bed, in the dark. This was the best way for me to remember my peoples' stories, and the only way for me to truly feel the stories pouring out of my grandmother, moving through me, and out of my pen onto my journal paper.

After breakfast the next morning, I headed out for my seven-minute walk to school, my seven minutes in "heaven" I called it, because I was alone with my thoughts which meant I could make up stories about what I saw. I very much-loved living in New Orleans, and especially loved that I had a best friend who was from the same part of Alabama as I. We met at Gilbert Academy, the premier colored secondary school in New Orleans, which if nothing else meant that everyone had high marks. It wasn't a premier preparatory school just because everyone was remarkably bright, it was that everyone belonged to a family that required them to be. As my mother often put it, "This is New Orleans." She said it just like that. There was no qualification or explanation. And yet we all knew what it meant. Excellence was required. And if we embarrassed our family, there would be hell to pay.

When we left Birmingham only a few years before, she gave us a similar talk. It was important that we listened to what she talked about the "decorum" expected of young colored people, how there were many groups of colored people like Creoles and Blacks and about a dozen other made-up names for us—it was if we hadn't traveled there several times a year for church conventions and the like. My point is this: My parents didn't expect me to know everything, but they expected me to know who and what I came from. And I wasn't Margaret. I was the daughter of Sigismund and Marion Walker. There was an "I" to be carved out when I was older (and famous, I surmised), but only one that was built on the foundation of Southern sensibilities, and Methodist faith. There were other things added on top which was out of a young Black girl's control. What I'm talking about here is the "Southern tradition" which was in code for color and caste, both of which age did not exempt me or anyone from understanding our place in the very concrete stratum that wove the fabric of everyday living in "Nawlins."

Lily was a girl from a similarly statured family of store owners and highly lettered athletes. She was a thin, fair-skinned girl with red undertones and red-brown hair that was surely kinky like mine without the touch of her mother's hot press. Lily sat on the last block to school off Dufassat Street, twirling her perfectly pressed curls which laid obediently pinned back at the nape of her neck. Lily was beautiful to me with her freckles and soft skin which she swore was not from her white grandmother but rather all that Gullah Geechee she had in her. I cherished the moments before I came upon our meeting place, but loved walking into school arm in arm, which everyone called our "sister act." As soon as we arrived at school, I went left, and she went right. It was probably best that we had different homeroom teachers because we were both very competitive. We had early dismissal at 11:30am due to it being the last day, and after three hours of cleaning out desks, hugging goodbyes, all the stuff that goes on the last day of school, we found ourselves again arm and arm, making our way down South Charles Street once again.

"Which one is your favorite, Meg? She said turning around, pointing to her curls that had survived the school day.

"Mmmmmm," I said under my breath as I ran my finger through the row. She had six of them laid in a perfect row. "This one." I pointed to the fourth from the left, scrunched it up and let it spring down and then up again before resting where it was.

"Don't touch it! My mother said the oil from our fingers will ruin our sheen. Between that and the humidity, New Orleans will be the end of every perfect hairstyle!" she said anxiously.

Lily's vanity was cute, but we were walking too slowly for me to be home fifteen minutes to the hour, which was the time my parents expected me to be home from school before they started worrying. I looked toward the sun to see if I could tell the time the way that my grandmother left her plantation shanty without a pocket watch. I didn't have to look for it. In New Orleans, the sun was always in your face unless it was storm season. I looked up and I unlinked my arms with Meg. I stood, cemented in the sidewalk, only half a block from school.

"Meg?" Lily asked as I continued toward the storefront. She bent over to pick up my tablet and pencil bag I dropped on the ground. That thud was about the last thing I heard from Lily or nearly anything, and after a half a block down the street I was inside a bay-windowed store front, knocking on the front window. I don't know why I was knocking; I just know that I felt like I did. This was one of the adages Grandmother taught me, which is that when you feel like you ought to be doing something for no reason at all, and it doesn't hurt anyone else, you should probably just do it. This was one way the ancestors spoke to us, she said, and if we ignore them, they might not be so keen to help us find our way next time.

By the time the first woman in white opened the door, the second woman in white came from behind the one bookshelf which stood tall in the middle of the room, with no books or papers on it. They stood with their fingers interlaced on front of their waists. I had forgotten all about Lily or the last day of school or getting back home at all.

I knew these women. I knew them from my Daddy and Mother's Friday church services, and I knew that I said, "Hello, ma'am," and "Blessings to you, ma'am," and that was about it.

When they came to hear Daddy speak on Friday services, and he alternated between calling them "Aunt So-and-So" and "Ms. So-and-So" every other week it seemed. Being a young Southern lady, I knew I was to call them Ma'am no matter who they were. Sometimes, they would ask me to come sit by them in the back row, never saying a word. My Mother never explained who or what they were, Daddy sure didn't either, although he knew what they were capable of. That's why he didn't want me around them.

"How are you?" the one with the brass bracelets asked me.

"I am well, thank you, ma'am."

"What have you observed this week?" The woman in white behind the first one had a long, velvet scarf thrown over her shoulder. The other wore a bone-white lace sash from left shoulder to right hip. Both their burnt sienna hair was pressed and curled like all the other ladies of her time, but she let out the unruly ringlets around her temples freely, despite their graying roots.

"This week I've observed that letters didn't come to the home." I said, quietly. Not arguing with what they were asking or if it was their business. They were an elder from church. It was best I answered politely.

"Who or what might be responsible for that?" the one with brass bracelets asked.

"Have you been reading or writing at all this week?" chimed in the other.

"Not as much as I'd like."

"Who or what might be responsible for that?"

"Neptune or Mars I suppose."

"Conjunct or opposed? Exact or inexact? Squared?" she pressed.

"I-, I-, I don't know, ma'am," I said, quietly.

"What do you *feel*?" she said, smoothing her skirt.

"I feel that it may have been opp–," I stammered.

"Why opposed?!" she bellowed. The door lock opened and shut with a *click* from the volume of her voice.

"Because I didn't know if I was coming or going. I moved down Dufossat Street, I lost Lily. Just now it happened." I said, turning around to see out the window. It was getting dark, and I had to leave before Mother came home from her Friday socials.

I was only nine years old when Grandmother gave me her ephemeris with all the planet's transits on it, but I don't know how they could possibly know that I had one. Maybe they saw me studying it in the pews, as I was desperate to always read most things. I loved looking at the dates and times that each planet moved into different parts of the sky called signs. It was old, but not worn. Grandmother kept it in the pages of her Bible, right next to Genesis 1:16: "And God made the two great lights—the greater light to rule the day and the lesser light to rule the night—and the stars." Grandmother told me that all these things went together. God created all the stars, and planets weren't nothing but one big star.

"I just couldn't find her, I said quietly.

"I think you know what they were both up to this week, Maggie. See you Sunday," she said, turning on her heel and walking off with perfect posture. The other elder followed not far after, but not before she stared at me, nonplussed. I could not tell if she was studying me or if she was disappointed.

"Before you leave, blow out the candle for me," the one with the purple sash asked, gesturing toward the long-wicked candle, dwindling in the glass holder. When I blew out the candle, something happened to me that has happened before. It's a moment when all the things in your life that confuse you come together to make perfect sense all at once. Sometimes the hair stands on your arm or you feel like you need a sweater before the chill that runs up your legs gets to your middle and forces the rest of your body heat out. I sometimes feel my face go pale, and other times, but fingers go numb and tingly until it travels up my arm, across my chest and down the other one til it comes out my pinky finger on the other side.

Others hear a ringing in their ear as if someone had removed all the water that had been clogging them up for who knows how long. When it all made sense, I watched the wick crackle, bend, and then pop once more before going out. The frosted glass cracked up one side, as if it could not stand the heat of the tiny flame. A small piece of glass flung on to the back of my hand as I stepped back. I looked up at the woman with the henna red hair.

"Congratulations," she said. I looked at my hands where the glass had lodged into my hand. There was nothing. No scar, no burn, no smell of flesh. I was untouched, on the outside. I took the ephemeris and left, the door closing firmly behind me. Lily was outside waiting for me.

"What did you get?" she asked.

"What do you mean what did I get?" I asked back, confused.

"You were only in there for a few seconds. I figured your mother wanted you to pick something up for her," she said, pleasantly, linking her arms again, and walking down the street.

That night after dinner of grits and sausage, I laid side-by-side with my Grandmother, waiting for my parents to come home. I listened to the whistle of her exhale as she fell asleep.

She told no story that night and I was fine with it. Outside, the smell of magnolia wafted in through the small crack she left in her open window. I looked out and saw only the small sliver of the moon which hung weighty on the bottom of its crescent.

Softly, she spoke again of when her mother moved from Alabama.

"Always plan to leave on a New Moon," she said, "Full Moons make everybody go crazy. You come up with your escape plan on a Full Moon. But you don't leave until the moon waxes and then turns new again."

I didn't wait until I heard the door's glass pane rattle to get into bed and grab my pencil. I realized while watching the moon that there are some things you know about life and there are some things you can write about and just hope to learn more about them that way. I intend to write about most of know and most of what I want to. Not children, husbands, teachers, or racists can keep me from doing what I want to do, God willing. Once under the blankets, I put my pencil to paper and wrote:

"I am Margaret Walker, daughter of Marion and Sigismund Walker. I am about to tell you a story about my grandmother and her mother before that."

This is for my brothers...

RAHEEM CURRY

Raheem is a writer out of Kensington, Philadelphia. He is inspired by James Baldwin, Malcolm X, Etheridge Knight, and Huey Newton. He hopes his writings does what writings did for him: changed the trajectory of his life. He is in the works of publishing his second book, and is looking forward to writing more poems in the new year

This is for my brothers who are dead and who are still here. The brothers who helped me become the man that I am today. I carry your truths like trinkets into my future. We were just brothers raising each other to be men.
Raheem Curry

My father passed
on when I was
fourteen
I learned early on
that heroes
in fact do
die.
When I was eighteen
my best friend
Basil taught me
how to tie
a tie.

I obtained a job
right after because
of this new
learned skill.

We lived in
a neighborhood
where we did
not know
when we would
be next.

We lived in
a neighborhood
ravaged by
oppression.
A neighborhood
devastated by
crack.

We were proud.
We were Black.

We raised each
other.
Our Fathers
were
under the dirt,
behind steel bars,
or still on
their trip to
the store for
milk, and also
their own pursuits
of Manhood,
but at the expense

When we could
be killed.

My brothers
and I would
have an economy
with each other
with our crisp,
but slightly
wrinkled
borrowed
dollars from
one another.

It was never
really "borrowed"
it was never
meant to be
paid back.

of a relationship
with their sons.

We got into
fist fights.
We stayed with
each other
on those dark
nights.
We invited
each other into
our homes
when one of
us did not
have one.
We gave money
we did not
have
We were the
proverbial route
to manhood in
the Hood.

Godspeed to my brothers.
Live brazenly.

Chantal James

Chantal James has been published across genres—as a poet, fiction writer, essayist, and book reviewer—in *Catapult, Paste Magazine, Harvard's Transition Magazine, The Bitter Southerner*, and more. Her honors include a Fulbright fellowship in creative writing to Morocco, a finalist position for the Alex Albright Creative Nonfiction prize from the North Carolina Literary Review for 2019, and a fellowship to the Vermont Studio Center. Her novel was one of Kirkus' 10 most anticipated fiction books of its year and one of Library Journal's top anticipated debuts of its winter as well as an Indie Next pick of the American Booksellers' Association.

Upon Alleyways
Fron the forthcoming novel *The Opening of the Mouth*

On days that would culminate in a party, Orlando often had some reason or other to meet with his business partner Roscoe. They'd met in a pool hall in Southeast one night soon after he'd left college. Orlando kept up with only a couple of the people he'd been in that school with because though he hadn't left town, his intention in dropping out and crafting a life that diverged from the destiny his father had laid out for him was to chart something new altogether. So he wanted new faces in his circle, new people to pal around with. He made friends in his neighborhood with the snap of a finger. Roscoe had asked to join his pool game with a couple of other friends that night and it was very easy for them to banter back and forth, and they fell into calling each other up to hang out and very naturally incorporated the partnership they now had that led to many of the most sought-after parties occurring around town.

They had a few last-minute details to work out. So after briefly stopping home, with the weather being nice enough that day, Orlando decided to take the thirty minute walk from his apartment to Roscoe's to sit down with him for a minute and get everything straight. A good party had the appearance of being composed of happenstance and a bit of chaos but Orlando and others behind the scenes knew it was in fact a deliberate orchestration, many elements coming together to produce a situation for a large group of people to gather and lose themselves in trance.

Orlando took a route through the backs of houses. He left down the front steps of the row house and it was only a few quick paces down the block before he inserted himself into the nearby alleyway. Flanked on either side by houses with stairs coming down from upper-level wooden decks, his feet pushed against cobblestone as he made his way. This was where raccoons would be at play come sundown, swaggering like they owned the place, and where the odd fierce opossum prepared to bare its ugly face with all its teeth at any creature getting in between it and the trash it intended to devour. In the alleys he went past trash can after trash can, kicked the butts of cigarettes that had been discarded and caused a syringe that had been left to clatter as his boot moved it out of the way. The alleys were the secret skeleton of the city that held it all together although they were not seen at first approach. To enter them was to enter a hidden network where the wiring and the messiness of the entire town was exposed. People left their trash here and they sat out in the back of their houses with citronella candles on summer nights and they strung laundry up between their houses sometimes and the clothes waved like the flags of a rag-tag nation in the wind as water was evaporated from them.

Orlando knew this route but was surprised to find himself lost all of a sudden, caught behind and in between homes he didn't recognize and unable to figure out which main street it led out to. His familiar way had shifted. He thought he heard an otherworldly mocking laughter at him rise up from one of the homes on the side. He couldn't see anyone, though.

His instinct was to move more quickly now, as though this would allow him to catch up to where he needed to be. He saw ahead of him that the street the alleyway intersected to led into other ways beyond it visibly and surely shifted to become another alleyway. Drink had never done this before. He was being toyed with by higher powers who were amused as he became increasingly bewildered at where he was, caught on every end between the back-ends of unfamiliar row-houses, and they sometimes seemed to narrow in on him which quickened his breath and his heartbeat with the fear of being trapped.

He would've called on the name of anyone who could come to his aid but when he searched his mind for who that would be, nothing came up, so a wordless sound trapped itself in his throat. Then as he grew more frightened the sound was released as a cry that barely sounded human. As Orlando's cry escaped into the heavens he heard a loud booming noise for a second and then the familiar world clicked into place around him and he realized he now recognized the homes he was behind. The trash cans were placed in the positions they should always be in, the cobblestone was marked with its familiar designations. He was now about ten minutes from Roscoe's place. That's how long it would take him to continue to make his way ducking through the alleyways, provided the landscape was finished shifting.

He took his hands and patted his whole body. He wanted to be sure he himself was still there because for a moment he was unsure he could even count on that. He felt the ridges of his clothing through his coat and it reassured him. Then he resolved to be on about his way trusting it could stay familiar to him. A paper towel on the ground was soggy and muddy and he nearly missed stepping in it. The smells were of garbage and faintly somewhere off of smoke from the cigar someone was having on their back porch.

Going through alleyways was generally a way to avoid seeing anyone familiar or many people at all. The people you passed back here along these routes were not eager to be seen because this was where private business was undertaken. Orlando's appetite for social stimulation was not inexhaustible and these moments of passing through ways where even those he passed didn't acknowledge him helped him keep the reserves of energy he needed to command the crowds at a party and see about their needs.

He exited the endless matrix of alleyways that would have and did go on forever at Roscoe's block. Roscoe lived in the bottom apartment of a row house. Seeing children playing outside who were the kids of Roscoe's upstairs neighbor he dug into his pocket, and found that he could produce a handful of hard candies he set out his hand to offer them. The three children, two girls and a boy all with skinny legs protruding from shorts, eagerly picked at the shining discs in his hands. When they left his hand empty he reached it out to muss up their heads one by one.

He shouted Roscoe's name at his window, then found a rock on the ground and chucked it up against the glass with an easy move of his wrist. Roscoe lifted the window. The kids scattered at the sound and resumed their game.

***

Gunter is no more a stranger to alleyways than his son had been. Not now. Since he's taken to wandering at night, he too knows of the pleasures of secrecy tucked between the back ends of people's houses, the forbidden pleasure there is in being somewhere private he is not supposed to be. Veiling himself by tucking into the system of alleyways that was the city's skeleton had been a way for Orlando to find respite and relief and recharge so that he could command a crowd again, but for his father these years later it is more or less to continue to be unseen. The butts of Gunter' Mavericks often joined the other random cigarette butts and refuse people left in these tunneled enclosures of the city's underbelly. Wandering the alleyways is a nice way to spend an evening. He'd wind up safely tucked and disguised in the back of some club until he'd tired himself out and was ready to dip into a brief sleep on the pull-out sofa before daylight found him working people's jaws for a living one more time. Gunter's mourning for his son did not often take the form of strongly craving Orlando's presence but when it did, it hit hard. It overtakes him as he is standing at the bathroom mirror shaving one morning as Martine had reminded him to do the day before when she'd noticed stubble on his face. He nearly stumbles under the impact of the sudden desire to reach out and touch his son's arm. He'd felt closer to his son when he'd offered bread and beer to the water, and he throws his razor down into the bathroom sink so that he can run into his bedroom and furiously scribble a note reminding him to do the same thing as soon as possible.

Until he could make his offering he'd console himself with the fact that his plans were coming together well. He'd have the mausoleum designed, he felt confident in the architect's abilities. He hopes there would be no questions as to why he wants the chamber unsealed but he can't concern himself with fear of that. He sees no other choice but to imagine things going well. Death and is not an option for him. He'd done the research to know the right charms Martine was to recite over his body as he lay dying. He'd recently begun researching the most effective poisons with which to end this life and transition into the new one. There is no way he could go wrong and no way he could be stopped.

After work he stops by Safeway again for a loaf of bread and beer. As usual he ignores the youths sulking in the corners and cracks between buildings and is unmoved by the sight of the warehouse whose windows had just been shattered by gunfire the night before. He steps into and out of the refracted light cast by the windows that had been broken in the patterns of spider webs. Today he will choose to cast the bread on the duck pond that was near his practice. He thinks he might be able to augur comforting signs in the reactions of the ducks to the presence of this source of food. He knows he is hearing confirmation, words of hope, in the sounds of the fizzing beer hitting the water when he poured it out. A little girl playing with her yo-yo a few yards from him stops her game to stare at him curiously. He disregards the fact that he has been observed. The girl is nobody. But anyway no witness could dampen the power of what he chose to do, he is utterly sure of this.

He accepts that his old life, his first life, is on its last legs. He is making the preparations now, getting everything in order so that in just a few short months he would rise out of his current mortal form into an immortal one. He is hesitating to discuss the final steps with Martine. He hasn't decided how large a role she'll play in ending his current life. He trusts her with almost anything but here he doesn't know what she could handle. As much as he hates to admit it there is a danger that anyone other than him could foil his plans. That was the trouble with leaving so much of this even in Martine's capable hands. But it is the option available to him. At night he stands at the window of his apartment above the dental office and watches pigeons flutter onto the power line outside, communing with each other wordlessly so that without even making a sound they are able to rise up as one cloud at the moment they had chosen. He watches the distant winter sun, white and lonely and small cloaked by the cold November fog, until it bursts into color and tucks below the horizon. He goes out nearly every night now to be hidden among crowds, in bars, in clubs. He thinks about what his moves tonight will be. Which sidewalks he'll pace down puffing smoke and hoping to be disregarded, which venues will accept him without noticing him too terribly much. The Channel Inn, The Flagship, the Fox Trap. It doesn't take much to prepare himself to go out. He wasn't even going to bother to change the clothes he'd been working in all day, he'd just throw his trench coat that was now rank with his body odor and stale smoke over them. He is not in the habit of looking closely into mirrors. It doesn't concern him that people he meets tonight might be making detailed judgments of him. His only concern is passing among them as invisibly as possible, close enough for the presence of other bodies to comfort him, but without making any contact with them as people that could interfere with his intactness. Everyone doesn't need to know him for him to be content pouring his all into living on forever. His status as a man of the white coat would be useful to him insofar as it motivated people to do as he said when he needed something but being highly visible in the here and now was not as useful for him. He would be his own living legacy as he continued on where others had no choice but to stop, past what for them was the final boundary of death. Others had to suffice with leaving something behind when they could live no longer. He'd take it all with him and speak his own name forever.

He sits on his sofa to gather momentum within himself for the night ahead, feeling the energy circulate within him. He could not remember if he'd left his door open or closed, and didn't hear anyone approach, so he is startled to suddenly see that the figure of a young man has risen before him. The form of the figure is sheer, so that through the body clothed in fashions of a decade ago he can see clear through to the wall on the other side of his apartment. Orlando. Gunter blinks several times to be sure his eyes aren't playing tricks on him out of his fatigue.

"Son," he calls. There is no answer. There are no words coming from the transparent mouth of the figure of Orlando who stands before him. Yet he feels that his son is urgently demanding something of him. He wants to know what it was. He searches the figure's vacant eyes.

"Orlando. What do you need from me?"

As soon as he utters the words he hears the door to his apartment loudly slam shut and turns towards the noise. When he turns back to the figure of his son, there is no one there. For a good while he is paralyzed sitting on the sofa, air from the open door raising hairs on his arm, running through whether or not he should tell Martine about this visitation. He knows there was a danger others sometimes sensed in the ideas he expressed. He could tell that by a fear in their eyes sometimes. But he doesn't know the codes to always be able to tell what those dangerous thoughts were, what was safe to share, when he'd be supported. His son needs his help in some way from the other realm. That is clear. Is he serving Orlando in his mission to live forever or is he just serving himself? He doesn't know. He makes a point to dedicate his mission to his son, whatever that looks like. He has the urge to spit and there is a glass coated with the remnants of juice sitting before him on his coffee table, so he takes it up and lets out a huge wad of saliva.

He commits this action to the intent that he receive a strong sign.

Thoughts of Orlando and the memory of the visitation prevent him from enjoying himself when he goes out that night. Determinedly after committing to his course of action he'd risen from the sofa to put his arms through the trench coat, and taken up his keys from where they were beside an ashtray.

He goes into a club on the waterfront he'd been to before after playing the admission cost. This night his separateness from the other patrons is painful. He can't stop himself from wondering if his every move is something that can help Orlando get what he needs or if his son is disappointed in what he did from beyond the grave.

He declines the offer of a woman whose Jherri curl soaked her shoulder pads to dance. He didn't usually dance with anyone when he came out, and feels self-conscious about the time the lady had spent eyeing him from among the crowd.

He wants to see his son again. He hadn't had the chance to say anything he needed to say to him. He would get another notebook to add to the many he now scribbled in throughout the day indecipherably to anyone else, and in this one he'd take notes on the things he'd tell Orlando if he was given the chance again. He knows he hadn't been the most expressive father. His father hadn't been, his father before that hadn't been. The way he knew was not to be forthcoming with his feelings but to sternly command. To set the expectation for the kind of behavior he wanted to see from his kids by accepting nothing less. He might be able to admit that had never worked with Orlando. But it is not too late for him to say those words that needed to be said, to pour himself out. Not with his son making himself known to him from beyond the grave like this. If it had happened once it could happen a second time, a third time. And he would even learn to call the experience to him. He would make peace and set everything right with Orlando before ultimately glorifying both of them when he achieved immortality soon.

C. Prudence Arceneaux

C. Prudence Arceneaux, a native Texan, is a poet who teaches English and Creative Writing at Austin Community College, in Austin, TX. Her work has appeared in various journals, including *The Academy of American Poets' Poem-A- Day, Limestone, New Texas, Hazmat Review, Texas Observer, Whiskey Island Magazine, African Voices* and *Inkwell*. She is the author of two chapbooks of poetry—*DIRT* (awarded the 2018 Jean Pedrick Prize) and *LIBERTY*. Her debut full length collection *PROPRIOCEPTION* is out 2025 from Texas Review Press.

Austin Police Department and Nazi Cowboys Meet 'N' Greet On the Far West Boulevard Bridge

The house across the street is backlit by morning shine, the Earth tilted against the celestial plane. Farmdogs beyond the reclamation pond, howling roosters, sunrise in black and grey. The house next door is guarded by grackles; they lateral line north, west, then north again.

If you'd trusted the griot in your blood, you would have understood the plague of frogs, as foretold, but they were miniature, desiccated. And if you'd ever believed in a grimoire, you could have read the loopy cursive the ants marched out of the chalky ink from those amphibian husks.

You warn the black mothers about what they put in their mouths: It's in your milk—the sorrow—settles into the bones of your young. The government feeds it to you, you say, in thick blocks, like cheese.

But you also missed the dying of the maroon mums. Sure, it was difficult to tell, their color already so like dried blood, but you remarked on how they seemed to be supporting each other, falling in together as a group.

Rittenhouse is unshackled to pledge to the rapiest mix of Greek letters, oozing poison slurp from his infected gut, keratinized spines immature, but present. Alex Jones and Steve Bannon scholarship him into Public Life.

You are studying your 5th degree burns when your nephew texts you at 2 am. He's watching a video of a video of police beating a black man in 1992. You know he is holding his newborn in one hand, her mouth newpink and nipple- ready, brain dizzy in formation, as he tries to text you with the other, his eyes blinking a Morse code of lividity.

REGINA HARRIS BAIOCCHI

Regina Harris Baiocchi is an African American artist whose Pushcart-nominated poetry, fiction, and creative nonfiction appear in *Black Women in America* encyclopedias, *Gwendolyn Brooks & Working Writers*, *The Encyclopedia of African American Music*, *Obsidian: Literature & Arts in the African Diaspora*, *Rat & Rooster Journal*, *Modern Haiku*, and other publications.

Scuppernong

Kill what needs to be killed

Ancestral weeds grow around our redbrick house in Tornado, Tennessee. They sway in the wind like old friends waving. Memories live in the underground storm house inside an adjacent hill. Our subterranean shelter is cool, dark, and safe. Even the angriest tornados respect our steel-reinforced door. Like the storm door my memory is solid.

Pecan trees smell of home. Warm breezes blow freely without

dodging high rises. I feel a million miles away from my Chicago apartment in my kinfolks' hometown. Inhaling deeply, I wade through tall weeds to my newly inherited house.

When I reach the front door, I turn back to survey the yard I just negotiated. The mailbox is leaning but announces our home address: 1 East Crooked Road, Tornado, TN, 38369.

Standing in the afternoon sun, breathing sweet air, I spy ghosts of workmen lined up at Gran-a-me's kitchen window. Gran-a-me sold sandwiches to stretch Papa's railroad pension. Aromas of potted meat, onions, and fresh biscuits linger.
Ghost-men wash their hands with Papa's water hose and find shady spots to eat.

Gran-a-me cranks up her scratchy radio or plays lively tunes on her mouth organ for entertainment. Gran-a-me's music made four-year-old me fall in love with the blues. Feeling *down home* safe I bask in the assurance that: "A safe human being stands confidently with a smile on her face: happy to bless what needs to be blessed, ready to
kill what needs to be killed…"

Fishing the skeleton key from my purse, I pray it works. Hallelujah! The door creaks open as I bump it with my hip. Resting my shoulder bag, I scan the modest home where Mother Rain and her four sisters were raised. Mother Rain and her sisters left home when they married, except the youngest. Aunt Mae went to the local A&M College to stay home with Gran-a-me after Papa died. Aunt Mae married James Brown. Not the Godfather of Soul, just regular ole Jimmy Brown from Tornado, Tennessee.

Aunt Mae and Uncle Jimmy's first child was stillborn. Their second child was miscarried. That's when Jimmy took up with a floozy. Rumor has it Jimmy needed to prove he was not shooting blanks. Then Booker was born. Aunt Mae said Booker was the best part of Jimmy. Aunt Mae died recently and left this place to me, the oldest child of the eldest daughter.

"Emma, is that you?" a man calls out.

"Who is it?" I am plugging my devices into chargers.

"It's Booker Lee." A tall, burly man enters the front room with my suitcase. I blurt out, "Hope you're not claustrophobic."
Booker looks puzzled.

"Your head," I point. "It almost touches the ceiling."
Booker's laugh is infectious. I laugh with him until his stare discomforts me.

"Thanks for covering up everything," I nod toward the furniture as I fiddle with the chargers. "How much do I owe you for the bills?"

Booker waves me off. "Not a dime. But I'd be obliged if you'll proofread Mama's memorial program."

I agree.

Booker hands me the mocked-up program and says, "Unless you have a hot spot, you're wasting time plugging in those chargers."

I ask, "Why?"

"Cell tower's quite a piece up the road," he explains. "The cell signal's weak." Having faith, I ignore his advice.

Booker breaks into a mock drawl. "Y'all northerners think all Down South folk are farmers. I'm Regional Information Technology Director for Bell South. So, I know a bit about chargers—By the way where do you want this luggage?" He handles my suitcase like it's empty.

"Put it where I can unpack it," I say. "It's too heavy for me to lift. I left it outside because the taxi driver wouldn't wade through the weeds to bring it in."

"I'll cut down those weeds," Booker offers.

I nod. "Can we eat first? I'm starving. Where's the closest restaurant?"
Booker says, "Follow me." He walks to the kitchen.

A bowl of fresh fruit is on the table. Booker opens the refrigerator to reveal my favorite staples. "I went shopping," he tells me.

"How'd you know I drink almond milk?"

"Same way I know you like tofu and chia seeds. There's hummus, Ezekiel bread, and berries—"

"Who told you I like—"

"I have sources," Booker smiles. "Have a seat. I'll whip up a veggie omelet."

"You don't have to cook for me."

Booker washes his hands and begins cracking eggs. He motions toward a chair. I sit at Gran-a-me's kitchen table. "You have grocery receipts for me?" I ask.

Booker waves me off again. "Tell me something good," he says.
I look around the kitchen. After so many years everything seems the same. Formica table and retro chairs predate me. Jell-O molds hang on the wall. Window sheers look familiar.

"What you been up to?" Booker asks.

I make small talk, "Since I last saw you, I've survived college, divorce, and career stuff." Avoiding eye contact, I search for plates and glasses to set the table. Bending to smell fresh flowers in a mason jar, I catch my stride. "What've *you* been up to, Booker?"

"Same song, different band. Went to Tornado High School, Fisk undergrad, Vanderbilt grad school. Married my college sweetheart, Aileen. Caught her with my ace-boon-buddy and—After that, I went my way, they went theirs."

Booker pivots to serve the prettiest omelet and yell, "Soup's up!" He sits, extends both hands, and asks me to say grace.

"Gracious God, thank You for this meal and the hands that prepared it. Amen." I release Booker's hands before he frees mine. He butters his toast. I pour scuppernong juice then raise my glass, "To cousins." We clink and sip.

"You know we're *not* cousins, don't you?" He announces. I am startled. "What do you mean?"

"I'm not your cousin, Emma."

I'm spooked but manage to ask, "Aren't you Aunt Mae and Uncle Jimmy's son?"

Booker's confession unravels me, "Jimmy's my father, but your Aunt Mae did not birth me. My birth mom abandoned me. Mama Mae raised me on the condition that Dad hit the bricks."

My voice is uneasy, "Are you serious?!" Booker confirms his story with a few nods.

We eat quietly, glancing up occasionally. Finally, Booker takes his plate to the sink.

"Better get to work," he says. He looks at my plate, "You don't like my cooking?"

"It's delicious. Guess I'm not as hungry..." A stammer betrays my nerves. It hits me: I am alone, with a man who is not my cousin, in a remote town where the closest neighbor is half a mile away.

Booker opens the back door. As if to read my mind, he says, "Blood's thicker than mud, Emma. But love and shared history make us kinfolks." He walks out.

I am glued to my chair until I hear chopping noises. Peering through the window sheers I watch Booker cut down branches, thistle, and selfheal.

Reading the program Booker wrote for Aunt Mae's memorial is a family history lesson. From four aunts (and their husbands) I have 13 cousins, all married with kids. Aunt Mae is the last of her generation. She would be proud of Booker's meticulous program book. Aunt Mae loved order. The cover photo shows Aunt Mae smiling in her garden. Neat beds of fruit, veggies, and flowers show off her green thumb.

The program includes Aunt Mae's memories of how people affected her life, such as: "Papa taught me, 'Never ask anyone to do what you can do for yourself...'"

Mama inspired me to nourish my mind, body, and Spirit... Rain assured me that everybody needs to be loved... Trudy and Nathan taught me how to be a friend... Booker, my heart, reminded me that *mother* is a verb...

Aunt Mae's Saturday-morning service is well attended. The choir opens with *One More Time*, the perfect gathering anthem. Auntie's cremains are in an urn encircled by flowers. Her larger-than-life headshot is on an easel.

Booker invites the audience to testify how Aunt Mae touched them:

"Mae was my best friend since kindergarten," Trudy cries.

"Auntie made the best corn pudding," Junior announces.

"Mae taught me to knit with two pencils," Earline shares.

Auntie loved teaching agriculture and mechanical engineering, I recall silently. I'm too self-conscious to stand and say it aloud.

Booker has the last word: "Mama inspired everybody and everything to flourish..."

A silent interlude follows the eulogy. The choir sings a rousing *Goin' Up Yonder* as the pastor leads mourners to fellowship hall. After a collective sigh, repast lines form. Booker thanks everyone personally. Aside from a warm hug and, "Good morning, Emma," Booker avoids me. Yet every time I look up, he is staring at me.

Mr. Nathan introduces himself to me by saying, "When I met Mae, she was double majoring in agriculture *and* mechanical engineering. Mae was our class valedictorian. She was happy-go-lucky until Jimmy broke her heart. Mae forgave him when she saw Booker's newborn face. Raising Booker was her main reason for living. Mae dumped Jimmy the day she adopted Booker. But she demanded Jimmy spend quality time with Booker because she wanted Booker to know his father...

"Lord, Mae would kill a brick for Booker—even on her deathbed!" Nathan's voice cracks.

"I knew Mae was sick when I saw weeds in her beautiful garden. She was so proud of her garden, but even prouder of Booker."

Out of the nowhere Nathan asks,

"Are you Booker's fiancée?"

After an aspirated sigh, I lie flat out, "We're cousins."

"Really!?" Nathan seems doubtful. Booker's stare must've caught his eye.

Nathan pats my shoulder and says, "Sorry for your loss, dear. Will you excuse me?" Others notice *the stare* too.

Kai whispers, "What's up with you and Book, Cuz?" I feign ignorance.

Cousin Kai asks, "Remember why we call him *Book*? 'Cause he always had his head in a book. Now Booker's studying you, Emma."

I do not react to the snickering. Before long I slip out and walk home. It feels good to be alone and outdoors.

Bless what needs to be blessed

The next time I see Booker it is Sunday morning. When he returns to the house, I am half asleep. I feel him before I see him. He wraps me in my bed sheet and carries me to the river in pitch darkness. Predawn air chills me. For some reason, I thank God I had not died in my sleep. Am I having a lucid dream? Did Booker take me outside in my nightclothes? Is he walking while carrying me?

What in the world is going on? I wonder.

Booker whispers, "I got you, Emma."

I am spooked worse than before. Friday night, when I uncovered the furniture, it was not Gran-a-me's but *mine*. My bed and sofa from Chicago. My chifforobe with *my* clothes—I had *not* packed. When I uncovered the piano it was not the spinet Papa won in a craps game, but the Bösendorfer Imperial I secretly dreamed of buying but never told a soul.

"Good morning, Sunshine," Booker's warmed-up voice is more awake than mine. He sets my body on the ground. A chill from the grass penetrates the bed sheet. "You're probably wondering why I brought you here." He pauses. "Emma, I need to tell you a story in the presence of the River.

"Since the Baby Boomer Age, planet rulers have been observing and tracking us through hypodermis chips."

Oh, God, I've been abducted by aliens! I think.

"It's not what you think, Emma. Please hear me out... Colonizers centralized banks, water, thoughts—you name it. To monitor everything, everyone is on the One World Chip System."

"Is that how you knew what groceries to buy for me?"

"Yes—but we're getting ahead of the story. Let's start at the beginning."

Booker continues, "I was programmed to track you from conception. I heard your music from Aunt Rain's womb. I put my ear on her belly when she was pregnant with you. At first that was the only way I could hear you. As time went by, I heard you from anywhere in the world.

"My Southern Bell IT group monitors chips in three States. We have triangulated bases in Biloxi, Chicago, and Tornado—"

"—Is this some kind of mind-control game?"

"No, Emma, I swear. Please hear me out…"

I don't believe him, but he has the upper hand. I hope this won't be painful—

"There's no pain involved," Booker says. "It's my job to take care of you, make sure you're happy."

The only thing that will make me happy is to be in Chicago, in my apartment. Alone. Away from this god-forsaken nightmare, I think. Then I try not to think. What's the use? He hears my thoughts.

Booker resumes his story as if I've said nothing, thought nothing.

"On the day you were born, the midwife shooed me out of the room because she believed children should not witness births. Your mother insisted I stay. When you came out, I reached for you. The midwife tried to steer you towards Auntie Rain, but your mom insisted I be the first to hold you because she knew I will be the last."

I have a sinking feeling that life as I know it ended Friday. Little did I know when I waded through that brush of weeds, I entered a twilight zone.

If I could see his face, maybe I wouldn't be so scared, I think.

"You *can* see me," Booker turns my body to face the River. Dew touches my feet.

The River's darkness faces me as if in a standoff.

Booker says, "Look into the River: with all your senses and intuition. Listen closely, the River knows all."

I listen to the River with closed eyes. Her southbound waters run gently to the gulf to be washed into the sea. I think of Lake Michigan's picturesque shoreline. Why isn't River more like Lake Michigan? If I could hear River's tide catch its breath against the shore, maybe I'd find comfort.

Then I hear River ask, "Why did you kill your siblings?"

I have no siblings, I utter frightfully.

"That's my point," River retorts, "and I have no Lake Michigan."

Booker says, "When you hear River, you'll see my face even in the dark."

I ignore Booker. River has my tongue. River has my ears, eyes, and all that I am. River volunteers, "If you speak to me, only I can hear you. Not Booker or Central Computers, no one else."

I see Booker even though his back is still pressed against mine. His body heat warms me. I ask River, *Is Booker for real? Should I trust him? Should I be afraid?*

"Yes… Yes… No…" River replies. "Booker was programmed to love you *and* his mission. You know him as well as he knows you. You searched for him in the men you courted. They felt Booker's presence. They knew you belonged together.

"Booker is your messiah, and you are his," River splashes and keeps running.

River is nature. I know I can trust nature, I think.

"Of course, you can, Emma," Booker assures me. "What did the River say?"

That's between me and River. I try to clear my mind. Booker smiles and thinks, *Now you can see me, Emma.*

"Finish my origin story," I plead. "Was Daddy there? What did he say?"

"Your dad was there. He questioned why your mom insisted I hold you while the midwife cut your cord. I was the first person to cradle your newborn head in my arm. The blood from your navel ran into my cupped hand. Instinctively, I drank it. Your flavor pleased me. I licked you from my fingers.

"You tasted like sweet scuppernong juice, from the female grape, and I love it! When the midwife saw this, she knew who we were to each other. Auntie Rain always knew. She told your dad you were her *wash-belly baby.*

"Your dad did not want to accept his firstborn as his last. Even though a girl child is a sign of fertility, your dad wanted at least one boy. But the moment he laid eyes on you, he knew you were every child he ever wanted."

"Why didn't my parents tell *me* about *you*?" I ask.

"It was not their story to tell," Booker says. "It's your story *and* mine. When your midwife inserted chips in your sea of qi and fontanelle, you never whimpered. You accepted each chip as your destiny. All you ever did prepared you for this moment.

"Even your birth zip code, 38369, stayed with you. Your Chicago address, 693 East 8th Avenue, Unit-3, begins with your zodiac number, then trinity (your favorite number), followed by the house of your moon, which leads back to the trinity. You are grounded by your *38369* roots."

My head nears implosion. A strong sleep comes over me. Hushing my thoughts, I embrace it.

Become what needs to become

I wake up in the same spot with Booker's back against mine.

His voice is comforting. "Did you sleep well?" I yawn and stretch.

"Emma, I don't mean to rush you, but if you take me as your husband, I'll be promoted from Director to Regional Vice President. I'll make Executive VP if we get pregnant on our wedding night, and Chief Executive IT Officer at our child's birth."

Thoughts pound my head. *I don't like fast friends. They're flashes in time.*

Booker's telepathy is strong, *We can recalibrate time*, he thinks. *One World Soul Mates can do that with each other.*

Recalibrating time intrigues me.

Booker speaks earnestly, "Emma, I have loved you forever."

I turn to River, *Booker's always been kind to me.*

River agrees.

I remind River, *We have always been each other's crush.*

"Since before you were born," River reveals.

Booker Lee does not envy people or covet things. River concurs.

What about Aileen and our parents? I ask River.

"What about them? Aileen ain't coming back. Your parents wanted the best for you and Booker. Mae prayed for Booker's happiness—yours too!" River assures.

Why would Aunt Mae pray for my *happiness?* I ask.

"She saw you were unfulfilled. Mae *and* Rain prayed for you and Booker to be with each other... But it's your decision, Emma." River is emphatic.

Things're moving too fast. Booker's just lonely and grieving.

"Booker loves you, Emma. Your love will ease his grief."

Booker *does* feel like my homecoming. I spent my life searching for this feeling.

Now I'm afraid to claim it.

I seek River's affirmation. *Booker is not boastful. He does not indulge in self-pride. He is not dishonest or self-serving in any way.*

"You know Booker better than you think," River says, "You deserve to be happy, Emma. Y'all were meant for each other."

He wants to start now. What if I'm not ready? I stall.

"*Now* is all you have, Emma. Give yourself to Booker. Let him love you a spell. If you don't love him—and I know you do—return to your windy city of wild onions." River's voice trails off.

What's so important about Booker's promotions? I think. *In the grand scheme of life isn't it more important to be happy than to be a* "Chief Executive Officer"?

Booker explains, "In the One World system c-level executives, their spouses, and their children are mindful beings with multi-realm passports. They can commune with ancestors from time immemorial and descendants beyond infinity."

What makes c-level so special? I wonder. *Who determines which people are promoted?*

"That's the beauty, Emma," Booker expounds. "Everyone chooses to be or not to be transformed." Leave it to Booker and the One World system to provide justice for all.

Basking in this transfigured morning, I turn to face Booker. He laces his strong fingers between mine. Our eyes meet. He kisses my cheek. His lips travel to mine. Booker takes me slowly and I take him. We interlock as day unfolds, tarrying until the planet shifts to recalibrate time. Our collective energy startles thunder and blinds lightning. Souls of our son and daughter breathe into my womb as Booker and I become One.

We are married. Before God and River.

WENDY MERCER

Wendy Isom Mercer is a freelance editor and columnist for the only Black-owned newspaper in Jackson, Tennessee. Wendy is a member of the Griot Collective of West Tennessee. She earned her bachelor's degree in print journalism from Clark Atlanta University. She received her master's degree in instructional and curriculum leadership with a concentration in special education. She is an active volunteer with several community organizations.

Young, Beaten, and Black

Talented
Young Black Man in Memphis
Ruthlessly beaten by Black Men with a badge
Eulogized by Rev. Al Sharpton who continues to shine the
National light on these unspeakable crimes as
Immediacy prompts a
Call to action for a
Halt to the brutality
Occurring before our eyes in a city where Dr. Martin Luther King, Jr.
took his last breath
Look, listen, and
Stop, please stop killing young Black Men who only want to live out their
American dream

ANGELA CLEAR

Ms. Clear is a fiction and poetry writer living in Delray Beach, Florida. She is a graduate of the Creative Writing Program at Florida State University and the National Book Foundation (NBF) Intergenerational Summer Writing Program. Her work was published in the NBF anthology, *Sounds of this House*. She is the daughter of proud HBCU grads, including a mother, a former English teacher, who came of age during the Black Arts Movement.

Lost Girls

Petite soldier
Camouflaged
As a frightened child.

On tiny shoulders she endures
Rubble stacked
Like fallen dominoes.

The fragile frame
Broken, but resilient
Her spirit rebels.

Thick eyeglasses
Coated with dust,
Seek sunlight slivers at dawn.

Raspy voice peeps
Like a baby chick
Tiny fist breaks free, birthing…

We inhale collective life
into those chalky lungs
Pry her up with our shared despair.

And yet, her fleeting
soul loosens its grip
on our fingers
rises high,
chases the
glory of
her given name…
Ana,
Ana,
Ana.

(for Anaika St. Louis, lost in the 2010 Haitian Earthquakes)

THEODORE HARRIS

Theodore A. Harris was born in 1966 in New York City and raised in
Philadelphia, where his art practice is based. Harris is Director and Founder
of The Institute for Advanced Study in Black Aesthetics, and in 2007 joined
the Visual Artists Network. In 1985 he co-founded the acclaimed Anti-Graffiti

Network/Philadelphia Mural Arts Program, and he has taught there since then. Harris is a collagist, poet, and author of *Thesentür: Conscientious Objector to Formalism*, and co-author of books with Amiri Baraka: *Our Flesh of Flames* (Anvil Arts Press) and *Malcolm X as Ideology* (LeBow Books); with Fred Moten: *i ran from it and was still in it* (Cusp Books); as well as *TRIPTYCH: Text by Amiri Baraka and Jack Hirschman* (Caza de Poesía). Harris has held residencies at the Ashé Cultural Arts Center, New Orleans; 40th Street AIR, Philadelphia; Hammonds House Museum, Atlanta; and the International Festival of Arts and Ideas, New Haven. His work is in private and public collections, including the Pennsylvania Academy of the Fine Arts, the Center for Africana Studies, the W.E.B. Du Bois College House, and Penn Libraries, University of Pennsylvania; Saint Louis University Museum of Art; and Lincoln University. Select exhibitions include the 9th International Conference, "Black States of Desire," Collegium for African American Research, Paris; *SURFACE POLITICS: Looking Beneath Aesthetics and Formalism*, a group exhibition curated by Harris at Salon Joose Studio Gallery, Philadelphia; and the solo exhibition, *Collage and Conflict*, curated by Klare Scarborough, La Salle University Art Museum, Philadelphia.

1999 COLLAGE EULOGY FOR AMADOU DIALLO

My memory
  Is you memory
``endless flag
   pretty blue
     done split
     done gone
     away

from under water
   rose we
     in it
       self

had be'd
    a flag
    of death

    Everything

Sick poison
     Gas is dawn
 Got a click teeth
Our space Death you cover
  Candy time. Holiday
   Cupid coffin Puck you
     No longer let it kill I
       Back. Them. Fire.
         Shoot. Stab them with
            They filth can't swing
             Don't sway   that's why
            They try to kill us
                This way

KALAMU CHACHÉ

Poetess Kalamu ChachÉ is a long-time and noted Cultural Arts Activist/ Advocate, Author, Educator, Event Organizer, Performing Artist, Producer, Promoter, Publisher, Songwriter, Vocalist, Recording Artist, and Writer. She has been serving as the East Palo Alto Poet Laureate since her community became the twentieth incorporated city in San Mateo County in 1983. She is the author of three volumes of poems: Survival Tactics; A Change Of Interest; and Survival Interest: A Collection Of Poem Revisited. She also appears in five book anthologies. As a vocal recording artist, Chaché appears on a total of seven record projects, namely with the Sons and Daughters of Lite and Daughters of Life for Ubiquity Records; as a Solo Artist for Undercurrent Records and SONWA Records; and as a featured guest on a Spoken Word CD recording by Hip-Hop Artist Know Expressions?.

Onetta Mae Harris
(January 6, 1925 - April 2, 1982)

If Onetta Mae Harris
Were alive today,
She would be elated
Over the community's way
Of paying tribute to her
For the many good deeds done
To serve the community
When she once lived under the sun.
She would be happy to know
That her sons and daughters
Committed themselves to growing
And passing on to their young ones
The beauty of her way
When she was so alive.
She was an inspiration to all she met.
She was really with us in our day.
If Onetta Mae Harris
Were here with us,
She would be proud to know
That she fulfilled her purpose.
She was an outstanding Afrikan woman.

She served a variety of people who lived
In the Belle Haven and East Palo Alto communities.

Justice, Freedom, Equality!

Justice, Freedom, Equality!
Justice, Freedom, Equality!
Justice, Freedom, Equality!
Justice, Freedom, Equality!

Dr. Martin Luther King, Jr. has been joined again
By Mother Rosa Parks, a loyal and devoted friend.
The Dreamer who used his life as a statement
Is with the Mother of the Civil Rights Movement.
They are comparing notes on
What's really been going on.
What do you imagine that they are saying?
For what do you think that they are praying?
Black Fire This Time, Volume 2 / A 2024 Publication 2 Original Poems
By Poetess Kalamu Chaché
Justice, Freedom, Equality!
Justice, Freedom, Equality!
Justice, Freedom, Equality!
Justice, Freedom, Equality!
I think Dr. King, Jr. and Mother Parks
Remain proud of their legacy and the sparks
That they ignited within the soul of each of us.
They left a great legacy of supreme purpose.
I think that they still want everyone
To always remember the work that they have done
For Justice, Freedom, Equality!
This is a call to action for all of humanity!

Justice, Freedom, Equality!
Justice, Freedom, Equality!
Justice, Freedom, Equality!
Justice, Freedom, Equality!

Before They Go Away

Did you hug an Elder today?
Oh, you must do so, before she goes away!
She has so much wisdom inside
That will have you bursting with so much pride
In knowing that what you're going through
Will be most helpful in your becoming a better you.
Being around an Elder will make you happy.
An Elder has stories that will help set your Spirit free.
Did you hug an Elder today?
Oh, you must do so, before he goes away!
He has a definitive way of being
That will clarify well what your eyes are seeing.
What he has to say will help you to fly
And know exactly the real reason why
You are here living upon this Earth.
You are born of greatness with value and worth.
Did you hug some Elders today?
Oh, you must do so, before they go away!
They have lived life in ways that you can't imagine.
They have paved a path to make greater things happen.
Elders demonstrate what it takes to carry on.
Their lived experiences will help you to be strong.
Honor them for all of your remaining days.
Treasure their gifts to you, always.

ASHLEY ROSE

Ashley Rose is a Haitian American multi-disciplinary artist and activist from Boston, MA. Her work within the arts has earned her multiple awards, including the ONEin3 Impact Award for Most Influential Person in Boston and Boston's Extraordinary Woman of the Year. She is mentored by writers such as 2023 American Book Award Winner Everett Hoagland, Dr. Soul Brown, Mel King, Askia Toure, Tontongi, Tony Meneilk Van der Meer and Aldo Tambellini.

America's Dried Up Well

Dedicated to those in Flint Michigan and across the world fighting
the war on water.

they were poisoned by poverty
souls of Black folk, slowly sipped cesspools of E.coli, mixed with your political lies
and you had no mercy

you stood in silence as our children cupped their hands under fraudulent faucets
watched as the possibilities of learning disabilities dripped into their sinks
educational dreams, down the drain
dark skin bodies drowning in tears of pain
our Black babies bathed in blisters,
casually you sat back and counted the casualties

but we should have known,
we would never draw water from America's already dried up well
revenge and a reckoning runs in the rivers
pay attention, these hurricanes start off the west coast of Africa,
and follow the same path as the slave trade
take it as a sign, that Yemaya has signaled it's a war for water
and we the people are thirsty for equity

and what happened in Flint Michigan
what happened in Standing Rock
what happened in New Orleans
what happened in Houston
what happened in Orlando

what happened in Puerto Rico
what happened in New York
what happened in the US Virgin Islands
what's happening in Sudan what's happening in Haiti
what happened in Roslindale in 1996

is what happens when justice is left dehydrated
when solidarity is left stagnant
when humanity is left parched
and your politics are allowed to pool

cuz this wouldn't be the first time that us Black and Brown citizens
have been forced to drink from black and brown fountains
would it?

we should have known...

Black Joy

Dedicated to Mel King the activist, poet and first Black mayoral
candidate to advance to the general election in Boston in 1983

&

Mayor Kim Janey the first Black person and woman of color
to become Mayor of Boston in 2017

They say, JOY cometh in the morning
but that's contingent upon if you can keep your faith through the night
It's taking the lows, with the highs
It's finding flight, after you fall
It's the hypotenuse of hope, dividing peaks from valleys
It's your ability to soar over the storm like an eagle
It's learning to dance, with both dusk and dawn
It's sunshine after a long New England winter
It's seeing Mel King on a bench in Copley
The Icy Lady on Martin Luther King Boulevard
2 sure signs that it's that start of a Boston summer

Black Joy

JOY is a Black Boy's smile
It's murals on the side of buildings that Breathe Life into the hood
Dare I say it, RADICAL JOY be revolutionary
It's Black Power fists on the top of Afro picks
It's being brave enough, bold enough, Black enough
to go underground for freedom
Being courageous enough to pitch a Tent in the City
and put JOY on the Black Market
It's making housing affordable
Rewriting school curriculums and textbooks to make our African
ancestors accessible
JOY is artists painting the city red, black and green
It's soul sisters saging the streets

JOY isn't gentrification
It's keeping Nubians in Nubian Square
It's going beyond your cliché terms, of equity, diversity and inclusion
JOY is a sacred circle
It's a hip-hop cipher
It's salmon, justice and jazz served over easy at Sunday Brunch
with a side of love and a cup of sweet hot tea

JOY is a Black man's praying hands
It's learning to thrive instead of survive
It's holding onto life
JOY is that teen that rethinks suicide
It's that mother who learns to mourn, but still believes in miracles
It's finding your laugh after loss
It's healing after harm
JOY is the brother of sorrow

It's a warm embrace after abandonment
It's Restorative Justice
It's learning to trust your discernment
JOY is the essence of forgiveness
It's underserved grace on bended knee
It's a brother's head nod, pound, or handshake ending gun violence
squashing decades of senseless block to block beef

JOY is a yellow trench coat earning wings
It's that Black child who looks in the mirror and sees themselves
as the future City councilor, State Represenative or
Kim Janey, Boston's First
Woman & Person of Color to ever become Mayor
It's warrior women like Ayanna Pressley in Washington politics fighting
for our children
to be able to rock beads, braids, cornrows, baldies and
afro puffs
It's changing polices, so our kids can attend school and graduation
and not be
singled out or reprimanded
for wearing their Kente cloth bow
ties or thier natural hair

JOY be resilient
JOY is progress after protest
It's us embracing our culture and celebrating these historic moments

And I know they say that, JOY cometh in the morning
But dare I say it...
TODAY, JOY be BLACKER than NIGHT

MICHAEL WARR

Michael Warr is Poetry Editor of the anthology *Of Poetry and Protest: From Emmett Till to Trayvon Martin* (W.W. Norton). His books include *The Armageddon of Funk*, called "a poetic soundtrack to black life" by the Black Caucus of the American Library Association, and *We Are All The Black Boy*. He is a San Francisco Public Library Laureate and recipient of the Creative Work Fund Award, PEN Oakland Josephine Miles Award for Excellence in Literature, Gwendolyn Brooks Significant Illinois Poets Award, NEA Fellowship, and more. He co-founded the English/Chinese poetry project Two Languages / One Community with poet Chun Yu.

Her Words (for Gwendolyn Brooks)

An archaeologist
not a lexicologist
figured it out.
The word was a woman.
Mingling among
the Oromos of Ethiopia
brandishing a painter's
brush in a dig
territorially defined by string
the archaeologist swept away
ancient crust and sediment
finding language alive
and agitated instead of
the fossilized femur
of a long-dead ramapithecus.
Words wrapped in rhythm
pleasure, knowledge, and pain.
Words as sharply defined
as an Ashanti sculpture.
Words of an African dynasty
made of peoples
not restricted to kings.
Words that survived
the Atlantic.
Words that survived Atlanta.
Words that survived migration
segregation integration
and false resolution.
Words worn as bracelets
amulets and weapons.
Words that were up
long before they were down.
Word Up.
Words that give more
than she has taken.
Children's lives reweaved
first through her poems

and then through their own.
Words that could weave a world.

Searching for Bob Kaufman

Hieroglyphic petals
illuminate an adolescent trek
through the paper fields, flat plains
and edited savannahs of
"3000 Years Of Black Poetry."
The traveling Trickster emerges
centuries of chapters away from
Africa's ancient poets Anonymous
spine-to-spine with those known:
Wheatley, Dunbar, Brown, Hughes, Brooks,
King, Jones, Evans, Giovanni and Cruz
bound to the sticky fingers
of this Black boy
seeking non-mystical space
between liberation and Ecclesiastes.
He never knew this sometimes
speaking-in-tongues saxophonius poet
except through sorcery etched in ether,
in improbable perfect juxtapositions,
in mind-bending visions manifest
in maddening unmarred stone, in gravity-
defying language turning the underground
upside down,
in silence deafening to those who want
to listen, in sonic waves of syllables
soothing the soul of Blue Whales,
in explosive lines fueled by heavy water,
in inaudible beats drowning out fascistic love-ins,
in inescapable jailbreaks from forced criminality,
in masses of massive solitude out in the open,
in iterations blocking unblocked iterations,
in revelatory secret acts of resistance.
Inside the mind of a Milky Way

a black hole absorbs our light
to be enlightened.

DASAN AHANU

Dasan Ahanu is an award-winning poet and performance artist, public speaker, community organizer, educator, scholar and emcee born and raised in Raleigh, North Carolina. He is an Alumni Nasir Jones Fellow at Harvard's Hip Hop Archive and Research Institute, resident artist at the St. Joseph's Historic Foundation/ Hayti Heritage Center, and visiting lecturer at the University of North Carolina-Chapel Hill. He has performed across the country, appeared on national radio and TV, published three books of poetry, been featured in various periodicals and released numerous recordings. He works with organizations and institutions to develop effective arts strategies to enhance their work in the community. Dasan is currently managing a grant funded initiative as the Rothwell Mellon Program Director for Creative Futures with Carolina Performing Arts. He swings a mean pen and represents the SOUTH.

To My People of Ash and Soot

To MY PEOPLE of ash and soot...
We know fire.
Lit gunpowder turned kin
into kindling. Ritual burial
the residue for resistance.
The rest taken in shackles and
bundled on cargo ships.
Anyone that knew how
combustible colonization was
sought water as refuge.
Those left were set in the sun
like stacked wood in the living room

of white supremacy. Overseers
like chimney sweeps making sure
the notes sung never reached
heaven or sent signals to those
in the woods who knew how
to read the message
along the skylines.

We know burning.
Cuz devils ain't never cared
what they poured kerosene on.
Just as long as they get
to see the flames.
Lit match to body.
Molotov cocktail to house.
Bomb to building.
What else can you say about
those who set crosses ablaze
in front of the blessed like they
trying sear away the truth
that melanin was crucified
for their sins.
Sometimes I think we got stuck with
a white Jesus because he needed
to be wrapped in gauze from
the third-degree burns.

We know ash and soot.
Can script prophecy in the smoke.

To My People of Ash and Soot

See a deadening as the
promise of renewal.
Know we got a covenant with the earth
and it will always help us
turn desolation into ceremony.
Just got to give our incandescent dreams
back to the mother who helped
helped inspire them.
Sit at her feet as she shows
us how to cook a phoenix
from scraps.
Then lay spread new hope
like resurrection Sunday.
Ain't we the ones who raised
glory in the clearing and then turned
that into a church?
So then everywhere we are
is a sanctuary.
Each breath is gospel.
We get so dressed up for Easter
because the ongoing will
to rebuild deserves celebration.
It's a coded affirmation. Like spirituals
told us how to get through. This pageantry
tells us how to get on.

Think about the black and grey
we cover ourselves in to send
our beloved goin' home.

Don't it seem so fitting for us?
I always wondered why the
church house smelt smoldering.
Why the wailing sound like sirens.
Why each tear, held hand, and I love you
seemed so necessary. Soil got to be
treated for a new blossoming.
We know what it is to work
the fields round here. Know what
is means to cull magic from the dark.
Know what it looks like to
build from brimstone.
Hell, they still mad they made us
craft this America and we didn't
pyramid their empire
an appropriate astronomy so
they shooting stars trying
to understand the resilience
of the night sky.

They believe they can
can win with fire, but
ain't no blaze
that can take our brilliance.
Can't take our purpose.
Can't erase our impact.
Can't remove our importance.
We still gone know joy.
Still gone cry and laugh.

We still gone create,
family and survival manuals.
Still gone dance with the same
legs that crumble in misery.
Still gone succeed in the same
madness they revel in.
Live full,
be so powerful.
We children of the sun
will never be afraid of fire.
We resilient wonderful
charred Genesis 1:2
will just make a movement
out of the light.

Family Affair

I step out the car
The door slams behind me
Look and see smoke over the back of the house
Take a deep breath
Smell chicken on the grill

we home

Ain't no hug like Autie's
perfume filling my nose
Soul music blaring through the speakers
Cousin trying to put a spoon of potato salad in my mouth

I see everyone's face frown and kindly decline

we here

Dap Unk up as I hit the back deck
Take a red cup and sip, almost die
Hear a card slap the table
Smell ribs being flipped
Look and see fish grease bubbling

we family

I ain't laughed like that in so long
Ain't seen joy like this in so long
My folks eating good food
Sweet Tea and Barbecue smelling like glory
My folks feeling free and loved

My folks feeling free
and loved
My folks
feeling
free

Protection

I always wondered where daddy was going
Face all steel, neck all hitch

To My People of Ash and Soot

Shoulders looking all trailer
So much, so much to carry
He kissed momma with necessity
Like gas stop before long road traveled
Told us goodnight with underlining message
like a bedtime story
So when the screen door closed behind him
Momma whisked us to our room,
went and locked up,
then came and tucked us in
Put palms together by our bedside
Prayed the morning sunrise would see
our family whole

I didn't know what that meant
Just knew that we never
talked monsters in the closet
The most dangerous were beyond
the front door
Outside was heaven and hell
Inside, we slept in faith
Woke to the smell of egg, grits, and grace
Daddy sitting at the table like God's response
We gave thanks and ate that amen together
What fun we had at that table
What favor
What a joyful noise

The first time I realized

Daddy had his pistol under his jacket
was from a hug he didn't see coming
My chest got tight
I was worried
Good thing I didn't know that he always
stopped at the shed to get his rifle too
That was the first time I was ever afraid
of the dark
Didn't know if it
meant we'd might have to eat
breakfast alone

I had no idea what this ritual was all about
Not until my cousin came to us with a truth
I wanted to be more folktale than gossip
Seems card play and moonshine way too loud
for maintaining innocence gave it all away
The night patrols
The shifts at guard at the end of town
The dedication and commitment
to protecting your own
The sacrifice made to make sure ghosts never
haunt your blessings
This was a cadre of fathers who knew that some
saw sheets as fitting regalia for crusades
to torture Black hope
So these men made sure there was enough
ammunition within reach to say no
and no more

To My People of Ash and Soot

That was the duty each father signed up for
To be peace in darkness
To say let there be light if better aim
was required
To know what to put in the dirt if need be
How to shed blood and build red clay
roadblocks out of the mud
This here was a means to an end
It rested in the hearts and hands
of the men who stood watch
Fully aware that to be a deterrent
required unwavering belief
Because falter might lead to any sense
of salvation hung
Might lead to houses set ablaze
as burnt offering to a devil of
an idea that ain't no way there
could be miracles that look like us
It was understood that there are some
who only saw us as tragedy

I remember the first house still dark
at breakfast
Heard the wailing through the neighborhood
Saw storm clouds hold just above the roof
for a week straight
Wondered why the night betrayed us
Held hands and shed tears that it even had

to be this way

Those men of the neighborhood

put flowers at the edge of the road

Part memorial, part warning

that folks round here would die fighting

That there won't gone be no retreat or cower

Not here

Round here we send ours gone home

Feed each other's bellies and spirits

Say thank you Lord

Then double check the ammunition

Clean the guns

Declare that that ain't gone be

any life be lost in vain

Fond memories and resolve ain't the

only way to honor the fallen

Another is target practice in an open field,

a alter call of scheduled resistance,

and some stump to help wash down

the pain

KIM MCMILLON

Kim McMillon, Ph.D., is a contributor to the anthology *Some Other Blues: New Perspectives on Amiri Baraka* (Ohio University Press). McMillon produced the Dillard University-Harvard's Hutchins Center Black Arts Movement Conference (2016) in New Orleans. McMillon was a guest editor for *The Journal of PAN African Studies*' special edition on the Black Arts Movement and contributed to the *Black Power Encyclopedia (1965-1975)*, a two-volume collection. McMillon was the editor of *Black Fire This Time, Volume 1* (2022).

Somebody Stole My History

Somebody stole my history
I looked for it in books
It wasn't there
I asked my people,
"Where is my history?"
They look down.
Too much Pain
Why do we deny our ancestors?
Listen
They want to talk!
The voices in our heads
are screaming
I want to know who I am!
Why do we walk past the living?
Pretending we don't see the lie
Pretending our truth is found in books
That we didn't write
Pretending
We don't need to know
We don't need to heal
How long
Do we sit at this table?
Till the ghosts of the middle passage rise
From waters
Too deep
with pain
That calls to us

Shouting bodies clad in the past
With words written
On the seafloor
Dark with tales untold
Begging to be heard.
Why can't we just say,
 "I hear you."
How long will
little black girls and boys
Be told
Just do what is right
Look straight ahead

Don't talk
Don't question
Particularly the dead
But we are
the dead
But we are not damned
We are here
Spirit warriors
Rising
Telling our truth
You can find us in the soil
You can find us in rooms long emptied
You can find us in your hearts
Open or closed
We are still there
We breathe in centuries
The first air of truth
We wish to hear our stories told
We have traveled with you for hundreds of years
We have built great cities
We have rebelled against injustice
We held our babies while
Inhumanity branded and burned
We have kneeled in prayer
Asking that our voices be heard
Our lineage is the past, present, future,
and worlds in-between

We speak words
To heal
To find
Lost parts of ourselves
Don't look away
We have been in corners
in dark places
We are moving towards the light
Whether you come or not
If you want to hear our stories
Sit
Question
Don't deny us
Don't deny
your history
It is everywhere
You have only to look
We are waiting.

Kofi Antwi

Assistant Editor Kofi Antwi is a writer of poetry, nonfiction, and fiction. He is a graduate of St. Joseph's College MFA Creative Writing program. He is a composition professor at SUNY Cortland. Born in Brooklyn and raised in Staten Island by parents of Ghanaian descent, Kofi's poetry has been published by *Writers Guild, Agbowo, Rise Up, Gumbo Media, Kalahari Review, Breadcrumbs, Rigorous* and elsewhere. He is the author of *Tidal Wave* (Kattywompus Press).

Akwaaba

to elongated nights in Accra'

devils have recounted

footsteps – in villages, like

Fante people purpose,

life sharpens horns & performative

measures under fainted breath,

fleeted fame is not for the week–

end, or no, but first; renounce

duality, double dare God's ordained

ministry. reap and destroy benefactors,

tyranny records manufactured bones

& tremble, weaken limbs communicate

yes

all hail the city of doom

downtown: we bypass ditches, potholes,

   engraved – a slender terrace, clench

   stenches of grinded coffee

   white boys and girls, squander

   forefather's commandments,

   construction workers squat

   aimlessly on dainty street curbs, laughing

bay street: pimps hustle work, selling perpetual

       sins – we, condemn & flood corners,

       we are all living in our last days

       the unholy man – rattles his cup,

       exposes hardships to

       privileged.   drunk or not,

north shore: peace, officers unlawfully stop

       and frisk, bash skulls

       unruly clergy men push dope – strike

       their wives, lie and cover it up.

       all hail the city of doom – an island

       constructed for not us, but choke outs,

       and the greater America, that doesn't include us

avotcja

Poet/Playwright/Multi-Percussionist/Photographer/Teacher Avotcja has been published in English & Spanish in the USA, Mexico & Europe, and in more Anthologies than she remembers. She is an award winning Poet & multi-instrumentalist who has opened for Betty Carter in New York City, Peru's Susana Baca at San Francisco's Encuentro Popular & Cuba's Gema y Pável, played with Rahsaan Roland Kirk, Bobi & Luis Cespedes, and John Handy.

I SING A SONG OF MAMIE TILL

I am the Child of a different time
A time when time had memory
A time
When time never forgets to remember
What time it is
A time when you better never ever
Forget the dictates of "our place" in it
Because
Forgetting what time it is
Was a luxury "we" were never allowed to forget
I was born in that time
A time
When forgetting "our place" in time
Could very well cost you & your family's life
But... Hey!
Wait a minute!
I'm getting ahead of myself
(Old age can do that to you sometimes)
OK!!!
I was born in New York City July 25th 1941
&
(my age mate)
Emmett Till was born July 25th 1941 in Chicago
Just two Black Babies oblivious of time
With Families
Who'd worked very hard to forget the horrors of "those times"
And protectively forgot to remind us of "our place" in it
&
The fantasy lasted 'til that day when
I accidently picked up that Jet magazine at my friend's house
&
I saw the brutality & inhumanity of Emmett's death
There was no way to deny the sadistic reality
Of
What had happened to that Boy & its message to us
&
With the terrifying power of that picture

I SING A SONG OF MAMIE TILL

The horrific ritual madness in the murder of Emmett Till
It's sickening evil
Stopped time, it killed our silence, it slapped us awake
It flipped the switch on lifetimes of acceptable passivity
&
The World finally knew what time it really was
So today
I sing a Song of Mamie Till
My dear courageous Sistah Lady
I woke up this Morning with your tears running down my face
I could feel the unbelievable horror you faced
When you looked at the mutilated, castrated body & face
Of the beautiful Baby that had nursed at your breast
The disfigured & desecrated body of your beautiful Manchild
&
When you screamed
"I want the whole World to bear witness!!!"
Mamie Till
You completely undressed America
&
I could feel the unapologetic fury of your rage
When you opened that coffin & screamed
"Let the World see what they did to my Boy!!!"
Mamie Till
I could taste every one of your tears when you screamed
"Let the World see what they did to my Boy!!!"
And with that one act
You ripped off all their sheets!!! You undressed America
You stripped the red, white & blue fantasy bare
When you opened that coffin you showed the World
The depraved evil ugliness
The self-righteous violent hatefulness
The perverse racist violence that "we" have always known was there
So tomorrow
I will sing a song of MamieTill
Because it's not over & it's dangerous to forget to remember
&
She is the example of courage I hope to find in myself
Truth is

I have 4 Grandsons & 5 Great Grandsons
Nine extremely good looking, hard headed rambunctious Boys
Nine Black Boys born with bull's-eyes on their backsides
Living targets
For impotent Zombies who've been dead so long
The only way they can get it up is by holding us down
But
Only succeeded in helping Mamie Till turn our fear into fertilizer
&
When she did what she did
We stood up … I say, we stood up

We stood up, we sat down, we came together by the thousands
We grew stronger
And now,
I want the whole World to see what they did to your Boy!!!
'Cause
Emmett, you are a whole lot more than one Mother's Son
You were always more than the Son of just one Mother
Emmett Till
You are my Brother
I want the whole wide World to know
That I know
Emmett Till… you are my Brother
You are
My Cousin, my Uncle, my Father, my next door neighbor
Emmett Till … you are
My cosmic Twin & your brutalized body
Embodies another part of me
&
Thanks to the unrelenting tenacity of your heart broken Mother
You, my Brother, will live forever
So
Yesterday I sang a song of Mamie Till
Tomorrow I will sing a song of Mamie Till
And because it's dangerous for us to forget to remember
Today & every single day of my life
I will sing a song of Mamie Till

&
Tell the World the story of you
Dear Sistah, you are the undisputed Mother of Mothers
The unacknowledged Black Queen of bravery
You are one of our greatest Heroes
&
For whatever it's worth
I will forever thank you for the strength it took to be you
I also thank you for
The strength it took to immortalize the name of your Son
&
An unforgettable job well done
Your example was the medicine I needed to grow & heal
It's because of
The beautiful unstoppable Mama power of you
That this Poem was born
&
Still I sing a song of Mamie Till

WALKING IN THE TRACKS OF THE WOLF
("Howlin' Wolf" AKA Chester Arthur Burnett 6/10/1910-1/10/1976)

Dear Wolf
I can
Still feel your fearless presence
The secure stance of your unbending pride
Standing tall
"Moanin' at Midnight"
In a world of small minded midgets
Your Spirit still sings to me
&
Your fiercely brilliant integrity
Still howls
Inspires courage
In the face of mediocrity
Wolf
You were

You are
And will always be
The example
That set the standard
That straightened the backs
Raised the heads
   &
Gave birth to a new kind of Bluesician
The unapologetic challenge of your swagger
The unashamed sensuality in your Song
  You
Completely reinvented reality
Your slow
Burning
Guitar magic
Was strong enough to demand respect
To command respect
From even the most disrespectful
  And I thank you Wolf
For moanin' the blinders off our eyes
Your proud Man's cry
Paid the price
The strength of your arrogant howlin'
Made ours a life worth living
You howled us into the light
  &
Made our world a better place
The intensity of your pride
Sung us awake!!!
And for that
I will forever be grateful

AL YOUNG

Poet, novelist, and professor Al Young was born in Ocean Springs, Mississippi. He attended the University of Michigan before moving to the San Francisco Bay area, where he earned a B.A. in Spanish from the University of California-Berkeley. Young often read to musical accompaniment, and his poetry reflected his interest in music, specifically jazz and blues, as well as his life in California. His collections of poetry include *Dancing: Poems* (1969), *The Song Turning Back Into Itself* (1971), *The Blues Don't Change: New and Selected Poems* (1982), *Heaven: Collected Poems* 1956–1990 (1992), *The Sound of Dreams Remembered: Poems* 1990–2000 (2001), *Coastal Nights and Inland Afternoons: Poems 2001–2006*, and *Something About the Blues: An Unlikely Collection of Poetry* (2008).

Young wrote several musical memoirs: *Bodies & Soul* (1981), winner of the American Book Award; *Kinds of Blue* (1984); *Things Ain't What They Used to Be* (1987); and *Drowning in the Sea of Love* (1995). He was also the author of five novels, including *Who Is Angelina?* (1976) and *Seduction By Light* (1988), and wrote several screenplays.

Young was a Jones lecturer in Creative Writing at Stanford University from 1969 to 1979. He taught at a number of universities, among them Bowling Green State University, the University of California-Santa Cruz, the University of Washington, and Rice University. He was appointed the 2002 Lurie Distinguished Professor of Creative Writing at San José State University and McGee Professor of Writing at Davidson College in 2003. He traveled widely as a cultural ambassador for the United States Information Agency and delivered lectures on literature and culture for the US Department of State. He received a lifetime achievement award from the Berkeley Poetry Festival.

Young received a Wallace Stegner Fellowship, a Guggenheim Fellowship, a Fulbright Fellowship, and grants from the National Endowment for the Arts. He served as poet laureate of California in 2005. He died in early 2021.

A Dance for Ma Rainey

I'm going to be just like you, Ma
Rainey this monday morning
clouds puffing up out of my head
like those balloons
that float above the faces of white people
in the funnypapers

I'm going to hover in the corners
of the world, Ma
& sing from the bottom of hell
up to the tops of high heaven
& send out scratchless waves of yellow

& brown & that basic black honey
misery

I'm going to cry so sweet
& so low
& so dangerous,
Ma,
that the message is going to reach you
back in 1922
where you shimmer
snaggle-toothed
perfumed &
powdered
in your bauble beads

hair pressed & tied back
throbbing with that sick pain
I know
& hide so well
that pain that blues

jives the world with
aching to be heard
that downness
that bottomlessness
first felt by some stolen delta nigger
swamped under with redblooded american agony;
reduced to the sheer shit
of existence
that bred
& battered us all,
Ma,
the beautiful people
our beautiful brave black people
who no longer need to jazz
or sing to themselves in murderous vibrations
or play the veins of their strong tender arms
with needles
to prove we're still here

untitled

ceiling fan makes in deep summer nights in

hot, unheavenly hotels—Oklahoma, Arkansas,

Tennessee—like the Mississippi River

so deep and wide you couldn't get a letter

to the other side, like Grand Canyon,

like Yosemite National Park, like beans and

cornbread, like rest & recreation, like love

and like, I know we last. I know our bleeding stops.

Who I Am in Twilight

Like John Lee Hooker, like Lightnin Hopkins,
like the blues himself, the trickster sonnet,
hoedown, the tango, the cante jondo,
like blessed spirituals and ragas custom-made,
like sagas, like stories, like slick, slow,
sly soliloquies sliding into dramas
like *Crime & Punishment*, like death & birth,
Canal Street, New Orleans, like the easy,
erasable, troubled voices a whirling.

Credits

Angelou, Maya. "The Mothering Blackness." https://www.poetryoutloud.org/poem/the-mothering-blackness/

Angelou, Maya. "Caged Bird." https://theater.emory.edu/documents/auditions/caged-bird.pdf

Aubert, Alvin. "The Revolutionary." https://journalchickenbones.blogspot.com/2014/05/poems-by-alvin-aubert.html

Bullins, Ed. *Claras Ole Man* (1968). https://library.ucsd.edu/dc/object/bb7748772r/_2.pdf

Cortez, Jayne. "The Oppressionists." https://conservancy.umn.edu/bitstream/handle/11299/166133/Cortez,%20Jayne.pdf;sequence=1

Davis, Thulani. "Backstage Drama." https://www.poetryfoundation.org/poems/52640/backstage-drama

Evans, Mari. "I Am a Black Woman" and "Who Can Be Born Black?" https://www.poemhunter.com/mari-evans/#google_vignette

Fabio, Sarah Webster. "The Hand That Rocks." https://folkways.si.edu/sarah-webster-fabio/the-hand-that-rocks/african-american-spoken-poetry/track/smithsonian

Garrett, Jimmy. *And We Own the Night* (1968). Reprinted by permission of the author.

Harper, Michael S. "Dear John, Dear Coltrane." https://diva.sfsu.edu/collections/poetrycenter/bundles/222879

Hoagland, Everett. "AN ELDER B.A.M. POET AT A BSU READING'S Q&A" and "AMIRI'S LAST SET:
SYMPHONY HALL, NEWARK, NJ, JAN. 17, 2014." *The Music: New and Selected Poems, 1973-2023*. Aquarius Press, 2023.

hooks, bell. (Gloria Jean Watkins), "Appalachian Elegy (Sections 1-6)" from Appalachian Elegy. Copyright © 2012 by bell hooks (Gloria Jean Watkins). Reprinted from The University Press of Kentucky.

Jackson, Angela. "Miz Rosa Rides the Bus." https://medium.com/the-forestry-of-prophets/in-december-b8fe530aa7b8

Printed in the USA
CPSIA information can be obtained
at www.ICGtesting.com
CBHW020731050624
9533CB00001B/1

Credits

Angelou, Maya. "The Mothering Blackness." https://www.poetryoutloud.org/poem/the-mothering-blackness/

Angelou, Maya. "Caged Bird." https://theater.emory.edu/documents/auditions/caged-bird.pdf

Aubert, Alvin. "The Revolutionary." https://journalchickenbones.blogspot.com/2014/05/poems-by-alvin-aubert.html

Bullins, Ed. *Claras Ole Man* (1968). https://library.ucsd.edu/dc/object/bb7748772r/_2.pdf

Cortez, Jayne. "The Oppressionists." https://conservancy.umn.edu/bitstream/handle/11299/166133/Cortez,%20Jayne.pdf;sequence=1

Davis, Thulani. "Backstage Drama." https://www.poetryfoundation.org/poems/52640/backstage-drama

Evans, Mari. "I Am a Black Woman" and "Who Can Be Born Black?" https://www.poemhunter.com/mari-evans/#google_vignette

Fabio, Sarah Webster. "The Hand That Rocks." https://folkways.si.edu/sarah-webster-fabio/the-hand-that-rocks/african-american-spoken-poetry/track/smithsonian

Garrett, Jimmy. *And We Own the Night* (1968). Reprinted by permission of the author.

Harper, Michael S. "Dear John, Dear Coltrane." https://diva.sfsu.edu/collections/poetrycenter/bundles/222879

Hoagland, Everett. "AN ELDER B.A.M. POET AT A BSU READING'S Q&A" and "AMIRI'S LAST SET:
SYMPHONY HALL, NEWARK, NJ, JAN. 17, 2014." *The Music: New and Selected Poems, 1973-2023*. Aquarius Press, 2023.

hooks, bell. (Gloria Jean Watkins), "Appalachian Elegy (Sections 1-6)" from Appalachian Elegy. Copyright © 2012 by bell hooks (Gloria Jean Watkins). Reprinted from The University Press of Kentucky.

Jackson, Angela. "Miz Rosa Rides the Bus." https://medium.com/the-forestry-of-prophets/in-december-b8fe530aa7b8

Jordan, June. "1977: Poem for Mrs. Fannie Lou Hamer." https://archive.org/details/passionnewpoems100jord

Knight, Etheridge. "The Bones of My Father" and "For Malcom: A Year After." https://www.poetryfoundation.org/poets/etheridge-knight

Lorde, Audre. "Poetry is Not a Luxury." https://makinglearning.files.wordpress.com/2014/01/poetry-is-not-a-luxury-audre-lorde.pdf

Lorde, Auddre. "Power" from *The Collected Poems of Audre Lorde*. Copyright © 1978 by Audre Lorde. W. W. Norton & Company, Inc.

Neal, Larry. *The Black Arts Movement.* https://nationalhumanitiescenter.org/pds/maai3/community/text8/blackartsmovement.pdf

Patterson, Raymond. "To a Weathercock." https://aaregistry.org/poem/to-a-weathercock-by-raymond-r-patterson/

Rodgers, Carolyn. "Translation", "U Name This One." https://mecopeland.wordpress.com/2013/02/28/poems-by-carolyn-m-rodgers/

Warr, Michael. "Her Words (For Gwendolyn Brooks", previously published in *TriQuarterly*, no. 96, Spring/Summer 1996. *gazelle pOets Anthology: Volume One, Number One*, 1998. *The Armageddon of Funk*. Tia Chucha Press, 2011.

Warr, Michael. "Searching for Bob Kaufman," previously published in the essay "Searching for Language" by Michael Warr for the Institute for Inquiry and Poetics, University of Arizona Poetry Center. Also performed by the poet in the video "Bob Kaufman's COLLECTED POEMS, a celebration AFTER his 95th birthday — The Poetry Center."

Printed in the USA
CPSIA information can be obtained
at www.ICGtesting.com
CBHW020731050624
9533CB00001B/1